Issue | 147

RADICAL *Review*
HISTORY

T0311441

The Political Lives of Infrastructure

Issue Editors: Wesley Attewell, Emily Mitchell-Eaton, and Richard Nisa

CURATED SPACES

THE SINEWS OF INFRASTRUCTURAL POWER

ROUNDTABLE II

The Political Lives of Infrastructure

Wesley Attewell, Emily Mitchell-Eaton, and Richard Nisa

The emergence of the COVID-19 pandemic in 2020 made it almost impossible for people to ignore the life-or-death role infrastructures play as arteries of community survival and as the material conduits organizing the abandonment of certain peoples and places. Some people wrestled with the highly localized labor shortages that disrupted the speed of an economy built on fragile, spatially expansive just-in-time supply chains. Others, now working from home, realized that they relied on so-called essential workers for survival. Those laboring away in the food processing and agriculture, warehousing and delivery, emergency and health care sectors, whose own precarity was framed as a necessary precondition for the maintenance of the status quo, were themselves vulnerable to reduced access to health care, higher rates of illness, and premature death. Still others endured bodily vulnerability and exposure while incarcerated, seemingly isolated *inside* carceral institutions but intimately connected to infrastructural circuits of abandonment that were simultaneously tearing through communities *outside* prisons.

As these crises unfurled, many saw their position within these different infrastructural spaces as a chance to reorganize their workplaces, build networks of community care, and make local demands about the provision of safety and security that resonated across space. Where populations of the elderly and immunocompromised lacked safe access to food or prescription medication, mutual aid networks emerged to extend these supply chains. In seeking to dismantle the excessive presence of police and prisons in their communities, abolitionists sought to build alternative pathways to harm reduction. In neighborhoods where racialized essential workers were extremely

Radical History Review
Issue 147 (October 2023)   DOI 10.1215/01636545-10637119
© 2023 by MARHO: The Radical Historians' Organization, Inc.

vulnerable to state infrastructures of expulsion and deportation, activists organized communications networks to preemptively announce the arrival of militarized immigration agents. These, too, are infrastructural projects.[1]

What these intersecting valences of the COVID-19 pandemic make plain is that infrastructures—as historically produced material and social systems of connectivity and relationality—establish lived relations of struggle that are embedded in particular places while circulating power across multiple, disparate scales. Further, many of the challenges exposed by the pandemic were themselves manifestations of previously constructed systems of connection and disconnection, integration and abandonment that distributed commodities and power unevenly. In these myriad junctions, imbrications, and circulatory arteries of infrastructural history, people sought to bring about a more survivable future.

A key challenge for these organizers was not to simply reject the power of the state but to frame alternatives in varying degrees of relation to state infrastructural power. Struggles to construct these new systems did not necessarily manifest through blockade, sabotage, or rejection, but also through organizing practices aimed at transforming the harms of dispossession and place-based capitalist abandonment into liberatory political movements. To paraphrase the abolitionist geographer Ruth Wilson Gilmore, these modes of organizing against the deprivations caused by global flows produce local materialities; they constitute a *presence*, not merely a rejection or a response to an absence.[2] Similarly, for Winona LaDuke and Deborah Cowen, survival and flourishing in these places—many of which have been intentionally isolated, disconnected, stolen, and poisoned by the settler colonial state—becomes a matter of imagining and building an "infrastructure otherwise."[3]

As the contributions to this issue of *Radical History Review* demonstrate, presence-making infrastructural practices like those above—all of which emerged in some kind of specific, place-based relationship to the state—are useful lenses through which to trace a longer history that takes shape across the twentieth and early twenty-first centuries. Our focus here is on exploring the historical production of infrastructures as places of resistance and world-building—for workers, for villagers, for migrants—across a century in which narratives about the role of infrastructure as a conduit for modernization, development, and the centralizing capacities of the state had broad purchase.

Given the intricate position infrastructures hold in framing and reproducing "how we live," states and communities alike continuously maintain, repair, and organize for the control of these systems.[4] Whether delivering violence or sanctuary, food shortages or community well-being, these incongruous outcomes play out *through* infrastructures and people's group-differentiated relationships to them. Infrastructure, in other words, channels us straight to the heart of political struggle across multiple scales of human action. By framing this issue around these political lives of infrastructure, we argue that it is imperative to understand infrastructure by focusing on the people whose organizing for survival coalesces around and against it, and by mapping the worlds that their endeavors call into being.

Approaching the history of infrastructure through this lens provokes two related questions about the political lives of infrastructure that each of the articles in this issue takes up in its own way. First, what stories can be told about the history of infrastructural power if it is delinked from master narratives tying it solely to state and state-backed centralization? While these essays clearly show that development, nation building, and extraction are all state-sponsored or state-backed projects, they also demonstrate that modern states were not the only wielders of infrastructural power in the twentieth century. Instead, in decentering the state as the only, or the most important, infrastructural actor, these articles also necessarily decenter the *nation*-state as a "natural" geographic scale of political analysis.[5] A second question extends from the first: How does this decentering of the state in infrastructural analyses in turn transform the stakes of radical political activity and the work of radical historical actors? Telling the history of large-scale infrastructures through more localized world-building practices opens up a different scale of political analysis, one that works both within and beyond the nation-state scale to position ostensibly disparate, small sites as central to larger politics and everyday strategies of "making do" and "getting by" as resistance.

Thus the articles in this issue offer a different proposition about infrastructural power, one that pushes back against the grand unifying themes that, across the twentieth century, have animated stories about state building, modernization, and development through infrastructure—dams, highways, radio networks, and flood-management systems, among many examples. To be sure, twentieth-century state projects to extract resources, labor, and capital and channel them in particular directions—away from certain sites and into others—were no less extractive than those of the transatlantic slave trade, or the centuries of formal European colonialism across the Americas, the Caribbean, Africa, Asia, and the Pacific (during which imperial state actors were often quite explicit about their aims to make matter move in the service of capital accumulation).[6] What *did* change in the twentieth century was the packaging. After the global wave of formal decolonization from the 1950s through the 1970s, state powers deployed a specific set of narratives justifying their ongoing redistribution of the potentialities of political lives, which is to say, the potential for life itself.

Throughout the twentieth century, states valued infrastructure-building projects for their potential to modernize rural peoples and integrate distant places into the regimes of accumulation preferred by the state (both capitalist and socialist). Under such conditions, large-scale state infrastructure projects offered a technocratic valence through which former colonial powers could depoliticize their ongoing regimes of dispossession and accumulation. This strategic depoliticization of infrastructure echoed states' similarly neutralized narratives about the role of development, modernization, growth, and progress. For states, that is, infrastructure was both a method and a means to obscure the ongoing work of empire, making it appear smooth, seamless, and even inevitable, rather than prone to political as well as logistical frictions. Instead of focusing narrowly on whether infrastructures delivered on these promises, or whether populations resisted state centralizations, the articles in this issue rescale the question of political struggle in infrastructural spaces. If all infrastructures aim to bring certain worlds or realities into being, what other types of worlds, publics, and political struggles emerge in the shadows of these state projects?

Given this capacity of infrastructure to facilitate multiple scales of politically transformative organizing, the articles are split into two groups, each exploring struggle and survival through different entry points. The first, "Political Lives in the Shadow of Infrastructure," highlights the tumult of lived human experiences as they intersect with and endure through (and beyond) the construction and provisioning of infrastructural projects. The second section, "The Sinews of Infrastructural Power," draws attention to the political work done by way of circulation and (forced) movement along infrastructural corridors themselves. Serving as a pivot between these two groupings is an image essay by the documentary filmmaker Solveig Qu Suess that accentuates the unresolved tensions between intimate family moments in a much larger technopolitical endeavor of optical engineering and state surveillance. The issue is bookended by two wide-ranging roundtable discussions. The first, a conversation between Deborah Cowen and Laleh Khalili, deftly navigates the ongoing frictional politics of the contemporary moment. The issue ends with a nod toward the future. In their conversation, Bench Ansfield, Rachel Herzing, and Dean Spade consider what it means—and what it might look like in practice—to build infrastructures premised on the belief that everyone deserves care and no one is disposable.

The authors attend to political lives of infrastructure that emerged during the twentieth and early twenty-first centuries across North America, the Pacific Islands, and East and Southeast Asia. In doing so, they turn to infrastructure as both *method* and *material* for thinking relationally across the diverse constellation of spaces and places that have historically served as key geographic reference or anchor points for what the historian Simeon Man describes as the "wider Pacific world." By exposing the densely layered colonial histories in geographic meeting-up places like Hawaiʻi, Guåhan, peripheral Shanghai, suburban Beijing, northern British Columbia, and rural Louisiana, these contributions promise to open up new spaces for dialogue among geographers, historians, and American studies and Asian (diaspora) studies scholars on the "global-imperial circuits" that have historically linked various sites of empire building and (settler) colonialism across the modern world. These conversations are inclusive of the inherently place-based movements for demilitarization and decolonization that have always resisted, slowed, and sometimes even reversed the rollout of these broader projects over space and scale.[7]

From a certain perspective, Robin McDowell's careful engagement with the histories of Black struggle for environmental justice and dignity in the heart of Louisiana's Cancer Alley seems like a bit of a geographic outlier. But McDowell insists that the struggles over and through infrastructure that animate St. Charles Parish in the present moment of crisis and emergency are also necessarily stories of how local communities continue to experience long-standing genealogies of racial violence, unfree labor, organized abandonment, and racialized refuge as an *inheritance* of prior plantation capitalism(s). These infrastructures of race war and counterinsurgency were never strictly domestic in their scope and reach. It is by now well known how plantation owners in Louisiana and across the US South turned to indentured Asian labor as a replacement for Black slaves and, by extension, a potential solution to the thorny problem of maintaining local economies in the immediate post-emancipation period.[8]

Louisiana's infrastructural connections to the wider Pacific world would remain significant throughout the twentieth and early twenty-first centuries. Mona Domosh, for example, emphasizes how infrastructures of technical assistance, rural uplift, and household management—infrastructures that played a central role in the US's Cold War on the forces of communism and decolonization in Asia—were first developed and stress-tested on southern Black communities in the early twentieth century.[9] Ann Ngoc Tran describes these infrastructures forcefully in her essay on the imperial and insurgent traffic in soap during the Vietnam War. Moreover, the displacements and dislocations set in motion by the Vietnam War also went on to shape the domestic geographies of everyday life in Louisiana, as exemplified by how New Orleans's eastern neighborhoods became a significant site of Vietnamese refugee resettlement from 1975 onward. As resettled Vietnamese refugees picked up the pieces of their shattered lives in largely Black neighborhoods like Versailles, they were forced to engage in a fraught and complex politics of relations with their new neighbors. These relation-making processes served, however uneasily, as the concrete scaffolding on which the two racialized and marginalized communities built interracial infrastructures of mutual aid and solidarity in the devastating aftermath of Hurricane Katrina.[10] It is precisely this refugee community that now finds itself in the crosshairs of the recently reinvigorated deportation regime that Jason Tuấn Vũ tracks in his essay on transpacific infrastructures of settler carcerality. All of this is not to suggest that the struggles and encounters mapped out by McDowell, Vũ, and Tran are somehow commensurable or directly related. Rather, we believe that the issue's more nuanced contribution is to open intellectual and political spaces where Louisiana, South Vietnam, Guåhan, and Hawai'i might be held together in the same frame of analysis. That is to say, what this issue offers is an opportunity to consider how seemingly localized insurgencies against "domestic" infrastructures of race war, racial management, and place annihilation might also help us better understand the everyday violence work of counterinsurgency and settler militarism in "foreign" sites such as South Vietnam and the Pacific Islands.[11]

When read together, these articles emphasize the historical role of infra-structures in enabling the global circulation of capital and commodities through the entrenchment of racial capitalism and the extraction of labor from racialized and marginalized communities. In her work, Katherine McKittrick insists that the slave plantation and its "attendant geographies," including "the auction block, the big house, the fields and crops, the slave quarters, the transportation ways leading to and from the plantation, and so on," have historically doubled as the geographic centrifuge that organized "various practices of spatialized violence that targeted black bodies and profited from erasing a black sense of place."[12] It follows, then, that public works infrastructures like the Bonnet Carré Spillway, which were built in Southern landscapes so thoroughly transformed by racialized modes of place annihilation, carry forward these legacies of bodily capture and unfree (Black) or indentured (Asian) labor, as McDowell emphasizes with such devastating clarity.

Similarly, as Desiree Valadares documents in her essay, the labor camp fig-ured centrally as a strategy of racial management during World War II, when the Canadian government interned Japanese men and forced them to work on various nation-building projects, constructing visions of white settler mobility and moder-nity as they built highways through Indigenous lands in British Columbia. Under such conditions of wartime settler militarism, it was precisely the labor capacity of racialized and marginalized bodies that gave meaning to infrastructures of race war and national security, yet also perversely laid the groundwork for a postwar turn to futures of racial liberalism and multicultural inclusion. In this sense, both Valadares and Yuan Gao—in his essay on the aesthetic histories of mass participation in social-ist China's spectacular hydro-engineering schemes—help us understand how back-breaking physical labor itself has historically been mobilized as an infrastructure for consolidating and developing a national consciousness.

Given the extent to which histories of labor are also histories of displacement, capture, and mobility, this issue foregrounds the long-standing centrality of infra-structure to the geographic management of circulations, both within and across bor-derlands.[13] Vũ's contribution is the most explicit in this regard, tracking how Hawai'i and Guåhan came to serve as "vital junction points" in broader transpacific infra-structures of (re)settlement, Indigenous dispossession, military transit, and refugee deportation, thereby ensuring the "rise and maintenance of the US's 'imperial archi-pelago' in the Pacific." In so doing, Vũ develops a framework of "settler carcerality" to explain how US imperialism across the decolonizing Pacific has historically used a combination of discipline and enclosure to enable the mobility of certain privileged groups, while restricting or controlling the movement of others.

Infrastructures of circulation of a different sort feature centrally in Ying-chuan Yang's essay on how the Chinese Communist Party developed radio networks into an "infrastructure of the masses" in and around rural Shanghai. By "attending to the everyday, technical aspects of one of the most ambitious—yet at the same time one of the most neglected—infrastructure projects in modern Chinese history," Yang considers the political lives of infrastructural development under state socialism. In his telling, the radio network built across midcentury rural China served as a "tool of inclusion" for the socialist state while also transforming life in the countryside in ways that "frustrated a completely top-down intervention" and "could become downright antirevolutionary." Much like Gao, Yang shows how socialist infrastructures were explicitly political from the outset, designed to discipline local communities while simultaneously interpellating them as members of a broader socialist nation.

Yang's comments on the affective dimensions and consequences of infrastructural development also draw our attention to the ways in which such projects invariably become wrapped up in the state management of intimacy, intimate relations, and (self-)care. Ann Ngoc Tran shows how US imperial state actors used the Vietnam War as a way to project their own visions of modernity—this time, as hygiene—through their violent management of Vietnamese and other Southeast Asian bodies and their traditional practices of cleanliness and self-care. During the war, US counterinsurgents and civic action cadres distributed free cakes of soap and other cleaning products to rural households, whose living conditions and personal hygiene practices were largely understood as slovenly and thus an impediment to future modernity and development. Through a deft reading of diverse archival sources, Tran tracks how rural communities "ruptured" these supposedly humanitarian practices of imperial gift giving with "acts of refusal and indifference," selling the cakes of soap on local black markets as a way of making ends meet.

Tran's focus on the everyday geographies of relation making and survival are picked up and carried forward by Suess's contribution to the "Curated Spaces" section of this special issue. In her visual essay, she narrates the process of piecing together a documentary about her mother's experiences working as an optical engineer for the Chinese government in the 1980s. As Suess demonstrates, her mother's story is not only a story of memory and (state-sponsored) forgetting, but also one of diasporic intimacy and transnational displacement. The power of Suess's engagement with family photography lies in her ability to show how even the most high-level state-based infrastructure projects—"the production of [optical] instruments for seeing at a distance and at night"—were necessarily experienced and lived at the scale of the intimate and the everyday. That is to say, she helps us recover how infrastructures of intimacy, care, and *relation work* have served as "the bedrock upon which empire rests and through which it reproduces itself."[14] It is precisely this infrastructural through line that connects Suess's essay to those by Tran, McDowell, Yang, and the rest of the contributors to this issue.

If infrastructures of intimacy, care, and relation work remain essential to securing the expanded reproduction of imperial, racial, capitalist, and settler colonial regimes of power and violence, this issue also emphasizes their enduring importance to the everyday work of building new or alternative forms of solidarity, collective well-being, and liberatory social transformation. As McDowell, Ansfield, Spade, Cowen, and Khalili all emphasize to varying degrees, organizing at its core involves constant relation work. It is, after all, relation work that undergirds or buttresses the various logistical aspects of organizing, community engagement, activism, and mutual aid: namely, the geographic management of who does what where, as well as the various flows of goods, funds, and other donations that are necessary to sustain and support the broader movement. The communities of descendants that are the protagonists of McDowell's essay, for instance, are sustained and invigorated in their fight to commemorate "the lives of Black people who worked the land beneath the [Bonnet Carré] spillway" by their affective investment and commitment to reclaiming and reasserting a particularly Black sense of place that has, over time, been constantly threatened by displacement and organized abandonment. "Like material infrastructure," McDowell writes, "the relationships formed through community organizing and storytelling and the kinship bonds between descendants and the larger communities to which they belong require maintenance."

These ideas are further developed by Spade and Herzing in their conversation with Ansfield, particularly when their attention shifts to the practical question of what "certain kinds of things we need to develop or build up in order for that practice—the practice of transformative justice or community accountability—to have the desired effect that we want it to have." While infrastructure, as Ansfield reminds the reader, is not a concept or framework that is typically used to explain and inform the everyday work of decolonization, abolition, and other forms of radical organizing, it nonetheless offers a generative way of thinking relationally, of doing "bridge work," across the "multiplicity of localized practices for addressing and preventing harm" so that they may be held together in the same frame of political analysis and praxis.[15] From this perspective, abolition becomes organized around and oriented to what Cowen refers to as the "collectively constructed systems that build and sustain human life."[16] In other words, abolition becomes *infrastructural.*

Each of the articles that make up this issue asks us, in its own way, to rethink the horizons and contours of radical politics under our current and ongoing conditions of crisis and emergency. All too often, the work of radical politics is narrowly understood—at least by mainstream publics—as limited to the work of dismantling carceral, imperial, capitalist, patriarchal, and settler colonial infrastructures. Radical work can, of course, take that form, often productively. But, again, the roundtables that bookend this issue remind us that radical movements like abolition or decolonization are about presence, not absence.[17] This radical politics of presence, in turn, must necessarily prioritize the hard, tedious, and occasionally joyful work of building what Cowen and her collaborators have collectively named "infrastructure otherwise."[18]

What the contributions to this special issue also clarify, moreover, is that such an infrastructural politics of radical presence has a long genealogy that continues to shape activism and organizing in the present. Whether we turn to the public history activism undertaken by descendant communities in St. Charles Parish, or the infrastructures of mutual aid and collective care that are both the prerequisite and the horizon of the broader abolition movement, marginalized folks are already building the systems they need to survive and move beyond broader geographic configurations of power, rule, and violence.

These political conversations, we argue, necessarily have intellectual implications for radical historians, as well as for their colleagues and comrades in cognate disciplines. What the contributions to this special issue teach us is the necessity of a theory of infrastructure that attends to the fundamentally *spatial* dimensions of struggle, organizing, and survival pending revolution. The "catastrophe of racial capitalism on a world scale," Gilmore helpfully reminds us, demands that we constantly think, act, and organize across geographic scales. All liberation struggles, she argues, are by necessity "specific to the needs and the struggles of people where they are." These struggles are, at their core, projects of radical place-making. Freedom, under such conditions, becomes a place that people *produce* through the everyday work of "building things, cleaning things, fixing things, teaching people, driving buses, whatever they do."[19]

And yet, if freedom is a place, it is one that necessarily transcends easy or narrow conceptualizations of borders and boundaries. As Gilmore has learned during her decades-long career as an abolitionist anti-prison organizer, social movements also require an "approach to solving problems that, however particularly local they are, have an international dimension, because it is an international problem."[20] What the humdrum realities of abolitionist organizing have clarified for Gilmore, in other words, is the fundamental importance of building (transnational) relations across highly localized sites of place-based struggle that might otherwise seem disparate and disconnected.

What the contributors to this issue all ultimately share is an investment in and commitment to using infrastructure as a framework for carrying forward this intellectual and political project. They are asking us how we, too, might contribute to the everyday work of building infrastructures otherwise.

Wesley Attewell is assistant professor of political geography at the University of Hong Kong. As a geographer of imperialism, decolonization, and diaspora, Wesley studies the global landscapes of US empire building from the Cold War into the present. His forthcoming book *Developing Violence: Disassembling the USAID Complex in Afghanistan* has been reviewed as a rich account of how the US transformed post-1945 Afghanistan into a key site for reimagining development into a liberal form of counterinsurgency. Wesley is currently working on a second book that maps the transpacific logistics infrastructures and the racialized labor regimes that the US assembled to supply its war in Vietnam.

Emily Mitchell-Eaton is assistant professor of geography at Colgate University. A feminist geographer interested in the politics of mobility and migration, she explores how racial meanings, laws and policies, military infrastructures, and emotions travel through space and over time. Her book *New Destinations of Empire: Transpacific Mobilities, Racial Geographies, and Imperial Citizenship* (forthcoming) examines the US empire's long-standing effects on the Marshall Islands and its role in producing a Marshallese imperial diaspora that stretches to northwest Arkansas. Her work has been published in *Political Geography*; *Environment and Planning D: Society and Space*; *Environment and Planning C: Politics and Space*; *International Migration Review*; *Gender, Place and Culture*; and the edited volume *Precarity and Belonging: Labor, Migration, and Noncitizenship* (2021).

Richard Nisa is special faculty in the IDeATe Program at Carnegie Mellon University, where he is the program lead in sustainability. He was previously an associate professor of geography in the Department of Social Sciences and History at Fairleigh Dickinson University. His current book project explores the transnational circulatory, political, and technological systems that constitute US-managed wartime detainment spaces. His work has been published in the *Journal of Historical Geography*, *Environment and Planning A*, and the edited volume *Algorithmic Life: Calculative Devices in the Age of Big Data* (2016).

Notes

1. In drawing attention to the distinctions between solidarity work like mutual aid and the idea of charity, Dean Spade makes an explicit case that "we should be working toward locally controlled, participatory, transparent structures to replace our crumbling and harmful infrastructure. Doing so," Spade argues, "helps us imagine getting rid of the undemocratic infrastructure of our lives—the extractive and unjust energy, food, health care, and transportation systems—and replacing it with people's infrastructure" (*Mutual Aid*, 20). From South Brooklyn Mutual Aid in that borough's diverse Sunset Park, Borough Park, and Bay Ridge neighborhoods to COVID-19 response networks in Hong Kong, many networks that crystallized across the globe during the pandemic were built on long-standing relationships and networks grounded in place.
2. Gilmore, "Abolition on Stolen Land."
3. LaDuke and Cowen, "Beyond Wiindigo Infrastructure," 246.
4. Cowen and LaDuke argue that the physical infrastructures that crystallize around things like "the economy" are inseparable from the intimate encounters that frame "how we live" ("Beyond Wiindigo Infrastructure," 262). Elsewhere, the historian of infrastructure Brian Larkin has helpfully referred to infrastructure as the material, social, and cultural systems "that create the grounds on which other" forms of power function ("Politics and Poetics of Infrastructure," 329). Though quite different, both approaches to infrastructures see them as social *and* material.
5. This reorientation away from the (settler colonial) state is informed by decolonial approaches that similarly pivot away from Eurocentric epistemologies and ontologies toward Indigenous ways of knowing and modes of world-building. See, e.g., Mignolo and Walsh, *On Decoloniality*; and Lugones, "Toward a Decolonial Feminism."
6. Hall, "When Was 'the Post-colonial'?"
7. Man, "Transpacific Connections," 451; See, e.g., Chang, *The World and All the Things upon It*; Banivanua Mar, *Decolonization and the Pacific*; Friedman, "US Empire."
8. See, e.g., Jung, *Coolies and Cane*.

9. These themes appear across Domosh's recent body of work. See, e.g., Domosh, "Practicing Development at Home."
10. Tang, "A Gulf Unites Us."
11. The foundations of this claim emerge from our engagements with the work of Stuart Schrader, Nikhil Pal Singh, and others. Schrader, *Badges without Borders*; Singh, *Race and America's Long War*.
12. McKittrick, "On Plantations," 948.
13. Loyd, Mitchell-Eaton, and Mountz, "Militarization of Islands and Migration."
14. Khayyat, Khayyat, and Khayyat, "Pieces of Us," 269.
15. On bridge work, also see Anand, Gupta, and Appel, *Promise of Infrastructure*, 14.
16. Cowen, "Infrastructures of Empire and Resistance."
17. Gilmore, "Abolition on Stolen Land."
18. LaDuke and Cowen, "Beyond Wiindigo Infrastructure."
19. Hayes, "Ruth Wilson Gilmore on Abolition."
20. Card, *Geographies of Racial Capitalism with Ruth Wilson Gilmore*.

References

Anand, Nikhil, Akhil Gupta, and Hannah Appel, eds. *The Promise of Infrastructure*. Durham, NC: Duke University Press, 2018.

Banivanua Mar, Tracey. *Decolonization and the Pacific: Indigenous Globalization and the Ends of Empire*. Cambridge: Cambridge University Press, 2016.

Card, Kenton, dir. *Geographies of Racial Capitalism with Ruth Wilson Gilmore: An Antipode Foundation Film*. YouTube video, June 1, 2020, 16:18. https://www.youtube.com/watch?v=2CS627aKrJI.

Chang, David. *The World and All the Things upon It: Native Hawaiian Geographies of Exploration*. Minneapolis: University of Minnesota Press, 2016.

Cowen, Deborah. "Infrastructures of Empire and Resistance." *Verso Books* (blog), January 25, 2017. https://www.versobooks.com/blogs/3067-infrastructures-of-empire-and-resistance.

Domosh, Mona. "Practising Development at Home: Race, Gender, and the 'Development' of the American South." *Antipode* 47, no. 4 (2015): 915–41.

Friedman, Andrew. "US Empire, World War 2, and the Racialising of Labour." *Race and Class* 58, no. 4 (2017): 23–38.

Gilmore, Ruth Wilson. "Abolition on Stolen Land." UCLA Luskin Institute on Inequality and Democracy, seminar, October 9, 2020. https://vimeo.com/467484872.

Hall, Stuart. "When Was 'the Post-colonial'? Thinking at the Limit." In *The Post-colonial Question: Common Skies, Divided Horizons*, edited by Iain Chambers and Lidia Curti, 242–60. London: Routledge, 1996.

Hayes, Kelly. "Ruth Wilson Gilmore on Abolition, the Climate Crisis, and What Must Be Done." *Truthout*, April 14, 2022. https://truthout.org/audio/ruth-wilson-gilmore-on-abolition-the-climate-crisis-and-what-must-be-done/.

Jung, Moon Ho. *Coolies and Cane: Race, Labor, and Sugar in the Age of Emancipation*. Baltimore: Johns Hopkins University Press, 2008.

Khayyat, Munira, Yasmine Khayyat, and Rola Khayyat. "Pieces of Us: The Intimate as Imperial Archive." *Journal of Middle East Women's Studies* 14, no. 3 (2018): 268–91.

LaDuke, Winona, and Deborah Cowen. "Beyond Wiindigo Infrastructure." *South Atlantic Quarterly* 119, no. 2 (2020): 243–68.

Larkin, Brian. "The Politics and Poetics of Infrastructure." *Annual Review of Anthropology* 42, no. 1 (2013): 327–43.

Loyd, Jenna M., Emily Mitchell-Eaton, and Alison Mountz. "The Militarization of Islands and Migration: Tracing Human Mobility through US Bases in the Caribbean and the Pacific." *Political Geography* 53 (2016): 65–75.

Lugones, María. "Toward a Decolonial Feminism." *Hypatia* 25, no. 4 (2010): 742–59.

Man, Simeon. "Transpacific Connections between Two Empires." *American Quarterly* 66, no. 2 (2014): 441–51.

McKittrick, Katherine. "On Plantations, Prisons, and a Black Sense of Place." *Social and Cultural Geography* 12, no. 8 (2011): 947–63. https://doi.org/10.1080/14649365.2011 .624280.

Mignolo, Walter D., and Catherine E. Walsh. *On Decoloniality: Concepts, Analytics, Praxis.* Durham, NC: Duke University Press, 2018.

Schrader, Stuart. *Badges without Borders: How Global Counterinsurgency Transformed American Policing.* Oakland: University of California Press, 2019.

Singh, Nikhil Pal. *Race and America's Long War.* Oakland: University of California Press, 2017.

Spade, Dean. *Mutual Aid: Building Solidarity during This Crisis (and the Next).* New York: Verso, 2020.

Tang, Eric. "A Gulf Unites Us: The Vietnamese Americans of Black New Orleans East." *American Quarterly* 63, no. 1 (2011): 117–49.

Inscribing New Infrastructural Relations into the World

Deborah Cowen and Laleh Khalili in Conversation

Wesley Attewell, Emily Mitchell-Eaton, and Richard Nisa

Few scholars have done more than Deborah Cowen and Laleh Khalili to upend the notion that infrastructures are the seamlessly integrated and largely unnoticed connective sutures that underpin everyday life. Infrastructure, of course, does facilitate movement. But Cowen's and Khalili's work unsettles the fantasy that this mobility is a metaphor or a smooth, productive abstraction. Instead, through the remarkable breadth of their scholarship, we see that infrastructures are materially consequential historical systems that give pattern and shape to—or spatially organize—the uneven connections and disconnections so central to capitalist accumulation. Through their career-long explorations of the circulatory contours of war, carcerality, and imperialism; ecology, oil, and extractivism; Indigeneity, resurgence, and resistance; and urban crisis, both have heightened awareness of just how incomplete and depoliticizing a frictionless framing of infrastructure is.

As has become clear in the three years since the onset of the COVID-19 pandemic, we are in a historical moment in which intersecting crises are playing out through the sociotechnical systems of circulation that give shape to the planet's uneven geography of life and death. Given the virus's continuing stresses on health care systems; the regional and transnational conflicts disrupting the spatial flows of life-sustaining food crops; the increased investment in border infrastructures to

Radical History Review

Issue 147 (October 2023)   DOI 10.1215/01636545-10637133

© 2023 by MARHO: The Radical Historians' Organization, Inc.

expedite expulsions; the police and vigilante violence accelerating the already-rapid speed of colonial and racial dispossessions; and the increasing intensities of storms, droughts, and lethal waves of heat and cold fraying already-stressed forms of community care and survival, we felt a real urgency in this moment to learn how Cowen and Khalili might together disentangle the snarled conduits shaping these vulnerabilities.

On December 19, 2022, and thanks to the transnational space-time (zone) compressions offered by Zoom's infrastructure, the issue's three editors were able to bring Cowen and Khalili together for what resulted in a remarkably substantive and wide-ranging discussion. As is evident in this discussion's easy, collegial tone, the two scholars have long been in conversation with each other and informed by one another's work. We were particularly interested in hearing how both scholars articulate the political stakes of infrastructure, how they map the organizing logics that infrastructures advance and curtail, and how they connect the forms of labor, protest, and "making do" that shape and are shaped by infrastructure's long shadows. That is, we wanted to encourage them to work through these issues together, hoping they would meld their diagnostic clarity about the evolving geopolitical and geo-economic underpinnings of infrastructural power with their shared commitment to highlighting the ways that people organize to build new and better futures.

The conversation—edited slightly for clarity and consistency—is a master class on the kind of capacious mapping of trans-scalar connections that is vital to understanding the complexity of this moment of crisis. At one point, Khalili connects the use of automated vacuum cleaners in people's homes with the financialization of urban real estate markets. Elsewhere, Cowen discusses how Indigenous communities engage in resistance and world-building while living with the legacies of land dispossession and the precarities of new and proposed pipelines. Readers will see that infrastructures can be hostile and destructive—both in their concrete materialities and in the lives that weave through them—and they can be insurgent and liberatory, not infrequently at the same time.

In all of this, one comes away from this conversation thinking anew about the importance of mapping the relations that stitch these contradictions together, and with an appreciation for the challenges these simultaneities—of the local and global political lives of infrastructure—set in place. This richness is perhaps most evident when Cowen and Khalili discuss the possibilities of world-building that moves us away from infrastructures of spatial containment that dispossess and toward infrastructures of freedom. What is also clear in this conversation is that myriad communities are differently (dis)organized by way of their many simultaneous struggles over the terms of survival: struggles over the terms of abolition and decolonization or for adequate housing, food, healthy living spaces, and education. These struggles are inextricable from particular, local, intimate geographies. Imagining what survival might look like, in other words, means imagining it *in a place*.

These ongoing, complex pluralities are what make simple claims about smooth and efficient infrastructure so problematic. As Cowen notes here, we should insist on thinking about infrastructures as mobile and ongoing, as "not impossibly firm or fixed." This spatial and temporal complexity matters if we are trying to set in motion interventions *against* empire, the extractivist state, and the prison industrial complex while simultaneously working to inscribe new infrastructural relations into the world, to build the bridges toward the future we want.

Emily Mitchell-Eaton: *By way of an opening, maybe we'll just start with a broad question: What is infrastructure or infrastructural studies to you right now, and perhaps more crucially, what are its political stakes? How do you define or understand infrastructure in your work presently, and have you found infrastructure useful in bridging the gap between intellectual and political praxis?*

Laleh Khalili: Deb, why don't you go first?

Deborah Cowen: I was hoping you would start us off, Laleh! Actually, one of the main reasons I really wanted to be here was to hear your thoughts [*laughs*], as always.

Khalili: Ok, I'll start! Do you want me to?

Cowen: Yes, please. I'll swim behind you [*laughs*].

Khalili: I don't know about that. I'm swimming behind you, actually. This is like a mutual lovefest. I'm much more of an empiricist when it comes to infrastructures. And although I think there's a lot of really exciting work that's being done on a whole lot of categories of things, people, ideas, etc., as infrastructure, I tend to stick to thinking about infrastructure as those sets of objects which underlie the operations of, nowadays, capital. And so, the objects don't obviously have to be made out of concrete and steel, although the stuff that I've worked on so far has been concrete and steel. But also, those things which virtually facilitate or act as lubricants for things like trade and capitalism. So everything from legal infrastructures, engineering and accounting standards infrastructures, and things like that.

I tend to think of infrastructure as this set of, as I said, objects that can be both concrete and virtual. And the interrelation between them is also constantly evolving, because what's considered to be virtual and what's considered to be concrete are also constantly shifting. For example, we're living in the age of crypto failures, and it is really interesting that crypto is a currency that is completely and totally detached from anything except for massive consumption of energy. And so, in a way, how do you evaluate crypto? I'm more hesitant to call people infrastructures, although I know that there are some really interesting critical approaches to that. But in part, for me, it immediately objectifies people, but also beyond that, I think there's a continuity with "human capital"-type discussions, which I find uncomfortable. But I can see why others would use it, and of course people like AbdouMaliq Simone are using it in particularly interesting ways. But again, as I said, I'm not particularly doctrinaire about who I include in the studies of infrastructure. The other thing is that I don't consider myself to be an infrastructure studies person, in part because I think what I'm interested in are relations of power across borders, and some of that plays through infrastructure, some of that plays through other things. And now I'm going to cede to Deb.

Cowen: Thanks, Laleh. I always appreciate and love what you share. And maybe just as a way of taking a different tack into some of the very same questions, I'll try and think a little bit maybe about the reasons why I think of myself as an "infrastructuralist" and what that brings to analysis and politics and action for me. It certainly centers the everyday for me, these kinds of questions around physical motion and the architectures or systems that support that motion—pipes and rails and cables that you've described in all their materiality. I think that this kind of motion corresponds in really vital and high-stakes ways to the politics that brings us here today, because I also am very much thinking about capitalism and infrastructure, and the role of motion within systems of accumulation or expanded reproduction.

A lot of my work is also thinking specifically about settler colonial capitalism, and in this sense it is really crucial to keep material systems like dams and bridges and railroads at the forefront. But there's another way of thinking about motion that is more about the movement and reproduction and forms of circulation that sustain life itself, intergenerationally. So thinking about the worlding or world-making, thinking about the whole literature on social reproduction and the ways in which motion is necessary and a precondition. But that it's not necessarily always limited to the everyday physical systems and structures that make people, bodies, substances, commodities move.

Lauren Berlant talks about infrastructure as the movement or patterning of social form, and insists that thinking infrastructurally helps us to see things as always in motion, and so not impossible.[1] Not impossibly firm and fixed. Hopefully that is already suggestive politically, as it is for me, because it opens up questions of the *how,* and not just disruption but other forms of motion that are incredibly necessary for not just fighting capitalist infrastructure, for instance, but of also paying attention to and hopefully helping to bolster and sustain radically different forms and systems of motion and reproduction. Thinking about motion in these expansive ways, and not just in terms of what gets where, brings in whole questions of systems and reproduction world-making [of the sort]. So noncapitalist and noncolonial forms of reproduction and motion are also vital all around us, and have their materiality. The discrete, sometimes more local, sometimes immediate or obvious physical infrastructures are vital politically, and they are what connects or links the everyday and the kind of wider forms of movement that constitute life and its others.

Khalili: Can I ask a question about that? Because I'm actually interested in something you just said, which I think is interesting and something that I'm thinking about, because Tim Mitchell was here and gave a talk last week. And obviously every time Tim Mitchell opens his mouth, absolutely just so many different kinds of ideas and configurations of ideas arise. But something you said: you said there are infrastructures that are not capitalist infrastructures. Do you think it is possible to have an outside to that, at this moment in time? An outside to capitalism?

Cowen: I mean, *outside* is a complicated word, right?

Khalili: Mm-hmm.

Cowen: So a lot of my readings and politics and involvements and projects definitely lead me to what I would say are noncapitalist forms of infrastructure, in that the kinds of relations, connections, and futures they're animating are noncapitalist, for sure. For sure. The "outside" . . . I guess I pause for a lot of reasons, but mostly because I don't think anything's entirely disentangled. I don't think there are any fully autonomous forms, and certainly, maybe even more importantly, a lot of the radical anticolonial or Indigenous or noncapitalist forms of infrastructure that I've encountered or been interested in often emerge or are reasserted in the process of refusal of capitalist and colonial forms. So yeah, the separation, I would be a little . . . I would want to think more carefully about, and certainly how that entanglement works is really specific in time and space. But I do. Yes, I do. I do think that those forms exist.

Khalili: Can I jump in again? I really like that, and I think that you're absolutely right. The separation is . . . there's kind of no "outside." But I guess what I'm curious about is what you consider to be . . . so your article with Winona LaDuke, I assign it in every class.[2] I find an excuse to set it in every class, because in everything I teach, it addresses that fundamental question of inequality and injustice but also of infrastructures and power. So what would be a noncapitalist set of infrastructures today for you?

Cowen: I feel like I'm in a comps exam or my own or something. It's great [*laughs*]. But my examiner is someone I adore, so this is great.

Khalili: I'm genuinely like, I really want to talk to you! There's no glass of wine here!

Cowen: [*laughs*] That's what I was going to say! That's what's missing is our liquid infrastructures. To keep things flowing! No, it's a great question, and maybe I'll come back to this question of motion, and not just infrastructure. Because I think what is defining in not just Marx but many, many thinkers of capitalism is that motion is organized. There's a great book by Thomas Nail that I came across last year that I really love on this question. It's called *Marx in Motion*. And Nail says something like, for Marx, capitalism is a regime of motion. Capitalism holds no monopoly over motion. It's a regime of motion, as we know, that is oriented towards expanded reproduction. That is a really, really helpful way of distinguishing or thinking through different kinds of infrastructures, and the kinds of motion they aim to support and sustain and expand. And that doesn't necessarily mean they achieve that. It doesn't mean that other forms of politics and projects aren't operating through them or on them or in refusal to them.

But expanded reproduction—accumulation and extraction—to me are distinguishing, animating principles for different forms of infrastructure. And I think, when I look at empirical cases, that's clear. For instance, I've had the opportunity to learn from nations in the "Ring of Fire," which is a mineral belt in Treaty 9 territory, otherwise known as Northern Ontario. Indigenous communities in this area are subject to immense mining speculation and projects. And it's a remote area, and so in order to access those resources, government and corporations are aggressive and gung ho about building infrastructure, especially roads. Now, the communities in these areas are also very much in need of access. They are remote fly-in communities mostly that have been really dependent on what are called "ice roads," which are only able to operate when the ground is frozen. And because of climate change, that period is shrinking quite dramatically. We have a season that's now weeks instead of many, many months, and it means . . . it's really defining in terms of, can housing get built, for instance. Can resources get brought to the community?

Many of these Ojibwe and Cree communities in Treaty 9 also need access and have been trying to think about roads. But the roads that are being pushed on them for mining purposes have a completely different route, design, and geography; have a completely different process and intention associated with them; and . . . seem to look very, very different as concrete infrastructures—even though both are desires for roads into the very same territory. For the Indigenous nations in this region, the desire for roads is largely about survivance. They're intended to connect communities for bringing in resources, but also access to hospitals, all those things that sustain life. The mining roads are obviously oriented towards something very, very different, which is extraction and accumulation. So, as a starting place, I hope that's something useful.

Khalili: Thanks so much.

Richard Nisa: *Thank you both so much. Your comments made me think a little bit about one of the things that we've been wrestling with: the idea that an infrastructure can be both life-provisioning and life-destroying, and that a political possibility exists to appropriate infrastructures and rearticulate their connections. Deb, the idea you mentioned that there are, in effect, multiple road systems points to this: one road is about the systematic or systemic destruction of a community and its environments, and the other is about motion in a very different context. In terms of* *trying to frame out different political stakes, in thinking about what the political lives of infrastructure might mean, this gets me thinking about how and if one can transform an infrastructure from one of death distribution to one of life distribution and how that might relate to the political and economic questions you were both just discussing. Or, thinking about organizing on the ground, what are the frameworks—or do they exist—for people to appropriate those deadly infrastructures in alternate ways?*

Khalili: Can I jump in? So, the reason I want to jump in is because actually, Deb, I don't think you were here when we first started. I'm sitting in the library of the Energy Institute, which used to be the Petroleum Institute, in Central London, and I'm doing some research on oil. And I've chosen a series of years to go and look at all of the oil journals for those years. And I've discovered this journal that's just amazing, and I was just telling these guys that the 1950s seems to be a moment in which there's decolonization going on, so there's a huge amount of interesting conflict that they're writing about, but at the same time, this is still the imperial moment, and so the journal editors are completely shameless about the sorts of interests that they're serving. And one of the things that actually emerges in part of this writing—and I'm going to go on ahead and talk about roads here—is, there is in one of the pages in a 1951 issue, they're talking about roads as "agents of development." And they specifically mention roads as being central to expanding the "backwards economies," and that's the term they use, the "backwards economies."

        And again, drawing on what Tim Mitchell said last week about development: Mitchell is arguing that the concept of "economy" emerges in the mid-twentieth century, and that "development" is that process by which the countries of the Global North, the colonizers, have an "economy," and they pass it on to the countries of the Global South. So they create an "economy" there as well. So there's this [presence] of development being this thing. So on the one hand, yes, roads are agents of development, which actually means agents of enfolding the whole world into this process of accumulation and extraction. But at the same time, one of the things that I discovered when I was doing my book on the Arabian Peninsula was that Britain, for example, was making so much money based on the oil that was being extracted from under the grounds of the countries in the Middle East, and yet they . . . United Arab Emirates didn't have anything but sixty miles of road, until it became independent from Britain. Sixty miles and that was it, and it actually connected Dubai to Abu Dhabi, and that was it. I mean, it went a little bit further north, but the bit that went further north was because Gamal Abdel Nasser had promised to build it, and so as a competition with Arab nationalists, they decided to build an extra bit that didn't have something to do with oil.

        So to me that is really interesting as well, because on the one hand, this is an object of economy in the way that Mitchell thinks about it, which is an object of folding the United Arab Emirates fully into that extractive, accumulative regime, because obviously they'd just discovered that Abu Dhabi has huge amounts of oil. But at the same time, those life-giving, important infrastructures simply didn't exist. And so there is this kind of an odd way where even in a place like the United Arab Emirates, which is a loyal servant of Britain and then later the United States, and a major producer of oil, which is destroying the world, and [completely and totally] working to undermine for example COP [Conference of the Parties], the anemic global negotiations around climate—even in an instance like that, you find these global inequalities, when it comes to the provision of infrastructure. And I think that that weird paradox is something that I really want to grapple with in my work, because it is the central paradox of pretty much capitalist production. The good things are also some of the things that will kill us. The "good things," you know.

Cowen: Yeah, so much to think about there, Laleh. Thank you. I want to come back to Rich's question: How can capitalist, colonial infrastructures be reappropriated, can they be used differently, can they be made otherwise? But even before that, I think your comments, Laleh, about the Emirates reminds me how important it is to consider vastly different varieties of infrastructure. I'll share another little anecdote to ground this and map it a little bit.

A good friend named Al Hunter is a medicine person in Treaty 3 territory—Rainy River First Nations. His community, between Thunder Bay and Manitoba, is not generally thought of as the center of North American capitalism, or anything else in the mainstream. And in fact, it seems remote or even peripheral to people in the context where I live, in Toronto. Rainy River's community logo is a map of Turtle Island with a Medicine Wheel centered on their territory, making their territory the center of the continent. Al explained to me the importance of rivers in precolonial transportation, and described the forms of trade that brought Indigenous peoples from the southern Americas and the Arctic to this site. He talked about artifacts that are found at the river from across this vast geography that show this. It was a really good geography lesson for someone who spends a lot of time in geography conversations but had never really been given any formal education in Indigenous geographies. Part of what was so interesting about it was not just that you can have a very different center and very different notions of space and periphery, but the scale of movement is enormous. I think there's an assumption that when we think of precapitalist or precolonial infrastructures or trade, that it would be fairly local. But there were these enormous forms of circulation and movement that took shape through other means of movement, which were rivers.

This question of movement is something that many Indigenous scholars are focusing on—cyclical and seasonal rhythms, nomadic lives. Leanne Simpson writes about the disruption of rivers with colonial dams, for instance, and how these dams disrupt whole ways of life that are human but not just human.[3] Michelle Daigle also writes on movement in the context of Indigenous lifeways.[4] Gerald Vizenor's writings on how "transmotion" anchors visionary forms of Indigenous sovereignty are incredibly powerful.[5] So the question of motion to me can be infrastructured in different ways, and while I don't want to just simply call a river "infrastructure," I think again the importance of thinking about motion otherwise to its capitalist and colonial forms . . . does insist that motion itself is not contingent on one particular kind of infrastructuring.

Some of the most inspiring examples for me of the repurposing of infrastructures come from the kind of question that, Rich, you asked at the outset of this exchange. And my mind immediately went to the transcontinental railroads. Just one infrastructure can allow you to think about so many different forms of reuse and repurposing. And here, it is not just disruption but different forms of political lives and world-making that can happen through appropriation or "misuse" of capitalist and colonial infrastructures. My mind immediately went to the Black railway porters who were employed to labor on the transcontinental railroads, first in the United States but then north of the border as well, in Canada. And the conditions of work were horrific and hard to distinguish from indenture. [Sarah-Jane] Mathieu wrote an excellent book about the porters in this northern context and emphasizes the ways in which the railroad allowed for particular kinds of political organizing and mobilization through circulation, so the Black porters or the Pullman porters used the railroads.[6] And not just to make a living but to share knowledge, to transfer culture and ideas, to organize.

That to me is just such an extraordinary example of occupying an infrastructure and doing something very different with it that we see all the time, in small ways or in bigger ways, like the porters. And of course, it wasn't just the porters themselves, but for the work that they and their families, often women in their lives, were involved in doing in communities across North America. Building community infrastructure, radical infrastructure for labor organizing, for community mobilization, for making space within Black communities, is kind of inextricable from the work of the porters. I could give more historical examples, an older example, but maybe I'll stop talking for a few minutes [*laughs*] and maybe we'll end up back there soon.

Mitchell-Eaton: *I think that's actually a perfect segue to a different question that we have. Deb, I'm really enjoying your example about the Black porters, thinking about your writing on labor and infrastructure, and also thinking back to Laleh's point about whether humans . . . How did you put it? Are people infrastructure? . . . is definitely something that we're continuing to grapple with. In the United States, we are also just coming out of a narrowly averted, but likely still building, railroad workers' strike, as of a couple weeks ago. And much of what was centered in the demands of the striking workers was articulated around questions of sick* *leave, in the context of the COVID-19 pandemic, but obviously concerns that pre-ceded the pandemic and that will continue. We'd like to ask you to speak to, then, how your own thinking around labor, protest, and unrest has shifted in the last cou-ple of years, during the pandemic. Generally, we're interested in how you see inter-sections between political lives and the lives of infrastructure morphing in these dif-ferent social and activist constellations in the present. We have a different question about social reproduction, but I'll leave that to the end, perhaps. Since you've both written about these labor circulations, and Deb, your work on essential workers speaks to some of these concerns, I'll stop there and turn it over to either one of you.*

Cowen: It's a great question, Emily. The pause is just because I always want to hear Laleh's thoughts [*laughs*]. I'll say something really brief, which is that I'm with Laleh on the question of people as infrastructure. I was suggesting earlier that Berlant's thinking around movement, the patterning of movement in relation, and connectiv-ity that's collective and assembled, to me that is where people can be part of infra-structure. Infrastructure is practiced, relational, and can certainly organize affect. Ruthie Gilmore offers a brilliant addition to [Raymond Williams's] "structures of feeling" when she introduces "infrastructures of feeling."[7] And labor is no doubt critical to the assemblage and maintenance of infrastructure. But I don't see people themselves as infrastructure.

Reflecting on what the pandemic changed in my thinking, what's pro-nounced for me is not that I think differently about infrastructure and labor, but that more people are thinking about infrastructure and labor in this context, and there's a lot more outright political struggle. The imagined technocratic nature of infrastructures as they support, especially, supply chains has been more easily chal-lenged as so many lives are contingent on how those infrastructures are organized, and the labor especially. The question of safety in a sector that is so premised on speed and accumulation and extraction has been the source of high-stakes struggle, insofar as we're talking about supply-chain infrastructure struggles that are particu-larly related to COVID-19. I mean, there's been so many forms of struggle over the last few years that are filled with that. Of course, the Amazon labor union has been one of the most visible in this part of the world, but there's so many versions of this and forms of contestation over the "how" of movement and containment. This, of course, in a context of lockdown was so extreme and so baffling in terms of how quickly life changed in some ways for so many people, and in some ways didn't change very much. I mean, I think for those who are in the most precarious forms of supply-chain labor, we saw that they weren't the ones who could stay home and stay safe, or anything of the sort. They were the ones on the very front lines. And there was that very brief moment where there was all this sort of . . . the loving vision of essential workers, but it really didn't extend very fast or far. And so those struggles continue to be incredibly vibrant and powerful, but also high stakes, and the, kind of, the visibility of them has not necessarily translated into the dramatic social change I think so many people were so hopeful for in the early pandemic days.

Khalili: Yeah. Yeah, it's interesting, because I think there's certain things . . . um . . . the pandemic kind of, on the one hand, showed who was being exploited, right? Like the supply-chain worker. Your Amazon delivery guy, your Deliveroo delivery guy, your nurses, obviously, who were working in hospitals, the train drivers who actually continued to work. And in some ways I think it's been really interesting, because the strikes that are going on in the UK right now—so the rail workers' strikes, the postal workers' strikes, and the nurses' strike, and actually there's also an Amazon warehouse strike that was just organized here in the UK—they all seem to be directly emerging as a result of the pandemic, because I think that . . . there's some really amazing spokespersons for these strikes, and Mick Lynch, one of them, actually talks extensively about the fact that when you needed us, we were there, but what about us now? And so there is a particular way that I think that those kinds of logistical workers, the importance of them, and the people that made the infrastructures work—the centrality of them was made clear by the— and Deb has written about this—by COVID.

When the pandemic happened, I kind of vaguely remember there were two kinds of big predictions. Everything has changed, and nothing has changed. But for me, only some things have changed. For us in the UK, it was really interesting that a Tory government opened the spigots of money, and there was so much money for people to go on furloughs and to support businesses and whatever. So in a way, it became clear that there is in fact a "money tree," which is often used as a rhetorical device in order to stifle demands for better wages or better working conditions. That turned out to be completely untrue. It was proven to be untrue. But I think something else also happened, which I think is quite interesting, and I don't know where it's going, but the idea of work changed. And you have the essential workers, who have to be outside, who have to move from one place to another, who have to do the kinds of things in order to keep the machinery of the economy, but also the machinery of the society, working. But on the other hand, you also had a lot of people who began to realize that the kind of work that you could do didn't need to happen with the same kinds of strictures. You don't have to appear in an office, you don't have to be surveilled, you don't have to be monitored, etc., etc., etc. And to me that was interesting because I think in a way it also . . . particularly in the UK . . . it changed the idea that there's sort of American-import bootstrap-ism, which is that you have to work sixteen hours a day in order for you to actually be doing anything worthwhile. I think some of that changed, and I think that has been interesting. The nature of work, the questions over the nature of work, have been really interesting. And part of the reason that they're particularly interesting is because it has become clear that the people who work with the infrastructures are considered to be essential workers in the way that some of us who don't work with the infrastructures are proven to be perhaps nonessential. The work that we do, what does it do? And I find that . . . as I said, I am not completely and entirely clear on what the implications of this are in the long term, but I do think that this has changed. This is the first thing.

The second thing that has been really interesting to me is watching what kind of mistreatments the world's seafarers were subjected to over the course of the pandemic, as obviously borders were shut. They couldn't get off the ships. Many of them were really, really ill, particularly on cruise ships, and they . . . they couldn't even in some places, they couldn't even get off the ship in order to get medical care. And so in some ways, the horror of that, the horror of . . . I mean, this is . . . it's like a . . . it is like a terrible kind of a dark myth of people just wandering on the sea, unable to come ashore . . . made clear also the extent to which the state is so central to this. Because at that point, corporations, shipping companies, unions, everybody, was saying please, please, let the seafarers in, and the states were saying no. And so the border regime ends up being this mode of attenuating movement. . . . This is Charmaine Chua's argument, which is that the border regimes not only facilitate but also attenuate movement in service of disciplining of labor.[8] And the attenuation that the border regime does enact ends up being so incredibly visible over the course of the pandemic. And I think the fact that the state was so central in so many different ways to defining what workers could be furloughed, to defining who had to continue working, to defining the parameters of who got to leave—to leave their homes but also to leave the borders—all of these things definitely made it clear that the state is, whether or not we like it, still this incredibly powerful actor that functions in really interesting and contradictory ways. Obviously to facilitate accumulation of capital even under conditions of extreme global distress, like in the pandemic, but also in ways that actually allows for the reproduction of the workforces for these places in ways that is contradictory. The reproduction allows for the reproduction of capital, but it also allows for the society to survive through what is horrendous devastation.

So essentially what I'm saying is that there's a lot of contradictory stuff, and I can't find my way really through it except to say that the state is much more visible than it was before, and the nature of work has really come under question in all sorts of ways. And my sense of that is also reinforced by my students, that since the end of COVID, I find their demands for recognition of the distresses and stresses they're under is much more vocal than it was before. So the work that they do is also now under question.

Cowen: So much there, Laleh, and thank you so much for really centering questions of the border. I mean, migrant work and migrant workers over the last few years and during lockdown—selective lockdown, right, because we still had farm workers coming and living in horrendous conditions and often dying here, in the

Canadian context—and the whole question of the state in that border regime, and the baffling multiscaled lockdowns that have taken place over the last few years are incredibly sobering. And I think some of the most important cases like you were saying, the seafarers, and migrant workers more widely, workers who move to work, as you said, there's a visibility to the fact that precarious and migrant workers have . . . they're essential work allowing society to survive. But the other side of that has been, what about the survival of those peoples? And I think the question of disposability has been so clear. When we think about bus drivers in upstate New York who died from pandemic exposure, who were mostly Black folks. And so we can see sometimes the incredible disposability that comes with what gets called essential work. And it's interesting, because the connection that you're drawing to some very . . . if not hopeful, then at least interesting potentials, with some of what's also very tied to that: the kind of unwillingness or refusal to take on certain kinds of work or to accept the reproduction of a way of life that's premised on that disposability can also come out of a context or condition of being made surplus. The education sector is a really interesting one for that, right?

And so many fields where people don't have meaningful work or don't have adequate work, or where those temporary forms of provisioning that at least some states did during the pandemic, when the economy was shut down, put into question . . . the hyperexploitation of their everyday. Surplus is full of potential for resistance. But the other thing that's very, very heavy on my mind these days is the ways in which the supposed health rationales for automation and the convenience of automation during the pandemic—the contactless—has persisted and intensified in just a few years. Of course, automation is not new. In our sector, the online teaching and the online everything . . . there's so many ways in which that has so rapidly transformed our practice. You can go an entire day and never interact with someone working, a human being working, right? It's all tap-tap-tap, tapping machines and self-checkout and all this. And that obviously has severe and complex repercussions for labor. This makes me a little bit more pessimistic. I don't want to downplay all the organizing and movement that you've described, because it's so important, and I really don't like thinking about events as successes or failures. But there's these ongoing afterlives. And so I do want to hold on to some of the radical potential that comes from the traumas, the losses, but also the incredible solidarities that have defined the last few years, and I think mutual aid at many scales can be part of that. But it also seems to me the rapid reterritorialization of extreme forms of hyperexploitation and inequality has just . . . is just very, very real as well.

Khalili: No, I think you're absolutely right about that. I mean, I think the way that . . . you know, certain things became very clear. That public investment, for example, in a vaccine could bring about a vaccine. But at the same time, it made it very clear that in parts of the world, no matter what they do, they can't have access to that vaccine. Things like intellectual property regimes were thrust forward. It became clear that you didn't need to be in a hyperexploited shared cubicle office. That you could work from home in a lot of different professions, and it could be fine. And then here at least we had all of these kinds of commercial property owners talking about the laziness of folks [because they wanted people to return to their office]. We had also, some of the other things, like the tap-tap-tap that you're talking about; it's actually one of the things that has been a kind of horrific outcome of this, has been that people don't carry cash. Homeless people can't ask for change. I mean, this has been one of the weirdest—we have a couple of people that are unhoused in my neighborhood, and we know them . . . we talk to them all the time—and that has been one of the most horrific outcomes of COVID. But at the same time, in the first few months of COVID, at least in this country, really good housing was suddenly found for the unhoused. So it's this really strange thing where it seems like we can . . . we are able to address these incredibly difficult circumstances, but people choose not to. And if . . . and they try to very quickly recuperate, as you say. Reterritorialize that system of hyperexploitation as it was before. But I do wonder about to what extent it might not be obviously . . . it may not be completely and totally obvious just yet. But the fact that, for example, in China people are protesting because they feel that without a set of social supports, a zero-COVID policy is essentially a form of disposability, is the extremely relevant term that you're using, is a form of instantiation of disposability . . . also to me tells me that there are echoes and afterlives to the, whatever, the two years of COVID global pandemic that I think is . . . we don't know yet what those afterlives are going to be. And it could go either way. I tend to be much more pessimistic than I am optimistic, but on the other hand, hope is a discipline, as Mariame Kaba says.[9]

Cowen: Absolutely. And I think it can go either way and it's going many ways [*laughs*], right? And the kinds of incredibly divided political communities at every scale are a sign of that. I mean, one thing that I wanted to mention because it was on my mind just over the last few days, in this context of thinking about labor and some of the more. . . I guess . . . the ways in which COVID and the last few years of many forms of colliding crises have changed not just conditions but subjectivities in ways that have complex articulations, some of which are exciting, around refusal and prioritizing life, prioritizing care, over various forms of either careerism or accumulation or just productivism, and that is genuinely exciting. But on the other hand, I am also seeing, especially, more precarious colleagues—contract faculty, pre-tenure folks, who are disproportionately women and people of color—who get COVID and work through it because they can teach online. The option people see, because of the pressures, the real fear of losing your wage, is often continuing online. But the idea of actually healing yourself? In terms of . . . health care, the body, and our capacities to think of ourselves as outside of just the workplace? The other thing I want to put on the table, that I think you've already pushed at, Laleh, but I don't think we've gone there explicitly or with adequate complexity: when you were talking about different forms of infrastructure and connectivity I always am thinking centrally about not just forms that connect us but the carceral forms. And I think with the border you also brought us to that important place. Carcerality in the context of the last few years has also been incredibly powerful, the emboldening of police forces, or carceral politics more broadly, and in the context of lockdowns the racialized policing of public spaces. . . . All of this, it's really critical for us to remember that those are also infrastructures. And forms of labor.

Wesley Attewell: *It's interesting that both Deb and Laleh are emphasizing, in different ways, how the home, over the course of the pandemic, has really become the site of work. And because we now work in the house, our homes have gradually become sites of logistical intervention that enable very particular forms of consumption and commodity circulation. This becomes significant when we think about Laleh's story about the migrant seafarers who get shut out by border regimes. I'm now living and working in Hong Kong, where . . . care work is fundamentally structured around the exploitation of migrant indentured labor. Domestic workers have, in all sorts of eye-opening ways, become so central to ensuring the proper functioning and expanded reproduction of the city's economy. A couple of weeks ago, I was teaching a class on how, at the very beginning of the COVID-19 pandemic, the city government asked employers to rescind the Sunday day off for domestic workers as a way of stopping the spread of the virus. This wasn't a legal command or anything like that, but it still meant that many employers took it upon themselves to lock their own helpers out of their homes. The net effect here is to expose how the home, at least for many Hong Kongers, became not only a site of (precarious) labor, but also an elastic site of border control, a space of bordering if you will. So I'm curious to go back to this question of social reproduction and work and infrastructure that Deb raised a little while back. I'd love to hear both of you speak on the political importance of these everyday struggles to survive, and their relationship to longer-standing and maybe more organized infrastructures of mutual aid and care. How might the everyday work of "making do," as Thuy Linh Tu puts it, serve as an infrastructural foundation or scaffolding for radical politics moving forward?[10]*

Cowen: There are so many directions to go with that. I think maybe even just starting with the question of home itself, right? Which, if there was ever such a condensation of extreme inequality, it was through the question of home during lockdown, right? On the one hand, we've had some amazing work done by geographers in our local context mapping evictions in the city and over the last few years and during the pandemic, and the skyrocketing evictions that are tied to the financialization of rental housing, for instance. And that's for homes that are already inadequate, that are already overcrowded, that have massive infrastructural failure in terms of heating and mold growth and such. So this housing is completely inadequate to begin with, and during the pandemic these were homes where you had many family members working in different "essential" sectors, so those homes were also very tied to overexposure and high risk of infection. But they remain so insecure. And some of the ways in which the shift from regular landlord-tenant hearings to online adjudication of these disputes, which are already stacked in favor of large corporate landlords. So we have these extreme inequalities just in thinking about lockdown and the home. Because on the other extreme, we have those who could stay home and order in, and had space, not just one home, but multiple homes, and homes with lots of private outdoor space.

So the home is already so fraught before COVID but becomes incredibly intensified in the last few years. And of course the question of work in the home has such a long, long history. Waged work and unwaged work that happens in domestic space or the private space of the home. There's already such an important politics around that, and I think, Wes, you've pointed to that in thinking about migrant domestic workers who are also caught up in the politics of bordering in many scales and many locations. So the home is a really vital way for us to think about these questions, and maybe the last thing I'll say before I pass it to Laleh regards the articulation of automation with these questions. As many of you probably know better than me, for the whole question of logistics and supply chain, the home had long been a "black box." The home was the "last mile," where not as much data was available, and that's why we've seen so much emphasis on surveillance and data collection of the larger logistical companies like the Amazons. But the ways in which the mass experiment with lockdown has led to a real extension of that, the logistics in and of the home, in a much more everyday way, I think is really incredible. I'm tempted to go to questions of social reproduction, but I think I'll pause there and see where Laleh takes us.

Khalili: So yeah, the question of the home is really interesting, in particular because Amazon has acquired Roomba, you know, those little automated vacuum cleaners. And so Amazon will have all of the data that it needs about your household layout. Because those things are essentially taking information down. Alexa is collecting everything that you have in your house. I mean, they're recording everything. The Ring is surveilling who comes to your door. Amazon is going to have all sorts of data on us, and from what I understand, they're also entering the health care sector, because of course that is a multi-trillion-dollar industry in the world, and a trough at which they would like to feed. One of the things that has been interesting, though, in the UK has been the extent to which the mechanisms for the processes of intensification of kind of landlord politics has partially been because of people shifting to work at home. So we've had a couple of sets of movements happening, particularly around London, which is that as commercial properties have become less profitable—for example, my husband's corporation has given up one of their big buildings, because not many people come in anymore—and what the effect of that has been, is a lot of investment in property has gone, has shifted from commercial property to residential properties. And then the residential properties are often being used as investment vehicles, often for people who have offshore corporations, which buy the houses, rather than anybody actually buying the place and living in it. So that intensification of commercialization of residential property in this country has had a perverse but completely and totally expected effect of essentially giving landlords whatever the hell they want, and so you're finding that prices are going up in all sorts of ways, and it's becoming more and more difficult for people to find an affordable place to live. It comes with all sorts of issues.

And again, Deb points to the ways in which this actually affects people in a very uneven sort of way. We've had the first kid who has died of mold spores in their terribly inadequate council housing, and of course it's a working-class Black kid, or a Black kid from a working-class family. And so these particular kinds of devastations that emerge out of this are also very unevenly distributed, and the same categories of people that are—from whom their labor is extracted, whose survival is subject to a lot more vulnerability, are the ones who are also being affected by this. A second effect, and this has been quite interesting, has been also a shift in the UK from London to other places. People suddenly decided they wanted to move to the country, because they wanted green space, etc., etc. But an effect of that in a country in which the rail services are absolutely and totally failing—it has nothing to do with the strikes, it has to do with the fact that there's no investment in the public-transport infrastructures—the effect of that is this kind of a situation where you have a lot of people moving elsewhere and then not having access to rail and therefore buying cars. And so one of the effects of this is also the intensification of road usage, pollution, congestion, and of course accidents that are concomitant with that. So there's all sorts of really quite problematic effects that are emerging out of COVID infrastructurally, and I suppose the most intimate areas, the notion of the home, is where you can see those effects really quite radically. I think I'm going to let Deb talk about social reproduction because I think she's way more eloquent on that than I could ever be, so I'm going to go ahead and cede to you, Deb.

Cowen: I disagree [*laughs*]. Rich or others, do you want to . . . can you sort of re-prompt us?

Nisa: *Sure. In terms of a re-prompt or maybe a closing question . . . It seems that a lot of the conversation today—from Laleh's point about the cashless economy's impact on connection in public space to Wes's observations about the home as a domain of larger-scale politics—touches on questions of scale and intimacy. Deb,* *you've written about the spaces of "intimate imperialism" and similarly the kind of crazy connections that you've both brought up today, there's a negotiation between the lived experiences of people and these humongous circulatory structures of power and accumulation, distribution, and so on. The issue of social reproduction is another question about the intimate scales of daily life or everyday life, as you were saying, Deb, and these broader forms of extraction or broader forms of accumulation. I don't know if this is a closing prompt to ask you to sum up two hours of conversation or if I'm just reframing what Wes has already asked—but if you could speak to that relationship between those intimate, bodily, personal, familiar even, scales of life . . . from the Roomba, from the fraught terrain of tidiness and domesticity all the way to the financialization of urban real estate . . . these connections across truly massive scales. They offer both an opportunity to think about infrastructure, to think infrastructurally, but also a chance to explore some of the perils underpinning the ways that our daily lives have been so exposed to these penetrations of capital, of surveillance, of carceral logics. So I don't know if I've added any clarity, Deb [laughs] . . .*

Cowen: Thanks, Rich, no, it was very rich . . . Rich [*laughs*]. I appreciate it. I was also keen to hear your voices, as much as I love the back and forth with Laleh. The questions are incredibly rich and the places that you're all thinking with are also really vital to hear about. I mean, social reproduction is in some ways such an old conversation and such an important one, but also one that I think is really important here. First and foremost, remembering that social reproduction isn't necessarily radical, right? Social reproduction is the reproduction of relations that can be centrally capitalist or colonial or both, right? Simultaneously. And so for me in some ways it's helpful in the context of thinking about infrastructure, because it points us to thinking about the "how" questions of a formation, down to a household, or even a singular body, continuing, reproducing at many scales itself.

So what are the conditions? And for me, that's material in the very expansive sense of the term, but it's a profoundly material question about everything from the water we're drinking, the heat that's keeping us warm, the internet connection that's allowing me to talk to you all . . . but those are also always, they're not just raw materiality, right? They take shapes and forms that are also tremendously affective and intimate, and the relations through which those things are provisioned or not are themselves sustaining or not. Social reproduction brings us to that materiality, but it also points us to a couple really key things for me. One is the question where we started earlier: Are there forms of infrastructure that are not capitalist or colonial? I think the question of social reproduction allows us to think that through. It allows us to think through what forms of life are being reproduced and how. And it reminds us that there are actually so many forms of reproduction that are possible, that exist, even if they're struggling to maintain space or time. And so the question of otherwise or alternative for me is anchored meaningfully and helpfully. It's in some ways very simple to me to ground a lot of these questions in ones of social reproduction because it immediately points to this: Are we just fighting for more or faster or slower or the same, or are we really talking about dramatically or radically different everyday lives? The relationship between questions of social reproduction and infrastructure, what kinds of worlds are we building or what kinds of worlds we are fighting for, in all their materiality, are helpfully illuminated through this way of thinking.

Khalili: I taught a module this year for the first time called Revolutions, and I got my students to read C. L. R. James's *Black Jacobins* in the first five weeks of the module. They're in the politics department, so they're uninterested often in older histories. But there was something about the book, and about the way in which it brought so much to the front, that the students were really engaged and came with all sorts of interesting things to say, and every session of seminars they had to talk about their favorite bit of what they'd just read, so some picked incredibly powerful political stuff. Some compared the circumstances to today's Tory government. Some chose passages because they were just utterly beautifully written. Some chose passages because they were really affecting or moving. And one of the things that was really interesting to me was that in one of the sessions, one of the students said, "I can't believe that we are not out on the streets." And I added, "With guillotines." It is entirely true. We're living in a time where I would have expected some way of completely and totally shifting the ground of where we are, because things are so bad everywhere, and yet, as Deb points out, the system socially reproduces itself. And it does so through a whole series of mechanisms of power. Race and gender, insistence on particular forms of gendering—or actually, in this country, no gender; they want sex, biological sex bullshit—and those kinds of systems, they're trying to reproduce an incredibly conservative, incredibly exploitative, incredibly hierarchical, incredibly unequal system. And so really, maybe the only way to not allow that form of social reproduction to happen is to demand for the guillotines to be out in the streets, like my students in the Revolutions class wanted.
[*pause*]

Khalili: It's not very reproductive.

Mitchell-Eaton: *I think that's how we call it! I think that's our finish.*
[*laughter*]

Nisa: *Do we just end it with that, and an ellipsis?*

Khalili: With guillotines?
[*laughter*]

Khalili: With like a little guillotine icon at the end of the article.

Cowen: Oh my goodness, I don't know about ending with guillotines. [*laughter*]

Khalili: No, it's a bit violent, but you know, one of the things that was really also interesting for the students to read *Black Jacobins* was that . . . I think that they have become accustomed to thinking that change will only appear through small motions or through peaceful agreement or through liberal means, and I think what was really powerful to them was that what they're looking at are titanic global transformations that emerge, whether or not you want them to, because of violence. And the violence is not necessary, but it is there, and so I think for them to understand the centrality of that was the thing that they really took away from the book. Because James, although he celebrates the incredible violence of the revolutionaries, is completely and totally open about how it's actually completely and totally destructive. So . . .

Cowen: Not to risk opening us up again, maybe for a last little blip, because it's hard to say goodbye . . . but it's not the violence necessarily that I don't want to end with. I think violence, what we're calling "violence," is a necessary part of social transformation that entails power and domination in its contestation. What I don't want to do is end without a sense of the possibilities and imperatives to world-building rather than just world-destroying or world-disrupting. And I guess I'm thinking very much . . . and not to say that you could ever say that about James, but just the image of the guillotine itself. Which can be an opening, certainly. But maybe I just want to put a little bit more weight there. I'm thinking about the work that Winona LaDuke is so deeply involved in, that kind of work that inspired our writing together, and thinking about these otherwise forms of infrastructure.[11] If we're talking about revolution and radical transformation, we're really insistent that part of what centering infrastructure does for us is push us to think in very, very expansive but also practical terms about how we live. Just saying "how we live" makes me need to cite the work of the Guyanese feminist Andaiye that Alissa Trotz has written about, and written with her about.[12] One of the central questions Andaiye asks is "how will we organize to live?" So when I go spend time with Winona on the White Earth Reservation, there is an extraordinary practicality. An extraordinary labor and an extraordinary care that comes with these sometimes mundane practices of feeding, or housing, of moving together. And given that this is not a community or an applied project we're sitting talking together about, but we're talking as and for an audience of people who largely spend most of their time thinking, I don't want to allow that separation. I think there was a question somewhere about intellectual practice or other kinds of praxis, and of course they have their relative autonomy [*laughs*], but the work that comes from making and building and organizing is not just work that needs to be done because it's important because we need to eat and drink, but to me it's the most instructive work.

I want to return to the importance of the learning that comes from infrastructure, for all the very expansive ways that we can talk about infrastructure, and that scholars like Lauren Berlant[13] offer us, of not necessarily only thinking about it in terms of, like, for instance, pipes and roads and cables, but also thinking about literature, movement building, film, poetry, as a way of organizing collective motion of organizing how we move together. . . . I think that there is a reason and a value in the kind of material form that becomes a kind of metonym for understanding infrastructure in these wider ways. There is so much to be learned through infrastructure's assembly, its defense, its disruption and occupation, and its removal. So maybe I'll just . . . maybe leave us there. From the guillotine [*laughs*].

Deborah Cowen teaches in the Department of Geography and Planning at the University of Toronto. Their work is concerned with the intimate life of war in ostensibly civilian spaces, the logistics of supply chain and racial capitalism, and the contested geographies of settler colonial infrastructure. Author of *The Deadly Life of Logistics: Mapping Violence in Global Trade* (2014) and *Military Workfare: The Soldier and Social Citizenship in Canada* (2008), Deborah also coedited *War, Citizenship, Territory* (with Emily Gilbert, 2008) and *Digital Life in the Global City: Contesting Infrastructures* (with Alexis Mitchell, Emily Paradis, and Brett Story, 2008) and, with Katherine McKittrick and Simone Browne, coedits the Duke University Press book series Errantries.

Laleh Khalili is Al-Qasimi Professor of Gulf Studies at Exeter University and author of *Heroes and Martyrs of Palestine: The Politics of National Commemoration* (2007), *Time in the Shadows: Confinement in Counterinsurgencies* (2013), and *Sinews of War and Trade: Shipping and Capitalism in the Arabian Peninsula* (2020). She is currently working on a project on the entanglements of oil in every aspect of modern life.

Notes

1.   Berlant, "The Commons," 393.
2.   LaDuke and Cowen, "Beyond Wiindigo Infrastructure."
3.   Simpson, *Dancing on Our Turtle's Back*.
4.   Daigle, "Resurging through Kishiichiwan."
5.   See, e.g., Vizenor, "The Unmissable."
6.   Mathieu, *North of the Color Line*.
7.   Gilmore, "Abolition Geography and the Problem of Innocence"; Williams, *Marxism and Literature*.
8.   Chua, "Circulation Revisited."
9.   Kaba, *We Do This 'til We Free Us*.
10. Tu, *Experiments in Skin*.
11. See LaDuke and Cowen, "Beyond Wiindigo Infrastructure."
12. Trotz, "Red Thread."
13. Berlant, "The Commons."

References

Berlant, Lauren. "The Commons: Infrastructures for Troubling Times°." *Environment and Planning D: Society and Space* 34, no. 3 (2016): 393–419.

Chua, Charmaine. "Circulation Revisited: A Forum on the Actuality of the Concept." *Zeitschrift für Medienwissenschaft*, no. 23 (2020). https://zfmedienwissenschaft.de/online/circulation-revisited-charmaine.

Daigle, Michelle. "Resurging through Kishiichiwan: The Spatial Politics of Indigenous Water Relations." *Decolonization: Indigeneity, Education, and Society* 7, no. 1 (2018): 159–72.

Gilmore, Ruth Wilson. "Abolition Geography and the Problem of Innocence." In *Futures of Black Radicalism*, edited by Gaye Theresa Johnson and Alex Lubin, 225–40. New York: Verso, 2017.

James, C. L. R. *The Black Jacobins: Toussaint L'Ouverture and the San Domingo Revolution*. 2nd ed. New York: Vintage, 1989.

Kaba, Mariame. *We Do This 'til We Free Us: Abolitionist Organizing and Transforming Justice*. Edited by Tamara K. Nopper. Chicago: Haymarket Books, 2021.

LaDuke, Winona, and Deborah Cowen. "Beyond Wiindigo Infrastructure." *South Atlantic Quarterly* 119, no. 2 (2020): 243–68.

Mathieu, Sarah-Jane. *North of the Color Line: Migration and Black Resistance in Canada, 1870–1955*. Chapel Hill: University of North Carolina Press, 2010.

Nail, Thomas. *Marx in Motion: A New Materialist Marxism*. New York: Oxford University Press, 2020.

Simpson, Leanne Betasamosake. *Dancing on Our Turtle's Back*. Winnipeg: ARP Books, 2011.

Trotz, Alissa, ed. *The Point Is to Change the World: Selected Writings of Andaiye*. London: Pluto, 2020.

Tu, Thuy Linh Nguyen. *Experiments in Skin: Race and Beauty in the Shadows of Vietnam*. Durham, NC: Duke University Press, 2021.

Vizenor, Gerald. "The Unmissable: Transmotion in Native Stories and Literature." *Transmotion* 1, no. 1 (2015): 63–75.

Williams, Raymond. *Marxism and Literature*. Oxford: Oxford Paperbacks, 1977.

"There Are Lives Here"

The African and African American Cemeteries
of the Bonnet Carré Spillway

Robin McDowell

It is late April 1975. Workers for the United States Army Corps of Engineers (USACE) stand in a muddy floodplain in St. Charles Parish, about thirty miles upstream from New Orleans along the Mississippi River. They are establishing drainage ditches in a nearly six-square-mile floodplain controlled by a mile-long wood and concrete weir. The entire structure, known as the Bonnet Carré Spillway, functions as a safety valve between the Mississippi River and Lake Pontchartrain. Spillways are a common form of flood control infrastructure that serve as outlets for excess water. The imposing concrete and metal structure looks like a low railroad trestle. Seven thousand vertical pieces of wood form a gate beneath the concrete, separating the Mississippi River from miles of open floodplain. Levees frame the sides of the spillway all the way to the lake, creating a giant earthen catch basin (see fig. 1).

When the river approaches flood stage, cranes remove the wooden pins and release river water into the basin.[1] This diversion of water out of the river's main channel lowers the water level downstream. The structure is hailed as a feat of engineering that "saves" New Orleans from flooding. This was the seventh time the spillway had been opened since its unveiling in 1935.[2]

The workers use backhoes and other equipment to open troughs through clay and sandy river silt to disperse standing water. But on this day, standard procedure

Radical History Review
Issue 147 (October 2023) DOI 10.1215/01636545-10637147
© 2023 by MARHO: The Radical Historians' Organization, Inc.

Figure 1. The Bonnet Carré Spillway looking east from Montz, Louisiana, with Shell refinery
in background, July 2014. Photo by author.

suddenly halts. In the northwest corner of the floodplain, a thick slab of wood, barely
visible, rises out of the silt. It is a coffin with human bones. This was the skeleton of
an enslaved person who toiled on one of several nineteenth-century sugar plantations buried underneath the sediment.

      The coffin held the last mortal remains of one of an estimated three hundred
enslaved and formerly enslaved African and African American people amid otherwise faceless territory, from Delhommer, Roseland, Hermitage, and Trepagnier
Plantations; Union soldiers in the Corps d'Afrique, and other free persons of color
interred in two cemeteries beneath the spillway.[3] Subsequent government-
classified archaeological studies determined that they were estimated to be in use
from 1820 up until the construction of the spillway began.

      These cemeteries are sites of ecological and racial conflict between flood
control and commemoration of Black history. On the surface, these histories appear
disconnected because the language of flood control and risk management allows the
project to conceal the ongoing political project of displacement and erasure of Black
life. By telling the history of both the spillway structure and that of enslaved and
formerly enslaved communities, I argue that a growing movement for commemoration of these cemeteries has the power to challenge and dismantle the political infrastructure generated by and for the preservation of physical infrastructure. This
movement is quieter than bulldozers and concrete mixers yet just as powerful.

Though the work of engineers has destroyed flesh and bone, the dearly departed also create community that is strengthened and continuously nourished by inter-generational Black kinship networks. These networks are steeped in centuries of shared struggle that, once exposed, extend culpability for current injustices back through those centuries to include sugar planters, traders of enslaved people, engineers, military leaders, and authorities and politicians on multiple levels of federal, state, and local government. Movements for commemoration are not quelled by home buyouts, public relations narratives, or empty promises in press releases. Enslaved labor was the power that made technocratic vocabulary possible.

My analysis of the ecological and racial conflict presented by the African and African American cemeteries of the Bonnet Carré Spillway proceeds chronologically. First, I provide the nineteenth-century historical context for Mississippi River flood control infrastructure, of which the Bonnet Carré Spillway is one part, and its dependence on an enslaved and formerly enslaved workforce. Second, I highlight details of the funerary culture of the people who lived, loved, worked, and buried their dead beneath the spillway area before and after emancipation. Third, I introduce a series of archaeological investigations triggered by the 1975 emergence of the bones and the USACE's subsequent attempts to trivialize the findings, despite an increasingly active community of descendants. Finally, I document key moments in the descendants' movement for commemoration that began in earnest in 1995 and continues to the present.

Disciplining the River, Disciplining Bodies

One can take a forty-minute drive out of metropolitan New Orleans down River Road, a historic byway that runs along the Mississippi River from New Orleans to Cairo, Illinois, and see the spillway for themselves. Manicured plantation homes framed by giant oak trees line the road, mere feet from petrochemical refineries and oceangoing tankers. Just beyond and often sandwiched in between, there are modest wooden houses, mobile homes, and churches. St. Charles Parish is in the heart of "Cancer Alley," a corridor that runs along the Mississippi River between New Orleans and Baton Rouge.[4] Throughout much of the eighteenth and nineteenth centuries, this region was home to the largest sugar plantations in the Americas outside of the Caribbean. Today, the same land on either side of the river is riddled with natural gas pipelines, oil refineries, plastic manufacturing plants, and shipping terminals that pollute the air, water, soil, and bodies of the many Black communities descended from enslaved people who had worked the land for generations before them.

Just before this dystopian road trip ends and the land dips down into the spillway basin, there is a USACE office. A retired or inactive service member welcomes the occasional guest and offers to play a video about the history of the spillway. The video begins with the Great Mississippi River Flood of 1927. About 27,000 square miles of land were flooded and 700,000 people displaced. This event spurred "a new strategy for fighting floods": spillways. The film continues by describing the engineering process and extolling the successes of the "remarkably efficient successful flood control structure."[5] Before signing off with a montage of brass bands, the narrator concludes that "the spillway's distinctive combination of utility and beauty shows us that it's possible to intervene in nature without damaging its character"[6]

This particular stretch of land—the site of this intervention—played a pivotal role in the story of flood control infrastructure of the entire Mississippi River. The spillway's location is very strategic. First, its position at the end of the entire length of the Mississippi River proactively protects the city and global shipping port of New Orleans. Second, its placement in proximity to nineteenth-century sugar plantation operations now protects the oil refineries on either side of the spillway.

Accordingly, describing the spillway as infrastructure may seem obvious. The term is most legible as physical armature in the landscape—a skeleton of human progress. It is "a material artifact constructed by people, with physical properties and pragmatic properties in its effects on human organization," or "something that other things 'run on,' things that are substrate to events and movements."[7]

While the spillway is infrastructure in this sense, it is also a site of racist use and abuse of people and land, made visible by "ways in which [it] can embody specific forms of power and authority" that endure over the course of centuries.[8] Control of landscape and accumulation of racial, social, economic, and political capital are cogenerated. The technology of the spillway, by way of its placement and operation, distributes both water and power unevenly across racial lines. The rich and the white live on dry land. The poor and the Black are expected to live with or under water. This racializing technology is tested during times of environmental disaster. In Southeast Louisiana, that means during floods. As snow melt and spring rains travel down the length of the Mississippi River from as far north as Minnesota, the volume and pressure of the water grows tremendously, causing flooding over the riverbanks and levees, and worse, levee breaks known as crevasses. Levees, the primary flood protection structures well into the twentieth century—and arguably to the present day—are earthen flood banks that skirt the sides of the river. Rising eight to twelve feet above water level, the Mississippi River levee system traverses nearly all of the river's edge from Minnesota to Louisiana. "Some of the larger levees have all the lines, angles, and strength of veritable fortifications," reported a *Harper's Weekly* correspondent in 1884.[9] Thirteen years earlier, an article in *Frank Leslie's Illustrated Newspaper* had described what happened when the river breached those fortifications. "Crevasses are formed in the banks, into which the flat-boats are drawn and whirled through the swamps. Levees are raised for the purpose of preventing these overflows; and even these levees are sometimes swept away."[10]

Two flood events in particular influenced the siting and racialization of the Bonnet Carré Spillway: the crevasse of 1850 and the Great Flood of 1927. These events that occurred seventy-five years apart demonstrate the enduring, deeply rooted racial logic of flood control infrastructure that preceded the USACE's narrative, which begins in 1927.

The Bonnet Carré Crevasse was one of the largest, most frequent, and most destructive of these levee breaches. In late 1849, the Mississippi River rushed to a small bend in the river, its tremendous force and momentum pummeling the levees. By December 29, 1849, the entire section of the east bank levee gave way, unleashing, as the *Chicago Tribune* reported, "a flood of water, one-third of a mile in width and fifteen to eighteen feet deep . . . pouring through the . . . Crevasse" thirty-three miles upriver from New Orleans (the current site of the spillway).[11] It remained open until July 1850.

Most of the testimony describing the Bonnet Carré Crevasse of 1850 and the dependence on enslaved labor as infrastructure comes from Oxley Plantation, one of the tracts beneath the spillway.[12] In 1850, 155 people were enslaved on Oxley Plantation. Some performed specialized labor such as gardening, blacksmithing, and driving, and most worked the sugarcane fields. Of all the plantations along the crevasse, Oxley Plantation would have been most impervious to flooding. Charles Oxley was known to implement new technologies on his plantation, notable among which was a pump for floodwater. But on January 2, 1850, Oxley reported that the "draining machine drowned out last night."

Oxley wrote in his log in a hurried script, "Crevasse this morning took the levees."[13] For the next two weeks, all enslaved people on the plantation labored on the levee. Women dug ditches in front of the levee, while men reinforced the levee itself. Oxley then began planting cane, only to be foiled again by a violent storm on January 20. The draining machine again proved futile. "Water rising, running over on Trepagnier side. Draining machine on all night, but water gaining height," Oxley wrote on January 21. A week later, the water was still rising over the rebuilt levees, despite assigning "his best hands to secure the plantation against the rising waters." By March, it seemed that the situation was under control. "Children and old hands planting cane. Men and Women working on levee," he recorded. Yet that same day Oxley also reported "another break in the dam." The next day, only the children were planting cane and "all hands were building up the levee." By three o'clock, the crevasse had fully ruptured once again. For weeks afterward, his log read roughly the same: "Crevasse at 11 o'clock a.m. . . . Crevasse at 3 o'clock p.m. . . . Damnation."[14]

Flood control was deadly work. Enslaved men and women attempted to rebuild the nearly obliterated levees with simple tools, wheelbarrows, sandbags, and mule carts. Many drowned in the perilously churning waters. Planters would later sue for indemnities from their parish governments for the loss of enslaved persons. These cases would eventually shape a very early progressive taxation policy in many flood-prone parishes, especially St. Charles Parish. Plantation owners within seven miles of a levee breach were required by state law to send all enslaved men between the ages of fifteen and sixty to repair levees.[15] Enslaved people who lived on the land beneath the spillway were thus doubly monetized, first as saleable commodities, then again as their bodies themselves served as flood control infra-structure and a means of disaster reparations.[16] At the Bonnet Carré bend, enslaved men and women, young and old, moved ceaselessly from cane fields to floodwaters and back again. Flood control, even before the design of spillways, was an example of a technology that is so "thoroughly biased in a particular direction that it regularly produces results counted as wonderful breakthroughs by some social interests and crushing setbacks by others."[17]

The Bonnet Carré Crevasse of 1850 made clear what many engineers and planters had known for some time. For planters to sustain the agricultural profits to which they had become accustomed, technological and ecological interventions besides levees and the manual labor of enslaved people were required. The crevasse set a major survey project into motion at the federal level in order to design a more robust flood control system. Andrew A. Humphreys, chief of the Corps of Topo-graphical Engineers, and the military engineer Henry L. Abbot completed a com-prehensive study of the Lower Mississippi River in 1861.[18] Using historical infor-mation on past floods and crevasses, including the crevasse of 1850, they proposed several options for diversifying the levee-only system.[19]

Humphreys and Abbot examined three options. The first was to create cut-offs that would redirect the main channel of the river into a straighter path, taking pressure off the levees and, debatably, creating a natural dredging effect, as faster-moving water would eventually form a deeper riverbed.[20] The second option was to create outlets, or spillways. Humphreys identified two possible sites with caveats for each. The first, a spillway at Bonnet Carré, would threaten the currently operational sugar plantations in its path. The second, a spillway on the other side of New Orleans that drained into Lake Borgne, would still leave the city at large risk for floods. Ulti-mately, though, Humphreys believed the cutoff and the spillway options to be pro-hibitively costly and ill advised. The last option was to raise and fortify the existing levee system.

In the end, no definitive recommendation was reached. Plagued by discord and disagreement among administrators at the federal and state levels, no new engi-neering projects at Bonnet Carré materialized. St. Charles Parish returned to rely-ing on the levee system.

The second major flood event in the history of the spillway, the Great Flood of 1927, however, spurred action. The events of 1927 are well-trodden by historians and geographers, memorialized by blues musicians, and often figure prominently into the infrastructure-as-savior narrative. The flood, the most devastating in the history of the North American continent, destroyed land from Illinois to the Gulf of Mexico and left hundreds of thousands without homes. Importantly, the Great Flood reached New Orleans, previously protected by the levee breaks upriver that relieved water pressure and volume. For the politically powerful, white suffering in a metropole typically catalyzes swift action.[21]

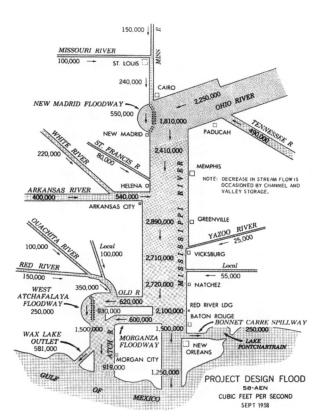

Figure 2. Diagram of Project Design Flood, showing the Bonnet Carré Spillway as the last outlet for river control before New Orleans, 1958.

The United States government promptly responded to the flood of 1927 by funding the Mississippi River and Tributary Project in 1928, a massive undertaking to control the entire river through public works. These plans were administered and implemented by the Mississippi River Commission, a federally appointed board that had been established in 1879. The commission, which is still active today, included USACE officers, a member of the National Oceanic and Atmospheric Administration, and civilians from the private engineering and business sectors. To develop the plan for this extensive system of flood control, the commission created several iterations of "Project Design Flood," a predictive model for the impact of river flooding based on historical data.[22] This time, the Bonnet Carré Spillway was a key element of the plan, along with floodwalls, dredging, and an enhanced levee system that ran from Cairo to New Orleans. The Project Design Flood diagram was startlingly simple for a production of such massive scale. Inlets and outlets were denoted by the flow rate of water in cubic feet per second. The Mississippi River resembled basic kitchen sink plumbing more than it did a highly complex alluvial system. As form follows function, objectives of ecological discipline are also achieved aesthetically (see fig. 2).

The Bonnet Carré Spillway was the last major feature of Project Design Flood, making it the last line of defense for New Orleans and all areas downriver against catastrophic annual floods. It was and still is the last opportunity for human intervention that can substantially alter the river depth and path. "You can still trace the history of the spillway through these globally induced processes of hydrological engineering, river management, modernist flood control," the political ecologist Joshua Lewis explained in a 2015 interview. "It is already an old story."[23]

Throughout the nineteenth century, then, the Bonnet Carré Crevasse embodied the fraught relationship between white plantation owners, enslaved African and African American people, and the constant specter of ruinous waters. In this way, the histories of flood control infrastructure and enslaved people at Bonnet Carré are inextricably bound together.

Transcending Plantation Boundaries

The lives of Black people who worked the land beneath the spillway consisted of more than digging, draining, ditching, and dying. Funerary artifacts recovered from the cemeteries shed light on social practices and kinship networks. Those lost to natural and unnatural causes were buried in these two cemeteries. Iron and wooden crosses were created for the burials, which were typically held at night. Some blacksmiths added initials to the crosses. Coffins ranged in size, with small ones for children and infants. Family members routinely sprinkled lime over the burials to keep weeds from growing.[24] Enslaved people on the plantations below the spillway visited one another, married, and started families. "It is not surprising," one of the USACE uncirculated reports reads, "that a social network which transcended plantation boundaries existed prior to the Civil War in the project area."[25]

After emancipation, formerly enslaved people either remained on the plantations as agricultural wage laborers, or pooled money to purchase land and founded the enclaves of Bell Town (Sellers), Jew Town (Sellers), Virginia Town, and Coffee Town (Montz) on the sites of Myrtleland, Roseland, and Hermitage (formerly Oxley) Plantations. In oral histories recorded in the 1980s, residents of Sellers (renamed Norco in 1934 after the arrival of the New Orleans Refinery Company) and Montz described how difficult it was for Black people to find work in the many years following emancipation. One woman recounted that her mother was lucky to find work as a laundress.[26] Another woman told a story of her mother working as a field hand. As a child, she took dinner to her every night in the sugar fields because she worked until after sundown. The same resident continued to recount her fear of the seasonal floods. During floods, her older sister would carry her on her back over the levee to reach their one-room schoolhouse.[27] Even with modest means, however, the Black community continued to organize funerals and processions. Civil War veteran Sanders Royal was marked by a headstone. Metal and wooden crosses were still standing tall on the eve of the spillway's construction.

When Bonnet Carré, the centuries-old thorn in the side of the white elite and foe to global capital flows, was finally selected as the site for the $13,266,000 flood control project, the price tag included "land acquisition."[28] The land "acquired" by the federal government was not vacant and never had been. During the spillway's construction from 1929 to 1935, the towns of Montz and Sellers, Louisiana, were demolished and partially relocated. Oral histories indicate that the USACE had made promises to move the two cemeteries to a nearby playground but never followed through.[29]

Construction began at the height of the Great Depression and offered residents a rare source of reliable work. The spillway project employed many locals as well as Works Progress Administration workers. *L'Observateur*, a biweekly newspaper distributed in the River Parishes, wrote in a 2000 article, "In the 1930s, most of the country was in the midst of the Great Depression. One wouldn't have noticed it around Norco."[30] Descendants of enslaved people were paid to bury their own towns and plow under their ancestors' resting places. By the time the spillway was conceived, it had been a cemetery of African-descended peoples for centuries. The land had already been steeped with memories of both white violence and Black joy that no flood would be able to completely erase.

Hidden in Plain Sight

From 1929 to 1975, the burials remained beneath the ground, washed further and further from their original locations with each opening of the spillway. Their haunting emergence set off a series of events that would bring much more than skeletons into the light of day.

When the bones surfaced after the 1975 spillway opening, the USACE commissioned an archaeological study and report on the history of the spillway land, a collection of oral histories, and an inventory of cemetery artifacts. Twenty-five burials were found at two cemetery sites, named Kenner and Kugler Cemeteries after the white families who most recently owned the plantations. Each cemetery was estimated to hold 150 burials. The remains of an infant, a child, and a young male were identified in the field.[31] All were confirmed to be African descended.

Jill-Karen Yakubik, the archaeologist who conducted the research for the report, recommended that the USACE share a "popular version" of her team's findings with the public in schools, churches, and libraries. The classified report, "Cultural Resources Inventory of the Bonnet Carré Spillway, St. Charles Parish, Louisiana," was completed in 1986.[32] A second report, "Phase 2 of the Cultural Resources Inventory of the Bonnet Carré Spillway, St. Charles Parish, Louisiana," was commissioned in 1987 and completed in 1988 by another team led by Eric C. Poplin. Yakubik's company, Earth Search Inc., was contracted in 2005 for a third report, "Background Research on the Kenner and Kugler Cemeteries, St. Charles Parish, Louisiana."[33] After Yakubik and her team conducted the first "Cultural Resources Inventory," the

Figure 3. Site of Kugler Cemetery, August 2014, looking north from River Road. Photo by author.

USACE identified approximately one hundred out of an estimated nine hundred descendants. They were contacted by mail and informed that cemeteries containing the burials of their relatives had surfaced in the spillway. Yakubik interviewed several of the known descendants for the 2005 report. Although the first two reports are now unclassified, USACE employees who are aware of these reports cited the prevention of grave robbing as the reason for secrecy during a site visit in July 2012. Figure 3 shows the site of Kugler Cemetery, hidden in plain sight, in 2014. As for the recovered artifacts documented in the reports, the Louisiana Division of Archaeology responded to inquiries about their whereabouts by warning that this would be "opening Pandora's box," and by doing so, it "will cause some of us to scramble to figure out what happened with these materials."[34]

This attempted erasure of a larger public memory by the engineered landscape of the Bonnet Carré Spillway is not purely a result of physical demolition in the 1920s or of administrative inaction over the past two decades. It is also a consequence of active and ongoing institutional practices of repression, accomplished through signage in the spillway, public marketing materials, and narratives circulated by print and online media. Hailed in recent years as a wetlands preserve and "Sportsman's Paradise," signs dot the otherwise flat, marshy landscape, directing visitors to ATV areas, bike trails, model airplane fields, and bird-watching areas.[35] "It is a shame that . . . ATVs and biking get more resources than African American

History," a St. Charles Parish resident wrote in 2012. "Monuments have been built for others who actually fought to keep people of color enslaved and disenfranchised in Louisiana."[36]

While the struggle for commemoration was about to begin in earnest, there were already sites of memory that stood the test of time despite and along with floodwaters, wreckage, and death. The stories of grandparents, parents, cousins, and neighbors recorded by Yakubik cannot be acquired like property deeds or monetized like "land acquisitions." The foundation for the movement was there all along.

Fighting to Exist: The Movement Begins

Several of the descendants were members of the African American History Alliance of Louisiana (AAHAL), an organization working to recover, honor, and popularize stories of heroic African American ancestors. They first called on the USACE to commemorate the cemeteries in 1995. The AAHAL organized descendants and parish residents into the group Concerned Citizens for Ancestors' Lineages (CCAL), which focused on the spillway cemeteries. In September 1997, AAHAL collaborated with the "Authentic Voices Project, an African Studies program chaired by Dr. Clyde Robertson and sponsored by the New Orleans Public School System,"[37] to bring Dr. Michael Blakey, then professor of archaeology at Howard University, to the site to study the skeletal remains and share his findings with teachers and students. According to Blakey, the interred were subject to some of the most brutal manual labor and extreme malnutrition the team had found in their studies, similar to enslaved people on the sugar plantations of the British Virgin Islands.[38] His evaluation of muscle and ligament attachments on upper and lower body bones showed extreme stress on the joints and muscles from heavy repetitive labor. Through study of dental remains, Blakey "noted that the enslaved had a very unhealthy and poor diet." Further "examination revealed the presence of scurvy, dental loss, and abscessing which was consistent with a diet in sugars and starches."[39]

In January 2012, the USACE announced that the cemeteries were listed on the National Historic Register. This story received only moderate visibility via the *Times-Picayune*, a New Orleans daily newspaper.[40] Later that year, in response to pressure from residents and the CCAL to further commemorate the cemeteries and share the history of the African American communities with the public, the USACE announced a plan for interpretive panels and a walking trail called Project Resting Place.

On February 8, 2012, the USACE held a meeting to present the plan and open a public comment period on Project Resting Place. At the meeting, Christopher Brantley, the spillway project manager, presented a brief history of the cemeteries and spillway, explanation of the 1975 accidental exhumation, and designs for informational panels, landscaping, and a brochure. He noted that the cemeteries were not disturbed by the original spillway construction (though Yakubik's report explicitly states otherwise).[41] Brantley then opened a discussion period followed by one-on-one meetings. During the discussion, Margie Richard, a descendant who was interviewed in Yakubik's first report, shared that "this oral history went on in the 1970's and I was told not to talk about it."[42] Other attendees expressed similar concerns and requested that the USACE make presentations and share this information with other residents, high schools, museums, and universities.

Brantley suggested that maintenance of the site "could be a Friends of the Spillway project. We would like to approach the Friends of the Spillway and possibly a sponsor to help with upkeep in the areas on a more frequent basis." Attendees and descendants were not familiar with the nonprofit and asked that membership be extended to the public. Concerns were also raised about the need for a private sponsor when the sites were part of the National Historic Register and under the jurisdiction of the USACE.[43]

Over thirty comment cards gathered from descendants and residents during the open comment period expressed disgust with Project Resting Place owing to its lack of detail and sensitivity to the legacy of slavery and the accomplishments of African Americans in the spillway area. The text of the panels to be installed along the interpretive trail omitted details about the enslaved people interred in the spillway, such as Sanders Royal and William H. Bolson, members of the Corps d'Afrique, the first Black regiment in the Civil War, and Hannibal Waters, a heroic rebel in the 1811 Slave Revolt. Instead, the panels offered a general history of plantations and frequently referred to enslaved people as "workers" or "laborers" and "residents."[44] Descendants of Sanders Royal and William H. Bolson submitted comments with additional detailed information about their respective ancestors.

Comments also addressed the design of Project Resting Place. The question of how and how many designers or museum professionals were solicited and consulted was raised. Community members and descendants offered specific ideas for commemoration, such as a "9 foot Black Civil War soldier sculpted in bronze."[45] Others included "an eternal flame" and "areas for meditation and remembrance," as well as "an interpretive center long advocated by the Louisiana Museum of African American history, a statue celebrating the Slave Revolt of 1811, and historic markers noting now destroyed communities like Sellars."[46] One particularly powerful handwritten card read, "It feels like a war is still being fought over the right to exist."[47]

The Louisiana Museum of African American History (LMAAH), the successor of AAHAL, proposed comprehensive revisions. The LMAAH chairman, historian, and descendant Leon A. Waters researched and detailed the oppressive system of chattel slavery affecting the daily lives of enslaved people, and the accomplishments of specific individuals known to be interred in the cemeteries. LMAAH also advised that the name of the cemeteries should be changed from Kenner and

Kugler—the last names of the white plantation owners—to African and African American Cemeteries in the Bonnet Carré Spillway. According to *The Stories the Bones Will Tell*, a self-published informational flyer distributed by LMAAH, all of these revisions and critiques were in service to the vision to "preserve, honor, and learn from the ancestors of these cemeteries. Through proper study, much information on work conditions, diet, and African identities of the enslaved could be revealed."[48]

"We would like to do this this fall," Brantley stated at the conclusion of the 2012 meeting. Project Resting Place never materialized. Given the violence enacted on this community for centuries, a walking trail was merely a down payment.

The Power of Memory Work

The descendants' fight is "less a reminder that ancestors must be commemorated than that we are continuing their commemorative work. Remembrance was a vital part of the politics of slavery, then no less than now."[49] As a descendant wrote of the need for commemoration, "It is the ability to honor our ancestors which is left somewhat less than fully accessible. It is the need to have a nexus, connected in a material way with our families, which is missing. It is important and necessary to keep the spirits of the ancestors present and honored for generations to come."[50]

Like material infrastructure, the relationships formed through community organizing and storytelling and the kinship bonds between descendants and the larger communities to which they belong require maintenance. Public history work in the form of a movement for commemoration has tremendous power to activate, mobilize, and sustain communities. The passing down and sharing of stories of those who came before us, particularly of one's own ancestors, is a supremely emotive and human act. Sharing institutionally repressed histories among community members and to larger audiences provides points of access that draw more people into activism and community organizing through a shared stewardship of history.

A phone call with the USACE Freedom of Information Act (FOIA) records manager, in November 2014 reveals the conflicting forces at work in this landscape and the true power of the descendants. The manager could not release reports on any known descendants of those interred in the cemeteries or minutes from community meetings regarding the spillway cemeteries because there were "lots of angry Black people out there." He was adamant, as if he needed to bar the door. "They want a golden arch over that cemetery, and we say to them, take it to your congressmen if you want anything."[51]

Since the report of known descendants remained classified, and the records manager had no intention of providing documents, LMAAH began a print campaign in November 2014 entitled "Do You Have an Ancestor Buried in the Bonnet Carré Spillway?" to find more descendants by working through churches, schools, nursing homes, and other community groups in the River Parishes. A poster and

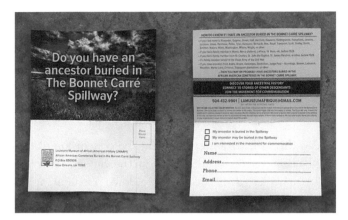

Figure 4.   Postcard and poster designed for the Louisiana Museum of African American History that includes a tear-off, mail-in portion. Photo and design by author, 2015.

detachable postcard with a list of last names of descendants was a new step forward (see fig. 4). Two possible descendants were found at the Second Louisiana Reconstruction Conference, organized by the Louisiana Public History Forum and hosted at Southern University at New Orleans. Neither descendant knew that their relative was interred underneath the spillway. Together, and slowly, the movement for commemoration continued to grow.

A young man studying at Chattahoochee Technical College grew up hearing stories from his grandmother about the vibrant, now-displaced community under the spillway. He remembers visiting his aunt in Montz, seeing the spillway in passing, but not venturing into the foreboding landscape or knowing about the cemeteries. His name is Christopher Smothers, a cousin of Margie Richard, the woman who was told to keep quiet about her oral history recording.

In 2019, Smothers began putting together the puzzle pieces of the spillway story by drawing on these family memories to trace his genealogy. He visited archives across the state of Louisiana, even traveling to the National Archives to find military pension records for one of his ancestors. They led him back to the spillway. He began to organize his family, friends, and community members and connect with other descendants. He has taken up the struggle for commemoration by locating more descendants around the country and advocating for an official landmark, history center, and memorial wall of stone. Two years later, on live television, he stood face to face with Jason Emery, an archaeologist for the USACE, and demanded a return of the remains and proper commemoration of his ancestors.

"Many years I spent trying to find the narrative . . . trying to find answers for my grandmothers," Smothers told FOX8 reporter Nicondra Norwood, herself a native of St. Charles Parish. "They were really robbed of a lot . . . not only did it help me build a connection to them, but it really gave them closure for a lot of the injustices they witnessed in their youth." He continued, "It's very emotional," as he described some of the documents he encountered in his research. "You can interpret the pain . . . How they really, really suffered."[52] The camera then cut to Emery, standing near a cemetery site. "Not making any apologies for it. The world was a different place in 1929," he says.

In 1929, the designs of white men ran roughshod over a finite earth. Levees were built higher, and the river was dredged deeper to protect the economic interests of the few. Crowds gathered to cheer on presidents preaching the gospel of infrastructure as evidence of a democratic, egalitarian society.[53]

In the Bonnet Carré Spillway, floodwaters still swirl, government authorities still spin platitudes, and white families picnic, drive ATVs, fly model airplanes, and ride mountain bikes. Meanwhile, in homes and churches, backyards and porches, sisters, cousins, uncles, and grandmothers tell and retell stories of Black life in Montz, Sellers, Bell Town, Jew Town, Virginia Town, Coffee Town, and in the Myrtleland, Roseland, and Hermitage Plantations. Generations of descendants reach back into the future, writing visions of statues, memorials, history centers, and reinterment ceremonies. Creating spaces in which they "would also be thinking of the dead," as "the dead already include the living in their own great collective."[54]

The Bonnet Carré Spillway is not the only example of Black communities being displaced for private and public infrastructure projects, of cemeteries of enslaved people resurfacing, or of people of color being sacrificed in the name of disaster prevention and recovery.[55] To name only a few: the Cross Bronx Expressway, constructed in 1948, displaced over sixty thousand residents, the majority of whom were Black and/or Puerto Rican; the town of Pinhook, Missouri, founded by sharecroppers, was demolished in 2011 to prevent the flooding of Cairo, Illinois; and the Monroe and Bruslie Cemeteries underneath the Shell Oil Refinery in Convent, Louisiana, resurfaced in 2013.[56]

The story of the Bonnet Carré Spillway cemeteries speaks to such struggles within and beyond Louisiana in that it raises questions of spiritual repair for the desecrated dead, intangible property loss through geographic displacement, and historical atrocities that belie "natural" disaster recovery and prevention. "A disaster," says the historian Andy Horowitz, "is at best an interpretive fiction, or at worst, an ideological script."[57] As such, resettling communities is not just about rebuilding homes and redrawing property lines, but about severing people from land that is not only created and maintained by their labor but also holds community memory. Commemoration of the lives of displaced, dispossessed, and enslaved peoples gets to the heart of the matter. To install a plaque is to acknowledge a crime scene. Taking into account the histories of places and struggles like Bonnet Carré, what does it mean for corporations and the federal government to grapple with a historical impossibility of repair?

. . . . .

The FOX8 interview drew to a close. "There were lives here. People who sacrificed their lives here," Smothers said. "There needs to be an official landmark designating the sacredness of this area." Emery responded, "I think we can get back to you. . . . I support it." As if permission to remember was ever his to give. Smothers swore to hold Emery to his word.

He does not stand alone. A legion of the living and the dead is not easily dispersed. Walls and weirs may temporarily allow the rich, white, and powerful to play God with Mother Mississippi, but because of forces they have unleashed, they cannot bury what they stole. There were *always* lives here. Indeed, there still are.

Robin McDowell is assistant professor of African and African American studies at Washington University in St. Louis. Her current research explores the history of bonds between race, ecology, and labor in Louisiana on a geologic time scale.

Notes

I am indebted to descendants Leon A. Waters and Christopher Smothers. Vincent Brown, Evelyn Brooks Higginbotham, and Travis Bost generously read early drafts, and Samuel Shearer and Amsale Alemu provided invaluable feedback. I thank the anonymous reviewers and editors for their helpful comments and support.

1. McCormack, "Tulane Studies Additional Diversions." The trigger point for operating the Bonnet Carré Spillway is a Mississippi River flow of 1.25 million cubic feet per second at the structure, which generally corresponds to a flood stage of seventeen feet at the Carrollton Gage in New Orleans. Bonnet Carré is designed to divert a maximum of 250,000 cubic feet per second of water from the Mississippi River.
2. Schleifstein, "Mississippi River to Crest Saturday." Throughout the mid-twentieth century, the spillway was used infrequently, about once every ten years (in 1931, 1937, 1945, 1950, 1973, 1975, 1979, 1983, 1997, 2008, 2011, 2016, 2018, and 2019), with a record twenty-three quiet years between 1950 and 1973. Since the 1980s, however, usage has increased, reaching a crescendo in 2019. February 27, 2019, marked the unprecedented opening two years in a row. The spillway opened once in April 2020.
3. McKittrick, *Demonic Grounds*, 95.
4. Canicosa, "Term 'Cancer Alley.'" The term can be traced to a newspaper interview with a St. Gabriel, Louisiana, resident in 1987. It gained more widespread visibility during the Great Louisiana Toxics March from Baton Rouge to New Orleans in November 1988.
5. Team New Orleans, "Bonnet Carre' Spillway Story," 2:45, 6:07.
6. Team New Orleans, "Bonnet Carre' Spillway Story," 10:08.
7. Star, "Infrastructure and Ethnographic Practice," 387.
8. Winner, "Do Artifacts Have Politics?," 121.
9. *Harper's Weekly*, "Mississippi Levees," 170.
10. *Frank Leslie's Illustrated Newspaper*, "Mississippi Crevasse," 145.
11. *Chicago Tribune*, "Crevasse at Bonnet Carré."
12. *Chicago Tribune*, "Crevasse at Bonnet Carré."
13. Yakubik, USACE, and Goodwin, "Cultural Resources Inventory," 114.

14. Diaries of Charles Oxley (1–6), Kenner Family Papers, Louisiana State University Hill Memorial Library; Diary of Martha Kenner, Kenner Family Papers, Louisiana State University Hill Memorial Library.

15. Louisiana Legislature, "Act No. 31, An Act Relative to Roads and Levees." In *Acts Passed at the First Session of the Ninth Legislature of the State of Louisiana*. New Orleans: John Gibson, State Printer, 1829.

16. Horowitz, "Acts of Men and Woman"; *Scribner's Monthly*, "How Uncle Gabe Saved the Levee"; Rose, "Fighting the Great Flood," 641.

17. Winner, "Do Artifacts Have Politics?," 125.

18. Pabis, "Delaying the Deluge," 447.

19. Humphreys and Abbot, *Report upon the Physics and Hydraulics.*

20. Pabis, "Delaying the Deluge," 451.

21. Barry, *Rising Tide*, 8.

22. Reuss, *Designing the Bayous*, 207, 223.

23. Schultz, "Keeping History Alive."

24. Earth Search Inc. and United States Army Corps of Engineers, "Background Research," 75.

25. Earth Search Inc. and United States Army Corps of Engineers, "Background Research," 60.

26. Yakubik, USACE, and Goodwin, "Cultural Resources Inventory," 177.

27. Yakubik, USACE, and Goodwin, "Cultural Resources Inventory," 176.

28. USACE, *Mississippi River Flood Control.*

29. Earth Search Inc. and United States Army Corps of Engineers, "Background Research," 85.

30. Gray, "Norco Town History."

31. Yakubik, USACE, and Goodwin, "Cultural Resources Inventory," 320. This 360-page public document is known to be held by only two libraries: the U.S. Army Corps of Engineers Library, for which special permission and research clearance is required; and Tulane University Archives and Special Collections, where its catalog entry reports it as "MISSING DUE TO KATRINA."

32. Yakubik, USACE, and Goodwin, "Cultural Resources Inventory," 334.

33. Poplin et al., "Cultural Resources Inventory, Phase Two"; Earth Search Inc. and United States Army Corps of Engineers, "Background Research."

34. Chip McGimsey, pers. comm., August 11, 2014.

35. USACE, "Hunting Guide to Bonnet Carré Spillway"; USACE, "Bonnet Carré Spillway Fishing."

36. Redacted sender, "Subject: Comments on Resting Place." Electronic correspondence with the US Army Corps of Engineers during public comment period, March 22, 2012. Included in attachment with author's electronic correspondence with the US Army Corps of Engineers, September 29, 2014.

37. Waters, "When Paying Homage to Our History."

38. Thibodeaux, "Slave Cemeteries Remain Unmarked."

39. Waters, "When Paying Homage to Our History."

40. Scallan, "African-American Cemeteries Plowed Over."

41. Yakubik, USACE, and Goodwin, "Cultural Resources Inventory," 325.

42. USACE, "Public Meeting Summary," 5.

43. USACE, "Public Meeting Summary," 4.

44. Kaser Design, "Bonnet Carré Spillway Interpretive Plan," 5a, 5b, 6a, 6b; Brantley, "Long-Term Management," 13.

45. Redacted sender, "Subject: Comments on Resting Place."

46. Redacted author 1, "Long-Term Management Comment Cards." Included in attachment with author's electronic correspondence with the US Army Corps of Engineers, September 29, 2014.

47. Redacted author 2, "Long-Term Management Comment Cards." Included in attachment with author's electronic correspondence with the US Army Corps of Engineers, September 29, 2014.

48. Concerned Citizens for Ancestors' Lineages, *Stories the Bones Will Tell*.

49. Brown, "History Attends to the Dead," 226.

50. Redacted sender, "Subject: Comments on Resting Place."

51. Frederick Wallace, pers. comm., November 2014.

52. Norwood, "Bonnet Carre Spillway Holds a Hidden History."

53. Winner, "Do Artifacts Have Politics?," 130; Thibodeaux, "FDR's Historical Visit"; Boak, "Biden Tells Storm-Ravaged Louisiana."

54. Berger, "Economy of the Dead."

55. Cheramie and Pasquier, "Lost Graves"; Lawrence and Lawless, *When They Blew the Levee*; Parker, "Three Weeks after Ida"; Burnett and Peñaloza, "Descendants of Slaves."

56. Segregation by Design, "Cross Bronx Expressway"; Jones, "Graves of One Thousand Enslaved People."

57. Horowitz, *Katrina*, 15.

References

Barry, John M. *Rising Tide: The Great Mississippi Flood of 1927 and How It Changed America.* New York: Simon and Schuster, 1997.

Berger, John. "On the Economy of the Dead." *Harper's Magazine*, September 2008. https://harpers.org/archive/2008/09/on-the-economy-of-the-dead/.

Boak, Josh. "Biden Tells Storm-Ravaged Louisiana: 'I Know You're Hurting,'" *WGNO*, September 4, 2021. https://wgno.com/news/biden-tells-storm-ravaged-louisiana-i-know-youre-hurting/.

Brantley, Christopher. "Long-Term Management of Historic Cemeteries in Bonnet Carre Spillway." Presentation at St. Charles Borromeo Catholic Church, Destrehan, Louisiana, February 6, 2012.

Brown, Vincent. "History Attends to the Dead." *Small Axe: A Caribbean Journal of Criticism* 14, no. 1 (2010): 219–27.

Burnett, John, and Marisa Peñaloza. "Descendants of Slaves Say This Proposed Grain Complex Will Destroy the Community." *NPR*, July 7, 2021. https://www.npr.org/2021/07/07/1012609448/descendants-of-slaves-say-this-proposed-grain-factory-will-destroy-the-community.

Canicosa, JC. "The Term 'Cancer Alley' Has a Long History in Louisiana—and Even a History before Louisiana." *Louisiana Illuminator*, February 5, 2021. https://lailluminator.com/2021/02/05/despite-sen-cassidys-critiques-louisianans-have-lamented-cancer-alley-since-the-80s/.

Cheramie, Kristi, and Michael Pasquier. "The Lost Graves of the Morganza Floodway." *Places Journal*, January 31, 2013. https://placesjournal.org/article/the-lost-graves-of-the-morganza-floodway/#.Yqz3m62xzg8.

Chicago Tribune. "The Crevasse at Bonnet Carré." May 12, 1871.

Concerned Citizens for Ancestors' Lineages. *The Stories the Bones Will Tell*. Self-published flyer, 2012.

Earth Search Inc. and United States Army Corps of Engineers, New Orleans District. "Background Research on the Kenner and Kugler Cemeteries, St. Charles Parish, Louisiana." New Orleans, Louisiana, July 2005.

Frank Leslie's Illustrated Newspaper. "The Mississippi Crevasse." May 13, 1871.

Gray, Leonard. "Norco Town History." *L'Observateur*, June 23, 1999.

Harper's Weekly. "Mississippi Levees." March 15, 1884.

Horowitz, Andy. "Acts of Men and Woman." *Tulane School of Liberal Arts Magazine*, Fall 2019. https://liberalarts.tulane.edu/newsletter/acts-men-and-woman.

Horowitz, Andy. *Katrina: A History, 1915–2015.* Cambridge, MA: Harvard University Press, 2020.

Humphreys, Andrew A., and Henry L. Abbot. *Report upon the Physics and Hydraulics of the Mississippi River; upon the Protection of the Alluvial Region against Overflow; and upon the Deepening of the Mouths: Based upon Surveys and Investigations . . . to Determine the Most Practicable Plan for Securing It from Inundation, and the Best Mode of Deepening the Channels at the Mouths of the River.* Washington, DC, 1861.

Jones, Terry L. "Graves of One Thousand Enslaved People Found near Ascension Refinery; Shell, Preservationists to Honor Them." *The Advocate*, March 18, 2018. https://www .theadvocate.com/baton_rouge/news/communities/ascension/article_18c62526-2611-11e8 -9aec-d71a6bbc9b0c.html.

Kaser Design. "Bonnet Carré Spillway Interpretive Plan Implementation Project." December 8, 2010. https://www.mvn.usace.army.mil/Missions/Mississippi-River-Flood-Control/Bonnet -Carre-Spillway-Overview/Cultural-Environmental-and-Natural-Values/Kenner-Kugler -Cemeteries/.

Lawrence, David Todd, and Elaine J. Lawless. *When They Blew the Levee: Race, Politics, and Community in Pinhook, Missouri.* Jackson: University Press of Mississippi, 2018.

McCormack, Frank. "Tulane Studies Additional Diversions to Reduce Bonnet Carré Flows." *Waterways Journal*, July 7, 2020. https://www.waterwaysjournal.net/2020/07/07/tulane -studies-additional-diversions-to-reduce-bonnet-carre-flows/.

McKittrick, Katherine. *Demonic Grounds: Black Women and the Cartographies of Struggle.* Minneapolis: University of Minnesota Press, 2006.

Norwood, Nicondra. "Bonnet Carre Spillway Holds a Hidden History." *FOX8 New Orleans*, February 25, 2021. https://www.fox8live.com/2021/02/26/flooded-hsistory/.

Pabis, George S. "Delaying the Deluge: The Engineering Debate over Flood Control on the Lower Mississippi River, 1846–1861." *Journal of Southern History* 64, no. 3 (1998): 421–54.

Parker, Halle. "Three Weeks after Ida Toppled Tombs in Ironton's Cemetery, Caskets Remain Scattered across the Community." *Nola.com*, September 20, 2021. https://www.nola.com /news/environment/article_461ec99c-1983-11ec-af74-476b04762451.html.

Poplin, Eric C., Paul C. Armstrong, Carol J. Poplin, and R. C. Goodwin. "Cultural Resources Inventory of the Bonnet Carré Spillway, Saint Charles Parish, Louisiana Phase 2." New Orleans, Louisiana, March 17, 1988. https://apps.dtic.mil/sti/citationspdfs/ADA203808.pdf.

Reuss, Martin. *Designing the Bayous: The Control of Water in the Atchafalaya Basin, 1800–1995.* College Station: Texas A&M University Press, 2004.

Rose, M. A. "Fighting the Great Flood." *Technical World Magazine*, August 1912.

Scallan, Matt. "African-American Cemeteries Plowed Over for Spillway Now Recognized as Historic." *Times-Picayune*, January 24, 2012. http://www.nola.com/environment/index.ssf /2012/01/corps_to_commemorate_african_a.html.

Schleifstein, Mark. "Mississippi River to Crest Saturday; Will Bonnet Carré Spillway Be Opened?" *Nola.com*, April 7, 2021. https://www.nola.com/news/environment/article _4666f03a-9717-11eb-9e2c-070305a8fb78.html.

Schultz, Heath. Unedited transcript of "Keeping History Alive: Notes on Memorialization, Identity, and the Bonnet Carré Spillway: Interview with Robin McDowell." *Midwest Compass Collaborators*, 2015. https://midwestcompass.org/.

Scribner's Monthly. "How Uncle Gabe Saved the Levee." 16, no. 6 (1878): 848–57.

Segregation by Design. "The Cross Bronx Expressway." https://www.segregationbydesign.com /the-bronx/the-cross-bronx-expressway (accessed October 2, 2022).

Star, Susan Leigh. "Infrastructure and Ethnographic Practice: Working on the Fringes." *Scandinavian Journal of Information Systems* 14, no. 2 (2002): 107–22.

Team New Orleans. "The Bonnet Carre' Spillway Story." YouTube video, April 4, 2013, 11:12. https://www.youtube.com/watch?v=CcusARVzcY8&feature=youtube_gdata_player.

Thibodeaux, Anna. "FDR's Historical Visit to Norco." *St. Charles Herald Guide*, April 8, 2019. https://www.heraldguide.com/news/fdrs-historical-visit-to-norco/.

Thibodeaux, Anna. "Slave Cemeteries Remain Unmarked, Underwater in the Spillway." *St. Charles Herald Guide*, March 25, 2019. https://www.heraldguide.com/news/slave -cemeteries-remain-unmarked-underwater-in-the-spillway/.

USACE (United States Army Corps of Engineers), New Orleans District. "Bonnet Carré Spillway." October 2014.

USACE (United States Army Corps of Engineers), New Orleans District. "Bonnet Carré Spillway Fishing." 2014.

USACE (United States Army Corps of Engineers), New Orleans District. "Hunting Guide to Bonnet Carré Spillway." 2014.

USACE (United States Army Corps of Engineers). *Mississippi River Flood Control: Bonnet Carré Spillway Constructed by Corps of Engineers U.S. Army 2nd New Orleans District.* 1938. https://play.google.com/books/reader?id=crwqrC-8nOQC&pg=GBS.PP7&hl=en.

USACE (United States Army Corps of Engineers). "Public Meeting Summary: Long Term Management of the Bonnet Carre Spillway Historic Cemeteries." February 8, 2012. https:// www.mvn.usace.army.mil/Portals/56/docs/MRT/Feb82012BCScempubmtg.pdf.

Waters, Leon A. "When Paying Homage to Our History, Remember Our Ancestors' Stories That the Bones Will Tell." *New Orleans Data News Weekly*, February 20, 2019. https:// www.postnewsgroup.com/when-paying-homage-to-our-history-remember-our-ancestors -stories-that-the-bones-will-tell/.

Winner, Langdon. "Do Artifacts Have Politics?" *Daedalus* 109, no. 1 (1980): 121–36.

Yakubik, Jill-Karen; United States Army Corps of Engineers, New Orleans District; and R. Christopher Goodwin and Associates. "Cultural Resources Inventory of the Bonnet Carré Spillway, St. Charles Parish, Louisiana." R. Christopher Goodwin and Associates, New Orleans, Louisiana, September 30, 1986.

Imperial Gift

Soap, Humanitarianism, and Black Markets in the Vietnam War

Ann Ngoc Tran

It is soap day at Sơn Hòa. A throng of Vietnamese villagers clusters around an American Division medic to receive gifts of soap (fig. 1). Their eyes and faces, most of which we cannot see, are eclipsed by their bodies' forward alignment, evidenced in the eager posture of bare feet raised subtly above ground and torsos lunging toward a hidden center. The only facial features visible with moderate clarity in the darkened photograph are the bright smile of a child to the right and the confused—perhaps skeptical—looks of the children gathered behind him. The medic, who towers above everyone, smiles congenially on the horde of bodies attracted to his bounty. The medic's visibility given his soaring height and the villagers' seeming (in)conspicuity in the shadowy aggregate of smaller, compacted bodies makes the representation of his humanitarian gesture suggestively partial. Here, it is not the implication of the villagers' needs that stands out but rather the portrayal of his benevolence. A woman's outstretched arm, the centripetal force of his promised charity, and the beaming smile of the small boy who looks up in gleeful anticipation evince an altruistic ethos that enhances the American's image of kindness and presupposes the recipients' gratitude for his gifts. Furthermore, it is against the very impression of "cleanliness" implied by gifts of soap that many of the children's bare, unadorned feet, pressing into the hard dirt, become readily apparent. Soap, a seemingly quotidian object, becomes more than a cleaning instrument in this regard. Its

Radical History Review

Issue 147 (October 2023)   DOI 10.1215/01636545-10637161

© 2023 by MARHO: The Radical Historians' Organization, Inc.

Figure 1. Villagers gather around an American medic to receive gifts of soap. Courtesy of Americal Division Veterans Association Collection (VA050742), Vietnam Center and Sam Johnson Vietnam Archive, Texas Tech University.

pervasive presence in the archives as a "gift" to the suffering people of Vietnam suggests its multifaceted purposes as a tool to subdue rural resistance by eradicating diseases (read: primitivism) and subversive political persuasions (read: communism) and in this way to work along with advanced military operations to destroy racialized forms of life marked as deviant.[1]

    While Marxist conceptualizations of the commodity have categorized its dialectic according to its attributed technical function (social use value) and market worth (exchange value), the transverse movements of soap in occupied South Vietnam unsettles this classical Marxist definition.[2] First, within the informal gift economy of US humanitarian aid, soap exceeds its immediate use value by circulating imperial desires to corral, subjugate, and modernize subversive elements, acting as a surrogate for Western civilization. Thus soap accrues value not for its functionality but for its structuring of hegemonic relations. Second, the appearance of soap on the black market, an illegible site outside of state governance, corrupts the unidirectional principles of humanitarianism by moving beyond the end point of a gift economy, since that economy negates the insurgent modalities of survival that arise in response to the violent occupation and militarization of native life. Pulled from its original place in the corpus of civic domestication programs, soap facilitates new social relations in elusive spheres of inverse capital extraction, enabling networks of exchange to persist outside of imperial time and state-run market relations. While the archives of US occupation idealize the qualitative powers of humanitarian soap in the absence of the market, soap's reemergence on the Vietnamese black market reveals natives' recognition of its commodifiable potential—and by extension, their challenge to American capitalist logics undergirding the pacification project of Pacific empire. Both insurgent and disruptive to the war-making enterprise, soap's secondhand recirculation on an illegitimate platform, operating as *excess* to US military objectives of democratization and imperial ordering, disavows the state's ability to accumulate capital and expropriate docile laboring subjects and their labor power.

The unruliness of soap and its circulatory poetics, therefore, gesture to its instantiation as both a commodity and an infrastructure in the American war in Vietnam. Heeding Brian Larkin's contention that "infrastructures are matter that enable the movement of other matter," "things and also the relation between things," I engage with soap as both material matter and as the basis for the movement of other things, specifically imperial fantasies of rural compliance and entwined logics of cleanliness.[3] During the war, soap not only operated as a tool to clean and sanitize those the US military deemed dirty and uncivilized but also brokered the ideological movement of empire from the nation-state to the distant hamlets and villages of South Vietnam. Analyzing soap as a sociopolitical infrastructure for the circulation of US liberal empire "reads against the grain" of the institutional Vietnam War archive, which has been preoccupied with the object's deployment as a means of fostering medical care and proper hygiene rather than as a conduit for the dissemination of military discipline and strategies of counterinsurgency.[4]

In the historiography of the American war in Vietnam, soap seldom appears in any substantial form beyond writings on its tactical use as an aid to "win hearts and minds," and when textually present it is quickly subsumed into broader discourses on the pragmatism of disciplinary soft power and civic action in Vietnam.[5] Alternately, histories of the war have attributed infrastructure primarily to the built environment—roads, shipping lines, weapons manufacturing, and chemical warfare—and have focused less on the elemental building blocks of empire that network racial ideologies, politics, and social hierarchies across time and space.[6] I see these two disparate threads braided in the mechanisms of wartime US humanitarianism, which proffer soap as both a counterinsurgent weapon of soft power and as an infrastructural poetic that moves empire from the US state to subjects in need of exigent rescue. These rhetorics were manifested discursively in the pamphlets and letters exchanged between medics in Vietnam and the American public and materially in tightly bound, paper-wrapped Ivory bars shipped by the ton overseas, imbued with desires to reform and sequester a racialized and intransigent demographic on the verge of revolutionary upheaval. The nation-state's visions of benevolent rescue, therefore, consolidated alongside securitizations of empire that undermined insurgent possibilities by propagating Eurocentric regimes of cleanliness and sanitation to those the US deemed compromised by medical and social ills.[7] When acts of personal autonomy eclipsed these motives, evidenced in incidences of native refusal and archival elisions, they gesture to what Neferti X. M. Tadiar terms "remaindered forms of life-making," or the creative and adaptive capacities of making life and other forms of sociality in times of war that may be unrecognized by the state but are nonetheless persistent in heterogeneous temporalities beyond the linear, homogeneous time of capitalist production.[8]

This article begins by "reading along the archival grain,"[9] in the words of Ann Laura Stoler, to identify the grammars of US humanitarianism that underwrite the transpacific conveyance of soap and its mobilization of unequal relations between the US military and South Vietnam's putatively infirm villagers, and which adjudicated the latter's racial propensity for reason and progress according to incommensurate degrees of public health knowledge. The article then moves to examine the anarchic practice of South Vietnamese black marketeering, which redeployed soap as an illegal market commodity to intercept the movement of US empire and, as a practice that arose in response to wartime capitalism and militarization, allowed natives to command new social relations at the cost of disrupting the Republic of Vietnam's flows of capital and the United States' ongoing war campaign. As an informal, opaque, and yet thriving infrastructure of its own, the black market fostered insurgent survival strategies that repurposed military supplies and gifts into versatile commodities, allowing even soap to escape its original containment as a civilizing agent for new uses and meanings. Mobile and untethered to the limits of the state, the black market developed illicit lifeworlds that persisted within US empire but beyond its jurisdiction.

Vietnam's Operation Soap

In 1962, a formal US Navy program named Project Handclasp began to bring educational materials, food, and medical supplies from American private relief donors to the war front as part of the US military's pro–South Vietnam civic action projects. Succeeding "Operation Handclasp," which waged the early Cold War on stated humanitarian principles, Project Handclasp used US Navy and Marine Corps transportation and administrative facilities to pass materials from American manufacturing firms and charity organizations to needy hamlets in occupied South Vietnam. Individuals and organizations donated the goods and supplies to warehouses in San Diego before the navy carried them overseas on a space-available basis. When the navy began to realize the growing need for civic action programs as the war progressed dramatically in 1965, space opened and the flow of supplies increased, with goods arriving at different ports of entry and filling post exchange (PX) stores and warehouses across Vietnam. By January 1966, the navy had transported nearly

sixty-three thousand pounds of miscellaneous basic commodities (e.g., food, clothing, medical equipment) to the Third Marine Expeditionary Force, an air-ground
task force partly responsible for conducting humanitarian assistance programs
alongside combat operations.[10] While soap was not the only commodity transferred
from American donors to rural villagers, the navy's "people-to-people effort"
stressed donations of medical necessities like soap in order to relieve the Vietnamese
from skin diseases and bacterial infections.

As pacification efforts intensified in the mid-to-late 1960s, physicians and soldiers poured into Vietnam in increasingly high numbers. They hailed not just from
the US mainland but also from decolonizing countries and territories impacted by
US militarist imperialism in the post–World War II period, and included Philippine,
South Korean, and Asian American subjects.[11] Civil action programs conducted by
different branches of the US military considered health assistance a crucial part of
the government's effort to win civilian hearts and minds and, more covertly, to
receive valuable intelligence on insurgent movements. Interactions between American medical personnel and Vietnamese civilians numbered almost forty million
between 1963 and 1971, during which projects like the Medical Civic Action Program (MEDCAP), the Cooperative for Assistance and Relief Everywhere (CARE),
Provincial Health Assistance Program, Military Provincial Health Assistance Program, Civilian War Casualty Program, and the American Red Cross were active in
South Vietnam to provide health care and resources to natives.[12] Within the big picture, these medical programs were only smaller building blocks of a larger civic
action infrastructure that also included the repair and construction of facilities like
schools, churches, and hospitals; nurses and physician training; assistance to sick
patients in orphanages and war zones; and voluntary gifts—that is, commodities
like soap and hygiene materials.[13] The US Army, Marines, Navy, and Air Force recognized the utility of civic action programs in the combat environments of Vietnam,
where expunging enemy forces from the Vietnamese body politic and the interior
body—both of which were presumedly diseased by mistrust and other social ills—
required the import of numerous commodities packaged as care and compassion.
Increased numbers of medics introduced thousands of bars of American-made
Ivory and Lux soap to Vietnamese civilians, offering what one military advisor
deemed "a luxury beyond comparison," for soap provided "a cleanliness to its
users that they never knew existed."[14] To medical professionals, the power of soap
as an instructional tool and a political conduit was not to be underestimated. The
distribution of soap as "presents" on Vietnamese national holidays, Christmas, and
other occasions, typically alongside other items like toothbrushes, toothpaste,
candy, and chewing gum, became a regular part of pacification rituals in hamlets
and villages surrounding suspected communist-run territories.

In a 1965 appraisal of health facilities in South Vietnam, the prominent
American physician Howard A. Rusk remarked plainly that "the level of medical

practice [here] is about as it was in the United States in 1875." If it were not for the material, technical, and logistical support provided by USAID (US Agency for International Development), Rusk argued, the incompetent South Vietnamese government and its people would surely continue to suffer.[15] In another morose review of the Republic of Vietnam's medical infrastructure, a reputable medic by the name of Captain Calvin Chapman noted that most of the existing Western medical practices in the region had been established by a few missionaries under French colonial rule. Compared with more capacious medical institutions in the West, Vietnam's hospitals and sanitary facilities seemed morbidly deficient. Chapman surmised that large pockets of the rural population did not have adequate access to proper health care: "Even in the cities drinking water was unsafe, sewage disposal facilities were inadequate, and no Vietnamese understanding developed concerning disease, hygiene and sanitation." The war in Vietnam, coupled with belligerent "Viet Cong activity" in the vicinity, had eliminated most of the medical services previously offered in the rural villages, where the majority of doctors had been drafted into the army. Chapman was particularly disgruntled by the Vietnamese villagers' overdependence on ancient Chinese medicine, which he described as mere sorcery.[16] The eradication of such erroneous beliefs, then, would entail American intervention through channels of medical assistance and soap distribution, and called for the displacement of atavistic Vietnamese medicinal practices and the adoption of modern science and medical care.

The physicians' concerns with Vietnamese vulnerability to illnesses and indigence raise questions as to what the US medical corps considered normal hygienic behavior and what they did not. The historian Nayan Shah has argued that "there is a persistent congruence between the public health logic of normal and aberrant and the racial logic of superior and inferior and their reconfiguration over time."[17] The normative public health knowledge that substantiated these racial logics found influence in Western medical philosophies that attributed Chinese medicine and other culturally specific practices in Vietnam to the incomprehensible, primitive, and thus dismissible realms of illegitimate quackery. The subsequent emergence of US medical infrastructures in South Vietnam not only overturned preexisting medicinal practices rooted in native lifeways but also instilled an institutional practice of cleanliness that disciplined unmodern subjects to display normative behaviors and codified what the US military and medics deemed proper hygienic conduct.

Humanitarian medical programs thereafter sprang up "on a repetitive basis" near Bien Hoa Air Base to offer vaccinations, medical treatments, and surgical soap to natives who were painted as filthy, inept, and indolent.[18] From June 1965 through May 1966, the Air Force implemented these programs in a leper colony, two orphanages, two refugee camps, two Vietnamese independent military clinics, and twenty-four hamlets and villages. MEDCAP teams spurred similar programs in other divisions by offering free surgeries, immunizations, and medical treatments, and they regularly distributed personal care kits that came with bars of soap and leaflets to instruct users on proper bathing and hygiene.[19] Soap was ubiquitous in these scenes, as was its normalization as an obligatory hygienic ritual. Of course, one should not fully discount the potentially meaningful experiences of the medics who participated in such humanitarian work, nor diminish the degree of relief that medicine and soap provided to the sick patients who received them. Objectives for soap, however, extended well beyond the benign and rather simplistic intent to cure antiquated diseases and impurities in the local Vietnamese, for military officials and medics had myriad reasons for its propagation, including raising support for the war in the United States.

Garnering material support for soap likewise drew extensive overseas participation. The gradual establishment of transnational networks for soap accumulation took place within the folds of letters, pamphlets, and newspaper columns that advertised and promoted the American medical mission to home-front audiences. The transfer of soap from the "clean" hands of Americans to the "dirty" palms of Vietnamese villagers mobilized soap as a concurrent infrastructure and commodity, politicizing medicine as a counterinsurgent imperative. In 1965, an article entitled "Our Town" in the *Eastchester Record* (New York) observed that the very well-known Captain Chapman, the army commander of the Third Tactical Dispensary, had received "thousands of cakes of soap" through the column's regular readers. Described as "the good doctor of Viet Nam, who flew through hailstorms of bullets to help the sick and dying," the captain had been fortuitously blessed with an outpouring of support from the newspaper's followers. In the previous year, Chapman's aunt began the process when she suggested in a column that people "send a cake of soap" to her nephew in Vietnam.[20] Her entreaty facilitated what eventually became informally known as "Operation Soap," a mission to proselytize Western hygienic rituals to the villagers of Vietnam and enable the transnational participation of Americans on the home front to the cause of civilian aid on the battlefront.[21]

The thank-you letters Chapman personally signed and sometimes handwrote to Americans who sent him boxes of soap were not simply receipts for the packages but also attempts to positively promote the American war effort in Vietnam. To boost civilian confidence in the war, Chapman frequently embellished his missives with patriotic messages that, addressed through the confidential, interpersonal epistolary form, enfolded his recipients in the grander cause of saving humanity in the derelict villages of Vietnam. Writing to a Mrs. Florence J. Barnaskey, who had sent him a gift of "fine English soap," Chapman claimed, "Thoughtfulness such as yours is a reminder that people do care about the many Americans who are doing a very necessary job 12,000 miles from home."[22] In another letter, he asserted that gifts of soap would begin the "long education process" to reform poor hygienic habits in rural villages, helping natives to "recognize the value of the fundamentals of sanitation."[23] By invoking their responsibility to do the necessary job of saving lives via gifting soap, Chapman assured Americans on the home front that their presents were not only magnanimous but also part of the larger war effort to cleanse and purify the Vietnamese people, whose bodies and minds were at risk of contamination.

The cause of medical rescue found greater impetus in the sympathies of Americans who sought to deliver the most innocent figures of the war—young children—from disease and other, invidious psychological dangers. Indeed, children figured prominently in informational letters reported to contributors in the nation-state, often in language that enunciated their victimization, vulnerability, and guiltlessness. As Miriam Ticktin maintains in the context of modern-day humanitarian borders, "their innocence is what qualifies them for humanitarian compassion."[24] Medical officers like Chapman encouraged church congregations, nonprofit charities, and even political groups to launch widespread campaigns for soap collection in schools, hospitals, and university campuses to save the children of Vietnam, who quickly became the target population for the US military's medical infrastructure and the core justification for the staging of its rescue narrative.[25] In one case, the Women's Auxiliary of the Plattsburgh Junior Chamber of Commerce explicitly stated its desire to donate soap as "we would like very much to especially help the Vietnamese children."[26] With children positioned as the centerpiece of his own medical mission, Captain Chapman forged a paternalistic intimacy between the American public and Vietnamese families, whom he painted as powerless and whose very salvation from disintegration and disease depended on American pity and dollars. "I can assure 2 dollars will go a long way," he wrote to a donor, "in helping to clean up . . . some of the pathetic adults and children we treat in our village medical programs here."[27]

Bathing children with soap was a common practice of hygienic paternalism in the militarized villages of South Vietnam. Alongside routine reconnaissance patrolling in the hamlets, which policed the bodily movements of natives within the confinements of barbed wire and armed surveillance, units like the Marine Corps distributed soap to families and held "sick calls" for the villagers with a designated corpsman and a medical team. The biggest issue with the young children and babies, the medical team and corpsmen surmised, was not some incurable illness or disease but their total lack of cleanliness. To resolve these deplorable conditions, several Marine Corps squads installed makeshift stations in the villages to give children baths. Sergeant Stephen Salisbury, an interpreter for the Civic Action Program, described the practice: "They [the squads] just had an assembly line set up of Marines and the people would bring children to the bathing spot and the men would just hand the child from one to the other and one would wash and one would rinse it. One would wipe it and so forth."[28] In the act of bathing the children, the corpsmen demonstrated to watching parents and guardians the utility of soap,

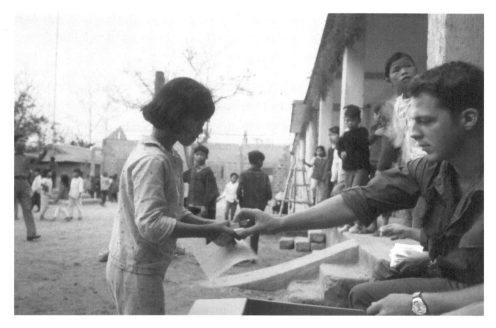

Figure 2. An American soldier gives a young girl a bar of soap after her immunization at a county fair. Courtesy of Mike McDermott Collection (VAS083173), Vietnam Center and Sam Johnson Vietnam Archive, Texas Tech University.

which the US servicemen hoped they would adopt in personal and daily practice.[29] These hamlet programs evidence the conjoined alliance of militarization with the soft power of humanitarian aid, or put differently, the integration of military control with the spectacle of civic action. Such actions were also highly gendered, as predominantly male soldiers engaged in the feminized acts of showering babies and children. Against the highly masculinized and hypervisible backdrop of violence and war, the soldiers' participation in traditionally femininized spheres of domesticity, channeled through the passive economies of soap, palliated the violent occupation of Vietnam by transforming death and injury into their recuperative obverse: health.

The infrastructure of Vietnam's medical humanitarianism depended largely on the pretext of soap as a free and luxurious "gift," which generated much-needed subjects for the expansion of US empire (fig. 2). Soldiers and medics alike indulged in profuse displays of Vietnamese gratitude for their volunteer work, and American donors were reminded of their altruism through Chapman's written accounts of local appreciation for the gifts of soap.[30] As a tactical weapon manipulated for different political causes, soap makes transparent the power relations between medics operating in the rural villages of Vietnam and the silenced but "grateful" recipients of their charity—a debt economy that continues to echo in postwar refugee epistemologies.[31] Soap's discursive character thus appears consistently as an infrastructure for political and ideological transmission. By imploring their fellow Americans to send soap to the Vietnamese peasants and children, medics and military officers created an attractive avenue for foreign remedial assistance that further engaged the humanitarian feelings of Americans on the home front to devote their financial capacities to aid vulnerable villagers in an ostensibly terrorized landscape.[32] And if such hearts and minds were already influenced by perverse political ideologies, these medics hoped that gifts of soap and lessons of hygiene could somehow alleviate such detrimental afflictions.

In rendering the villagers as passive and grateful recipients of humanitarian aid, the US military largely overlooked their capacities for self-determination. Replete with state reports on US civic and governmental intelligence programs, the archive does not show how soap moved from the caches of humanitarian supplies to the black market. However, the scattered appearances of medical soap in documents on South Vietnamese black marketeering open apertures for our speculation on the clandestine activities and desires of people eclipsed by archival recognition. As Noel Buttigieg has noted in relation to black-market intrigues in Malta during the World War II–induced food shortage of 1942, civilians who participated in illegal dealings often had to negotiate between what constituted "moral" and "immoral" consumer practices, given the collapse of their wartime economy, and black markets allowed many to reclaim a limited sense of control over food in times of scarcity.[33] Likewise, mobilizing soap as an insurgent commodity through its entry into the black market would have allowed some Vietnamese to reclaim a small measure of authority from their imperial benefactors and to seek alternate ways of survival beyond laboring or dying as proxy soldiers for the war, thereby disrupting soap's infrastructural logic as an imperial broker. In the next section, I attempt to delineate the contours of the wartime black market by following the trail of missing and stolen soap, examining both the instability of US capitalism in the war and its antithetical form in the black-market economy.

Apathy, Black Markets, and Refused Benevolence

Although the infrastructure of humanitarian aid to the indigent Vietnamese was cloaked in charitable language, the problems that some medics faced in the villages did not always mesh coherently with the archetypes of the Western humanitarian and the grateful yet impoverished Asian subject. Hidden or less visible within the material reproductions of capitalist and imperial hegemony were uncertainties that civilians themselves displayed, ambivalences fleetingly captured in refusals to wash, groom, and mimic the hygienic demands of empire. A 1967 special to the *New York Times* reveals an illuminating instance of refused benevolence. When American medics attempted to teach a Montagnard village of Indigenous Djerai (Jarai) people, described as "[living] their immemorial lives in squalor, sloth, and disease," about soap and its antibiotic uses, many were disheartened to find that "despite repeated instructions, the Djerai steadfastly refuse to use the soap." Brigade commander Colonel James Adamson admitted in disbelief that "we even take mothers down to the stream and show them how to wash babies, but they never do it again after we leave."[34] Why did the Djerai people refuse, and what does their denial of soap and, by extension, American aid suggest?

Regarding the activities of the US Medical Corps in Vietnam, Thuy Linh Tu has argued that "whether any of these [Vietnamese] subjects consented in a meaningful way to their treatment is unclear. Patients, especially children, likely did not know or could not without repercussion refuse the offer of care, even as the use of their body (and its image) remained outside their control."[35] Acts of refusal and indifference, therefore, rupture understandings of commodity culture as simply an imposition from above with little room for personal negotiation. Timothy Burke's argument regarding colonial commodities in Zimbabwe widens this script: "The consumption of commodities [in Zimbabwean society] was also shaped by individual acts of will and imagination, engagement and disinterest. It was also a part of struggles and practices that were tangential or peripheral to the central political and social issues of colonial life."[36] Although the archive does not privilege incidents of refusal and chooses instead to hypervisualize the grateful and obsequious recipients of US aid, these barely traceable glimpses of defiance undermine the projects of hygienic reform that prevail in humanitarian narratives. Though voiced through the disappointment and annoyance of American medics, these acts convey the incompleteness of imperial desires to administer social change and program racial orders.

Despite the widespread and systematic distribution of cleansing agents that proliferated hegemonic ideals about cleanliness and ideological purity to native villagers, the appearance of "gifts" of soap in the black markets of South Vietnam, predominantly on the streets of Saigon, Hue, and Da Nang as well as within hamlets and villages, reveals another node of resistance to US aid that elided the constraints of the law because of the pervasiveness of the black market and its diffuse form. On sending Captain Chapman four cases of soap for the people-to-people program, the US Operations Mission to Vietnam issued a warning: "Suggest each cake be cut in two pieces," a representative advised, "otherwise soap may end up on the black market."[37] The statement hinted that soap became more covetable as its quantities grew. In another source, a physician recalled "seeing cakes of soap in the marketplace that had been used as barter, because not enough time had been devoted to showing the people what it was for and how beneficial it would be." Although he interpreted this occurrence simply as "the apathy of the Vietnamese," the summation of their denial as solely the result of inadequate training and ignorance misses the subjective negotiations of value that arbitrated these decisions.[38] Rather, they reflect what Tu calls a project of "making do," which are "tactics of everyday life, of use, reuse, and other innovations that turn people from 'mere' consumers into actors and producers."[39] Vietnamese who bartered soap that had been distributed for humanitarian purposes in effect *recycled* the material into a means of monetary subsistence that breached its original enclosure as a gift, transforming it into a commodity and medium of exchange for other goods—what Jeong Min Kim calls a *quasi*-currency.[40]

Scholarship on the prolific growth of black markets in areas besieged by war has attested to their informal and inherently insubordinate nature, occurring in the absence of state regulations and periods of government laxity due to weakened wartime or postwar economies.[41] Within the historiography of black markets in imperial and postwar Japan, numerous scholars have demonstrated how alternative urban markets arose out of the inability of state authorities to regulate basic goods, leading to "criminal" commercial activities that handed power and choice back to the people.[42] Transactions on black markets take place between both skilled and unskilled suppliers, vendors, and intermediaries and sometimes draw into their orbit soldiers and government officials who turn a blind eye to the operations or purchase items furtively from sellers for personal use. The destabilizing power of these markets lies in their quotidian exchanges and chaotic assemblage, gesturing to the internal breakdown of state infrastructures and the instantiation of a new social order.

Several factors enhanced the desirability of soap as an extralegal commodity on the Vietnamese black market. During the war, the South Vietnamese government imposed high taxes on "luxurious" goods like soap, cigarettes, liquor, and gasoline. If these items arrived as imports from foreign countries, they incurred hefty customs duties that Vietnamese locals were forced to pay to provide income for the national government. However, under international agreements established with the GVN (Government of Vietnam), US military personnel were freed of obligations to pay any taxes on imported goods. Because a significant portion of the sales price on imported commodities was just the government tax, prices of American-owned commissary merchandise, PX goods, and military supplies like soap were often cheaper than equivalent products on the local market.[43] To avoid the surcharge, unauthorized black market resellers would acquire American goods by hijacking delivery trucks and manipulating inventory sheets, forging or stealing ration cards, or purchasing untaxable American imports directly from GIs, who might give away the commodity in question "out of the kindness of his heart" or in return for services.[44] Some articles reported that American GIs simply could not meet the demand for soap after sharing their small rations with the natives, a deficit that gradually triggered more campaigns to send soap to Vietnam.[45] As one MACV (Military Assistance Command, Vietnam) report alleged, "If just one in every ten people [above-average GIs] give an extra box of soap to their maid during a month, that means 100 boxes of soap per day into the [black] market. That soap is worth 20,000 piastres a day, or 600,000 piastres a month."[46]

The operations of black marketeers vis-à-vis the sale of untaxed goods induced a sizeable loss of revenue for the GVN and, by close relation, a loss of credibility for the US imperial state. As William Allison has argued, the black market demonstrated one of the "fundamental challenges the United States faced in a land peopled with a truly foreign set of cultural mores that matched poorly with American liberal democratic values."[47] An obstacle to the liberal claims of the US empire, the black market became a laboratory for opportunism by Vietnamese civilians and American military personnel alike. It became, in its dissident yet methodical ways, an insurgent infrastructure that remained deliberately opaque, difficult to trace, and impossible to dismantle even after US troops withdrew in 1973 and the American embassy in Saigon closed in 1975.[48]

In conjunction with the shipment of medical supplies that commenced under the banner of civic action work, the US Commercial Import Program (CIP) established by USAID had been injecting large quantities of commercial goods and American capital into South Vietnam since the end of French colonization in 1954. As US dollars trickled into the country's national treasury, a select number of businessmen were granted import licenses that allowed them to purchase dollars with South Vietnamese piastres below the market rate, which they could then spend on consumer goods to boost the economy.[49] The Saigon government then pocketed the profit it made from selling US aid dollars to fund the war and the national police.[50] Unsurprisingly, the program resulted in South Vietnam's artificial dependence on US sponsorship and material aid.

The distribution of profits made from the sale of American commodities like soap was not an equitable process. CIP importers and resellers in the cities enjoyed far greater financial and material gain than their counterparts in the countryside—a wealth disparity that led to increasing revolutionary fervor and anti-US/GVN sentiments among the rural population.[51] While the influx of things like refrigerators, soda, and soap expanded the upper and middle classes and contributed to inflation and gross materialism in a budding society, rural villagers continued to suffer from poor living conditions, which were exacerbated by military incursions and unending warfare between Vietnamese communists and US forces in the countryside. Increasingly resentful of the government and these abhorrent wealth disparities, this most vulnerable population of Vietnamese was targeted by humanitarian programs for reform and cleansing due to their proximity to communist influences, which only heightened revolutionary fervor in the population.[52]

The importers and entrepreneurs who benefited from CIP shipments differed from black marketeers, who moved and repurposed goods as independent, nonstate actors. Primarily army deserters or jobless transients who attained goods to be sold in the rickety stalls of Saigon and smaller cities, these black marketeers designated by the US military as "unauthorized persons" were not associated with nor contractually bound to the US or South Vietnamese government due to the illegality of their trade.[53] Operating in the underworld of Vietnam, they were marked as unregistered and illegitimate in the capitalist structures of power that controlled and maintained the hierarchy of racialized labor, and the profitability of their exploits unsettled both the nation's internal economic stability and US confidence in South Vietnam. I clarify this difference between CIP importers and black marketeers to bring attention to the divergent, if overlapping, desires of insurgent activities based on survival versus profiteering based on capitalist greed, which benefited only a few Vietnamese connected with the US state.

While valorizing the actions of black marketeers is not my intention, I entertain the ambiguities of the wartime black market to probe its entanglements with formal war economies that structured US racial liberalism and the imperial logistics infrastructure constructed under "just-in-time imperialism," which Wesley Attewell has argued "[manages] the transpacific flows of commodities and bodies between the US and South Vietnam" to produce "new nodes of racial capitalist anti-relationality."[54] As the war progressed and the CIP expanded, Vietnamese workers along with those from South Korea and the Philippines became racialized cheap labor in logistical supply-chain work that offered little compensation for their bodily expenditure. With the supply of commodities readily available, however, the black market posed intractable problems for the management of a wartime empire. By selecting to become underground resellers, barterers, and unauthorized stall vendors instead of unfree labor on the docks, military bases, and warehouses, the Vietnamese and other racialized Asian workers essentially withheld their labor from the military-industrial complex. In addition, women who participated in the black market could escape the financial binds and gender restrictions that limited most Southeast Asian women to extractive forms of social reproductive labor such as domestic, entertainment, and/or sex work—labor intimately connected to the wartime logistics of empire building away from the fields.[55] Counterproductive to the progress of the war, the withdrawal of black marketeers from sanctioned work made transparent the needs of empire to constrain devalued life and also showed the subversive ways in which the black market allowed resellers to upend such valuations by disrupting the flow of capital and labor back into the economy.

Indeed, the US military discouraged participation in the black market, but condemnation did little to curb the wayward enterprise. Multiple "fact sheets" published by the MACV between 1965 and 1972 labeled the unauthorized sale of commodities on the black market as illegal and corrosive to the Vietnamese economy, accompanied by graphics containing soap bars that stressed, "Do Not Support the Black Market" in all caps. Posters addressed both American GIs and Vietnamese civilians, who were cautioned to avoid trading PX goods if they did not want to jeopardize their own economy, government, and futures.[56] The potential for US economic goods and greenbacks to fall into the hands of communist forces, moreover, could become a prevalent risk in the eyes of the US State Department and the Department of Defense. According to a speech by Congressman Gerald R. Ford, state leaders initially turned a blind eye to black marketeering in Vietnam but were forced to acknowledge the situation in 1966 when the capturing of AID supplies in rural villages by "Viet Cong" insurgents became more frequent and out of control. Even then, the United States knew it could not halt its shipments of commodities without risking the imminent fall of South Vietnam's feeble economy. With the war worsening and no visible end in sight, Ford's cantankerous description of subversive black-market activities as a mushrooming "smelly mess" would seem a somewhat appropriate representation of the situation to those in command.[57]

The black market, illegible as a legal structure yet self-sustaining as an alternative economic practice and insurgent infrastructure, emphasizes what Tadiar aptly terms "remaindered life-times," which, in addition to remaindered forms of life-making, points to the "uses, experience, actions, and effects of reproductive life-times made and lived that are *not* absorbed into the processes of production and maintenance of the life-form of value nor into the processes of generating value from waste."[58] Put differently, practices of survival on the black market circumvent the value-making processes endemic to the political economy of capitalism, which has long consumed and exploited the labor power of the dispossessed and disenfranchised for its social and economic reproduction. The remaindered life-times encapsulated by black-market operations evade capitalist serviceability by animating other spaces of native life that state authorities may consider disposable or illegitimate. In such a way, they become untraceable in linear time, marked by evasions, elisions, and refusals that reject total transparency, including archival legibility.

While archival records do not contain the voices of its participants, the black market could have been a person's second chance, last resort, or new beginning. US military officials believed black-market sales were largely responsible for damaging the fragile economy of South Vietnam and blamed them on several "bad" GIs and unscrupulous Vietnamese, but these nongovernmental economic transactions imply considerable levels of disinterest and perhaps even disfavor toward Saigon's warmongering and anticommunist regime, breeding the seeds of opportunism that as a result forged an inscrutable and burgeoning underworld. Fed by war and sustained by need, the parasitical market found an an unwilling yet abundant host in US aid; this relationship formed one of many untenable unions that would write the war's eventual doom.

Conclusion

A Department of the Army Special Photographic Office video clip from 1967, shot by army photographer William Foulke, begins with grainy footage of Rome plows clearing brush, trees, and bamboo in a nondescript Vietnamese countryside. The giant plows destroy vegetation to root out enemy positions, but their sprockets cut and tread deep scars into the bruised jungle landscape. Minutes later, the video cuts to a MEDCAP worker scrubbing a young child's head with soap as his mother cradles him, her eyebrows furrowed in distress. The suds color the boy's skull a bubbly white hue. In the next frame, a group of medics passes out bars of Ivory and Lux soap to a crowd of villagers who eagerly await their gifts. Then one by one, babies and adults are treated for skin diseases, hot spots, and rashes while others loiter, simply observing. The camera pans out for the last scene: vast fields blemished with bomb craters, pockmarked and desecrated—the injuries of war on earth's alluvial skin. Even as scenes of soap distribution and medical aid cleave the video's opening and ending clips, violence marks and surrounds the affable gestures of humanitarian work, the true outcome and full reality of the US empire's pretensions to benevolence.[59]

Soap thus gifts and takes, for while it bestows cleanliness and good health, it also racializes and destroys. Seeking to ameliorate the poor hygienic conditions of rural Vietnam, physicians and soldiers introduced soap to those they deemed vulnerable to diseases of the body and the mind to construct a complacent society of grateful subjects. These projects, although valorized by military leaders as necessary and venerable work, were unsettled by their contradictory resonances of military violence and ideological coercion. Against these given terms, Vietnamese villagers who refused the soap for personal needs and sought economic profit through the illegal sale of soap exposed the volatility of the American humanitarian mission. Hygiene may have been the central priority for the American medics, but for the locals who bartered and sold on the black market, soap became a multipurpose commodity operating across modalities of individualism, monetary desires, and co-ethnic sociality.

Attentive to the structures of power in the archive, I aver that undoing the infrastructure of imperial militarization begins with the recognition of soap's multivalent reproductions in South Vietnam's myriad and intensely problematic wartime economies. As an infrastructure and technology of "civilization," soap reaches beyond its technical capacities to deaden disease and sustain viable life by interpolating both imperial *life-gifting* and minoritarian *life-making* into frictional and coexistent frames. Even against the hegemony of the historical archive and its prioritization of Western humanitarianism, by which the ungrateful, disobedient, and recalcitrant subject is expelled to the margins of US memory or relegated to the nonhuman status of the "Viet Cong," the transformation of soap and other material goods into commodities with extralegal mobility on the black market evinces the untenability of US benevolence. Where an imperial gift disappears into the illicit void, the script of humanitarian giving is rewritten into insurgent life and reclaimed.

Ann Ngoc Tran is a PhD candidate in the Department of American Studies and Ethnicity at the University of Southern California. She works on critical refugee studies, maritime Southeast Asian studies, and multiethnic histories of the US Gulf South.

Notes

A version of this article was presented at the conference "1972: The War between North and South Vietnam," hosted by the Vietnam Center and Archive in April 2022 at Chapman University. I am grateful to Nayan Shah for being my first interlocutor for this article at its very beginnings, and to Mariam B. Lam for her thoughtful questions and feedback at the conference. Thank you to the editors of this issue, specifically to Wesley Attewell, and the two anonymous reviewers for their generosity with this article, and to Adrian De Leon and Jason Vu for their brilliant insights, encouragements, and shared struggles on every step of this journey. All mistakes are my own.

1.   In this article, I use the term *natives* to refer to the people of occupied Vietnam, while recognizing that being native to a particular locality does not represent Indigeneity in the land. As a multiethnic society, Vietnam is composed of the majority Kinh (Vietnamese) people, who hail from northern Vietnam and southern China. While the current Vietnamese government does not label its fifty-three ethnic minority groups as Indigenous, the Montagnard peoples from the Central Highlands, of which the Jarai (Djerai) people are part, are indigenous to the mountains of modern-day Vietnam. I also maintain the Americanized use of names like *Vietnam* to be consistent with the source materials and scholarly literature on civic action and black markets in the war; however, as I am cognizant of the ways in which such uses are also US-centric, I use quotation marks around terms like *Viet Cong* to signal their hegemonic construction.

2.   Marx, *Capital*, 125–30.

3.   Larkin, "Politics and Poetics of Infrastructure," 329.

4.   For the purposes of this project, the predominant archive for the primary source materials is the Vietnam Center and Sam Johnson Vietnam Center Archive at Texas Tech University. When I began this paper during the pandemic, the institution's large digital database allowed me to access most of the materials I needed without an in-person visit. I did, however, come to the physical archive in July 2022, where I located additional materials to supplement my previous findings. Other sources come from newspaper archive databases, and Wesley Attewell has generously lent me access to important documents from the USAID Commodity Import Program, which I reference later in this article.

5.   See Wilensky, *Military Medicine*.

6.   An exception to this infrastructural trend is Keva X. Bui's study of napalm in wartime Vietnam and its cultural afterlives, in which they examine the ways in which napalm provides both material evidence of war's violence and acts as a political signifier for Cold War racial politics ("Objects of Warfare," 299).

7.   Large-scale hygienic reforms in the Philippines at the turn of the twentieth century following the defeat of Spanish forces in 1898 precipitated the US military's entrance into South Vietnam's rural villages in the 1960s. Warwick Anderson has detailed how American military and civil health officers who arrived on the archipelago attempted the burden of cleansing natives of bodily and behavioral impurities they believed were impeding the locals' optimal performance as modern citizen-subjects of the newly installed US empire (*Colonial Pathologies*, 2–3). Moon-ho Jung has connected these projects of imperial management to the ways in which the US "secured empire" across the Pacific region in the early twentieth century (*Menace to Empire*).

8.   Tadiar, *Remaindered Life*, 70.

9.   Stoler, *Along the Archival Grain*, 271–72.

10.   U. S. Marine Corps Civic Action Effort in Vietnam March 1965–March 1966 (1968), 0720803001, Box 08, Folder 03, John Donnell Collection, Vietnam Center and Sam

Johnson Vietnam Archive, Texas Tech University (hereafter cited as Vietnam Center), https://vva.vietnam.ttu.edu/repositories/2/digital_objects/95866.

11. As Simeon Man makes evident in his investigation of racialized and colonized workers, medics, and soldiers across Asia and the Pacific who participated in military activities in search of opportunity during the US war in Vietnam, US militarization constituted humanitarian civic action under the guise of racial liberalism and the political banner of "an Asia for Asians." Nonwhite medics and nurses, as early as the 1950s, took part in counterguerrilla and counterinsurgent humanitarian programs in rural Vietnamese villages to accelerate the "transformation" of South Vietnam into a modern nation modeled on the examples of the Philippines and South Korea. In Hawai'i, in particular, the Twenty-Fifth Division's "Operation Helping Hand" linked the public drive to collect soap for Vietnamese children to Hawai'i's liberal multicultural inclusion into the nation-state, obscuring US military violence and Kanaka Maoli dispossession on the islands. See Man, *Soldiering through Empire*, 84–87.

12. "Medical Assistance to Vietnamese Civilians," AMEDD Center of History and Heritage, https://achh.army.mil/history/book-vietnam-medicalsupport-chapter13 (accessed June 7, 2022); see Wilensky, *Military Medicine*, 4.

13. Report - Bridge to Understanding the US Civic Action Program - re: The 9th US Infantry Division (undated), 12730101002, Box 01, Folder 01, Donald Stiles Collection, Vietnam Center, www.vietnam.ttu.edu/virtualarchive/items.php?item=12730101002.

14. *Burlington Free Press*, "Soap Becomes a Secret Weapon."

15. Rusk, "Vietnam's Need for Medical Aid."

16. Comprehensive Medical Care in Vietnam (October 26, 1967), 0380104003, Box 01, Folder 04, Dr. Calvin Chapman Collection, Vietnam Center, www.vietnam.ttu.edu/virtualarchive/items.php?item=0380104003.

17. Shah, *Contagious Divides*, 30.

18. US Air Force Humanitarian Medical Programs for the Vietnamese (April 14, 1967), 0380114005, Box 01, Folder 14, Dr. Calvin Chapman Collection, Vietnam Center, www.vietnam.ttu.edu/virtualarchive/items.php?item=0380114005.

19. Report - Bridge to Understanding the US Civic Action Program, 42–43.

20. Our Town, newspaper (1965), 0380105006, Box 01, Folder 05, Dr. Calvin Chapman Collection, Vietnam Center, www.vietnam.ttu.edu/virtualarchive/items.php?item=0380105006.

21. Other unofficial soap-collecting missions under similar titles began under the command of other individuals like Marine Cpl. William C. Deans. See *Los Angeles Times*, "Operation Soap" (photograph).

22. Letter to Florence J. Barnaskey (February 17, 1966), 0380215085, Box 02, Folder 15, Dr. Calvin Chapman Collection, Vietnam Center, www.vietnam.ttu.edu/virtualarchive/items.php?item=0380215085.

23. Chapman, Letter to J. J. Reid (February 16, 1966), 0380215083, Box 02, Folder 15, Dr. Calvin Chapman Collection, Vietnam Center, www.vietnam.ttu.edu/virtualarchive/items.php?item=0380215083.

24. Ticktin, "Thinking beyond Humanitarian Borders," 257.

25. *Crowley Post-Signal*, "Soap for Vietnamese Children"; *Daily Herald*, "Vietnam Soap Drive"; *Los Angeles Times*, "Hospital Sends Soap"; *Herald News*, "Packages for Vietnam."

26. Chapman, Letter from Mary E. Grant (May 16, 1966), 0380215145, Box 02, Folder 15, Dr. Calvin Chapman Collection, Vietnam Center, www.vietnam.ttu.edu/virtualarchive/items.php?item=0380215145.

27. Chapman, Letter to Mrs. Henry Hunt (May 16, 1966), 0380113071, Box 01, Folder 13, Dr. Calvin Chapman Collection, Vietnam Center, www.vietnam.ttu.edu/virtualarchive/items.php?item=0380113071.

28. Interview with Stephen Salisbury (n.d.), USMC0013, US Marine Corps History Division Oral History Collection, Vietnam Center, https://www.vietnam.ttu.edu/items.php?item=USMC0013.

29. Interview with Paul Ek (January 24, 1966), USMC0046, US Marine Corps History Division Oral History Collection, Vietnam Center, https://www.vietnam.ttu.edu/virtualarchiveitems.php?item=USMC0046.

30. Chapman recounted in a letter to an American couple who sent a large package of soap, clothes, and toys to the children of Vietnam that "they [the gifts] have all been taken to the many villages and hamlets we visit and given directly to poor, dirty but very grateful Vietnamese" (Letter to Melody and Bruce Guiver [May 23, 1966], 0380215149, Box 02, Folder 15, Dr. Calvin Chapman Collection, Vietnam Center, www.vietnam.ttu.edu/virtualarchive/itemsphp?item=0380215149).

31. See Nguyen, *Gift of Freedom*.

32. Neda Atanasoski has articulated "humanitarian feeling" in the context of Vietnam War photojournalism and documentary footage of violence, which contributed to moral outrage in post–Vietnam War US culture (*Humanitarian Violence*, 74–76). I invoke the term here to gesture to the ways in which the language of destitution and poverty also fostered a humanitarian affect in the American population, who subsequently felt the need to save innocent Vietnamese from the diseases of premodernity and communism.

33. Buttigieg, "Breadways and Black-Market Intrigues," 254.

34. Wicker, "Tribal Village."

35. Tu, *Experiments in Skin*, 114.

36. Burke, *Lifebuoy Men*, 10.

37. Soap for the People-to-People program (October 12, 1965), 0380215034, Box 02, Folder 15, Dr. Calvin Chapman Collection, Vietnam Center, www.vietnam.ttu.edu/archive/items.php?item=0380215034.

38. Physician recalls experiences in Vietnam (February 13, 1967) 0380223033, Box 02, Folder 23, Dr. Calvin Chapman Collection, Vietnam Center, https://www.vietnam.ttu.edu/virtualarchive/items.php?item=0380223033 (accessed March 26, 2021).

39. Tu, *Experiments in Skin*, 151.

40. Kim, "From Military Supplies," 12.

41. See Steege, *Black Market, Cold War*; Roodhouse, *Black Market Britain*; Fuller, "Black Markets and War Booty"; and Regev, "'We Want No More Economic Islands.'"

42. See Chinn, "Staple Food Control"; Griffiths, "Need, Greed, and Protest"; Solt, "Not an Easy Road"; and Hatsuda, "Tokyo's Black Markets."

43. Fact Sheet, Provost Marshal - I FFORCE V: Blackmarket - Record of MACV Part 1 (undated), F015800360629, Box 0036, Folder 0629, Vietnam Center, www.vietnam.ttu.edu/virtualarchive/items.php?item=F015800360629.

44. Fact Sheets, Office of Information: Command Information Division, Black Market, Alcohol, Drug Abuse, and First Aid - Record of MACV Part 1 (September 15, 1971), F015800090718, Box 0009, Folder 0718, Vietnam Center, www.vietnam.ttu.edu/virtualarchive/items.php?item=F015800090718.

45. *Los Angeles Times*, "Hospital Sends Soap."

46. Fact Sheets, Office of Information: Command Information Division.

47. Allison, "War for Sale," 135.

48. Allison, "War for Sale," 136.
49. Report, Joint Economic Office - Economic and Financial Data (undated), 19600122008, Box 01, Folder 22, Gary Larsen Collection, Vietnam Center, www.vietnam.ttu.edu /virtualarchive/items.php?item=19600122008.
50. United States House of Representatives, Committee on Government Operations, Illicit Practices Affecting the US Economic Program in Vietnam (Follow-up Investigation), Fourth Report by the Committee on Government Operations, 90th Congress, 1st Session (Washington: Government Printing Office, 1967), 3–4; Jacobs, *Cold War Mandarin*, 99–100.
51. United States Senate, Committee on Government Operations, Improper Practices, Commodity Import Program, U.S. Foreign Aid, Vietnam, 91st Congress, 1st Session (Washington: Government Printing Office, 1969), 1–2.
52. United States Senate, Committee on Government Operations, Improper Practices, Commodity Import Program, U.S. Foreign Aid, Vietnam, 91st Congress, 1st Session (Washington: Government Printing Office, 1969), 1–2.
53. Fact Sheets, Office of Information: Command Information Division.
54. Attewell, "Lifelines of Empire," 910–12. See also Attewell, "Just-in-Time Imperialism," 1330.
55. N. Attewell and W. Attewell, "Sweating for Their Pay," 185–86.
56. Graphics, Provost Marshal - re: Black Market - Record of MACV Part 1 (undated), F015800360649, Box 0036, Folder 0649, Vietnam Center, www.vietnam.ttu.edu /virtualarchive/items.php?item=F015800360649.
57. Vietnam Black Market, May 20, 1966, Box D20, Ford Congressional Papers: Press Secretary and Speech File, Gerard R. Ford Presidential Library.
58. Tadiar, *Remaindered Life*, 71.
59. Philol Rubber Plantation, video (January 24, 1967), 1040VI0783, William Foulke Collection, Vietnam Center, www.vietnam.ttu.edu/virtualarchive/items.php ?item=1040VI0783.

References

Allison, William. "War for Sale: The Black Market, Currency Manipulation, and Corruption in the American War in Vietnam." *War and Society* 21, no. 2 (2003): 135–64.
Anderson, Warwick. *Colonial Pathologies: American Tropical Medicine, Race, and Hygiene in the Philippines*. Durham, NC: Duke University Press, 2006.
Atanasoski, Neda. *Humanitarian Violence: The U.S. Deployment of Diversity*. Difference Incorporated. Minneapolis: University of Minnesota Press, 2013.
Attewell, Nadine, and Wesley Attewell. "Sweating for Their Pay: Gender, Labor, and Photography across the Decolonizing Pacific." *Journal of Asian American Studies* 24, no. 2 (2021): 183–217.
Attewell, Wesley. "Just-in-Time Imperialism: The Logistics Revolution and the Vietnam War." *Annals of the American Association of Geographers* 111, no. 5 (2021): 1329–45.
Attewell, Wesley. "The Lifelines of Empire: Logistics as Infrastructural Power in Occupied South Vietnam." *American Quarterly* 72, no. 4 (2020): 909–35.
Bui, Keva X. "Objects of Warfare: Infrastructures of Race and Napalm in the Vietnam War." *Amerasia Journal* 47, no. 2 (2021): 299–313.
Burke, Timothy. *Lifebuoy Men, Lux Women: Commodification, Consumption, and Cleanliness in Modern Zimbabwe*. Durham, NC: Duke University Press, 1996.

Burlington Free Press. "Soap Becomes a Secret Weapon." March 14, 1966.

Buttigieg, Noel. "Breadways and Black-Market Intrigues in 1942 Malta." *Global Food History* 7, no. 3 (2021): 238–59.

Chinn, Dennis L. "Staple Food Control and Industrial Development in Postwar Japan, 1950–1957: The Role of the Black Market." *Journal of Development Economics* 4, no. 2 (1977): 173–90.

Crowley Post-Signal. "Soap for Vietnamese Children Being Sought." April 1, 1967.

Daily Herald. Vietnam Soap Drive Scheduled." April 16, 1967.

Fuller, Robert L. "Black Markets and War Booty." In *The Struggle for Cooperation: Liberated France and the American Military, 1944–1946*, 119–43. Lexington: University Press of Kentucky, 2019.

Griffiths, Owen. "Need, Greed, and Protest in Japan's Black Market, 1938–1949." *Journal of Social History* 35, no. 4 (2002): 825–58.

Hatsuda, Kōsei. "Tokyo's Black Markets as an Alternative Urban Space: Occupation, Violence, and Disaster Reconstruction." *Journal of Urban History* 48, no. 5 (2022): 1046–65.

Herald News. "Packages for Vietnam." October 4, 1967.

Jacobs, Seth. *Cold War Mandarin: Ngo Dinh Diem and the Origins of America's War in Vietnam, 1950–1963*. Lanham, MD: Rowman and Littlefield, 2006.

Jung, Moon-Ho. *Menace to Empire: Anticolonial Solidarities and the Transpacific Origins of the US Security State*. American Crossroads 63. Oakland, California: University of California Press, 2022.

Kim, Jeong Min. "From Military Supplies to Wartime Commodities: The Black Market for Sex and Goods during the Korean War, 1950–53." *Radical History Review* 2019, no. 133 (2019): 11–30.

Larkin, Brian. "The Politics and Poetics of Infrastructure." *Annual Review of Anthropology* 42, no. 1 (2013): 327–43.

Los Angeles Times. "Hospital Sends Soap to Vietnam's Needy." September 15, 1966.

Los Angeles Times. "Operation Soap." June 12, 1966.

Man, Simeon. *Soldiering through Empire: Race and the Making of the Decolonizing Pacific*. Oakland: University of California Press, 2018.

Marx, Karl. *Capital: A Critique of Political Economy*. Vol. 1. Translated by Ben Fowkes. New York: Penguin, 1990.

Nguyen, Mimi Thi. *The Gift of Freedom: War, Debt, and Other Refugee Passages*. Durham, NC: Duke University Press, 2012.

Regev, Ronny. "'We Want No More Economic Islands': The Mobilization of the Black Consumer Market in Post War U.S." *History of Retailing and Consumption* (Abingdon, England) 6, no. 1 (2020): 45–69.

Roodhouse, Mark. *Black Market Britain, 1939–1955*. Oxford: Oxford University Press, 2013.

Rusk, Howard A. "Vietnam's Need for Medical Aid Appraised." *New York Times*, September 18, 1965.

Shah, Nayan. *Contagious Divides: Epidemics and Race in San Francisco's Chinatown*. Berkeley: University of California Press, 2001.

Solt, George. "Not an Easy Road: Black Market Ramen and the U.S. Occupation." In *The Untold History of Ramen: How Political Crisis in Japan Spawned a Global Food Craze*, 43–71. Berkeley: University of California Press, 2014.

Steege, Paul. *Black Market, Cold War: Everyday Life in Berlin, 1946–1949*. New York: Cambridge University Press, 2007.

Stoler, Ann Laura. *Along the Archival Grain: Epistemic Anxieties and Colonial Common Sense.* Princeton, NJ: Princeton University Press, 2009.

Tadiar, Neferti X. M. *Remaindered Life.* Durham, NC: Duke University Press, 2022.

Ticktin, Miriam. "Thinking beyond Humanitarian Borders." *Social Research* 83, no. 2 (2016): 255–71. http://www.jstor.org/stable/44282188.

Tu, Thuy Linh N. *Experiments in Skin: Race and Beauty in the Shadows of Vietnam.* Durham, NC: Duke University Press, 2021.

Wicker, Tom. "Tribal Village in Vietnam's Highlands Just Squalor and Sloth." *New York Times*, January 27, 1967.

Wilensky, Robert J. *Military Medicine to Win Hearts and Minds: Aid to Civilians in the Vietnam War.* Lubbock: Texas Tech University Press, 2004.

The Human Tide

Hydraulic Engineering and the Aesthetic
of Corporeal Infrastructure in Socialist China

Yuan Gao

On January 21, 1958, more than ten thousand people gathered at the foot of Tian-shou Mountain to build a dam, 29 meters (95 feet) high and 627 meters (2,057 feet) long, in suburban Changping of Beijing Municipality. Having no advanced tools but using shoulder poles, shovels, and wheelbarrows, they were determined to industrialize local agricultural production with a modern hydraulic edifice. When the completion of the dam—named Ming Tombs Reservoir by Mao Zedong—was announced in June that same year, almost four hundred thousand people were counted as participants in the construction. Among them was Tian Han (1898–1968), a playwright who wrote the stage drama *The Caprice of the Ming Tombs Reservoir* (*Shisanling shuiku changxiangqu*, 1958) to portray the manpower of the revolutionary masses. Giving center stage to characters who demonstrate the Chinese people's passionate commitment to dam building, Tian Han's engagement raises questions critical to examining mass participation in socialist China's hydraulic engineering: What drove people to voluntarily take on the technological, environmental, and physiological challenges of the country's pursuit of hydropower? Was there a mode of labor that would enhance the productivity of the masses while giving them physical delight in the backbreaking construction work? How could this delight be cultivated, shared, and strengthened as the norm of infrastructural labor when there was little material reward?

Radical History Review
Issue 147 (October 2023)   DOI 10.1215/01636545-10637175
© 2023 by MARHO: The Radical Historians' Organization, Inc.

To answer these questions, this essay investigates the theatrical performance for the Ming Tombs Reservoir and the documentary *Red Flag Canal* (1960–70) as two examples of Chinese cultural works that served socialist hydraulic engineering by maintaining the masses' vitality, optimizing their productivity, and reinforcing people's biological delight from developing labor power by effectively managing their corporeal bodies. Both the drama and the film represent a political aesthetic that I call *corporeal infrastructure*. This notion conveys the extensive scale of hydraulic projects in New China, the great number of participants in building hydraulic infrastructure, and, above all, the forging of the socialist laboring body through evocative representations of collective and intensive infrastructural work. Different from "the technological sublime" in the United States,[1] corporeal infrastructure did not induce a sensation of awe by displaying the majestic shape of infrastructure. Shifting focus from the built structure to the building process, corporeal infrastructure highlighted the images and sounds of the working masses transporting dirt, digging tunnels, and diverting water—the actions that altered the landscape as well as the laborers' corporeal properties. Central to this aesthetic was the construction of an energetic, self-aware, and technologized model of the laborers as "the human motor" that could surpass the mechanical machine.[2] For many Chinese cultural workers, to portray infrastructural construction was not meant to create symbolic meanings for the materiality of the hydraulic edifice or to reinforce thought reform based on class consciousness.[3] Instead, they designed theatrical cues to inculcate new ways of working the body as a corporeal machine, new visions of seeing the land as a stock of resources, and new ears to absorb the rhythm of infrastructural labor. Activating the physical body as technical and political matter, the aesthetic of corporeal infrastructure renews our understanding of revolutionary culture not only as propaganda for indoctrination but also as a cultural device to fulfill the state's developmental plans. In China's socialist history of hydraulic engineering, I argue, the aesthetic of corporeal infrastructure was charged with the task of extracting human resources by training the masses to bear rural China's infrastructural modernization.

Approaching infrastructure from the perspective of labor and its transformative power complicates the existing analytical paradigms. Infrastructure has been conceptualized either as invisible technological systems tucked away in the mundane background of the economically advanced countries,[4] or as hypervisible artifacts that monumentalize a society's socioeconomic prowess.[5] Stephen Graham and Simon Marvin have theorized the coexistence of these views as the "dialectics of invisibility and monumentalism" that govern the everyday users of infrastructural services.[6] Between these two poles, however, socialist China's prioritization of construction over consumption propels an alternate paradigm to push the political meaning of infrastructure further. While scholars have observed that infrastructure is a technological object of developmental promise that separates the undesirables from the ideal citizens,[7] they have nonetheless assumed that infrastructure becomes a tool of social control only by provisioning resources and reshaping spaces for the inhabitants, thus often limiting their inquiry to the areas already equipped with modern infrastructure. Taking the building process for granted, the conventional dialectics fail to consider that infrastructural construction requires human resources that are never easy to organize and manage. Making the environment yield space, access, and energy to facilitate production is premised on drawing and sometimes even squeezing corporeal energy from laborers. Making infrastructure work depends first and foremost on putting humans to work.[8]

The socialist aesthetic of corporeal infrastructure expands the horizon by drawing attention to China's building of dams and canals as a project to vitalize the rural areas where Chinese peasantry had lived without sufficient technological apparatus for flood control, water supply, and electrification. From the 1950s to the 1970s, Chinese cultural workers joined the hydraulic projects by continuously delineating mass labor in building hydraulic systems. They visited the construction sites and re-created the building processes in their works to transform the nature of labor to compel China's hydraulic development. When monetary incentives had become ideologically suspicious in the country's planned economy after 1949, how to recast labor as an essential component of life hinged on normalizing a bodily propensity toward hard work by cultural pedagogy. Having taken on the mission of cultivating the masses' momentum in their struggles with hostile environments, equipment inadequacy, and bodily vulnerability, the cultural works not only displayed the spectacular forms of socialist infrastructure but more importantly brought the acquisition of the industrial body to the countryside. Through cultural mediation, where revolutionary vision and infrastructural imperative converged in the laboring bodies choreographed on stage and screen, China's socialist hydraulic engineering exerted power first and foremost on the builders rather than the users; at the same time, it reveals infrastructural politics not only in the regulation and contestation of access but also in its technopolitical command of the labor force.

To analyze the cultural training of infrastructural labor from the high socialist period to the middle of the Cultural Revolution, this essay situates the reservoir drama and canal documentary in the dual context of socialist redefinition of labor and the nationwide hydraulic campaign. I begin by discussing the early years of the People's Republic of China (PRC), when the revolutionary state instituted a labor reform to reshape people's attitude toward their bodily devotion to nation building and when mass mobilization became a policy for developing water conservancy projects. I then delve into a close examination of the Ming Tombs Reservoir drama, paying attention to how the plot and performance strove to merge the audiences into the theatrical mise-en-scène through which the imagination of a body without fatigue and pain was disseminated in and beyond the theater space. I go on to analyze the documentary *Red Flag Canal* with a focus on the screen presentation of the geometrically regimented land as visual training, the sequences of labor scenes as exemplary demonstrations, and the use of the rhythmic sound of construction work as a sonic scheme to penetrate the spectatorial ear. Instead of considering what cultural representations *mean* symbolically or metaphorically, my analysis illuminates what they *do* in teaching audiences how to tax their bodies to the physiological limits. If infrastructure, as Brian Larkin suggests, refers to "objects that create the grounds on which other objects operate,"[9] then the socialist hydraulic culture should be seen as art produced to excavate and mold the mass bodies as infrastructural "raw material."

Revitalizing Labor

Labor as toil was a tenet of Chinese left-wing politics before the establishment of the People's Republic of China. Xu Xian (1922–2015), an official in the Chinese Labor Association founded in 1935, summarized the social conditions that all laborers lived with: "The money workers earn with their labor cannot provide sufficient food or clothing, cannot support their families, cannot give them care when they are ill, cannot sustain their life when they are old."[10] Xu, in his plain language, characterized workers' lives of deprivation and insufficiency as "the problem of labor."[11]

After 1949, the communist regime took on the mission of transforming the perpetual transaction between meager income and tolerance of toil into an enterprise of empowerment and fulfillment. Labor in New China was soon redefined as a self-conscious, self-motivated, and self-supervised practice. These connotations were condensed into the notion of "awakened labor" (*zijue laodong*), a Chinese term derived from the Soviet Stakhanovite movement. Named after Aleksei Stakhanov, a coal miner who, in a six-hour shift on August 30, 1935, miraculously dug 102 tons of coal, fourteen times his individual quota, the movement attracted a great number of emulators in metalworks, textiles, transportation, and other industries and professions across the Soviet Union.[12] At the Stakhanovite Conference in 1935, Joseph Stalin praised the models for giving life to a series of labor virtues. Workers, in his description, cherished every minute and second, updated production standards, corrected conservative estimates of workload, mastered the latest technology, and, most importantly, initiated this labor movement on their own, from the bottom up, without any orders imposed by the managerial levels of industry.[13] It is the last feature that set socialist labor apart from labor's previous mode of conduct.

Embracing Soviet labor management, theory-informed writings in the early years of the PRC stressed that people had misunderstood labor as a shameful burden on the body because they were misguided by capitalist exploitation and prejudice against manual laborers. To change the status quo, the philosopher Yan Beiming 嚴北溟 (1905–90) argued that labor in a society freed from monetary exchange should become "a vital necessity of the healthy and strong body."[14] Citing Lenin and Engels,

Yan emphasized that socialist labor was not a means of survival but a vital necessity for the healthy body. Characterizing this "necessity" as a habit built by changing one's attitude, Yan suggests that the ideal form of labor should come from a biological impulse of the body, which, once revitalized, would rehumanize the workers in a socialist system. Echoing this relocation of labor in people's voluntary expenditure and generation of their kinetic power, several small manuals went on to develop the biological impulse as a liberation of human nature.[15] The socialist writers believed and prescribed that a radical reconceptualization of labor would eventually lead the Chinese masses to find happiness and joy in building a socialist society.[16]

The body in this sense was historized as an agent that compelled China's fundamental shift to the socialist era. It manifests what the French sociologist Marcel Mauss called "the social nature of the '*habitus*,'" the idea that people's quotidian movements (talking, walking, swimming, etc.) are not ahistorical but conditioned by the social environment. Defining the habitus as "a social idiosyncrasy," Mauss argued that it is not "a product of some purely individual, completely psychical arrangements and mechanisms" but always involves an acquisition process that makes the habitus adoptable on a mass scale.[17] To form a bodily habitus is therefore to perpetuate the way the body behaves. In Mauss's observation, for instance, the way French girls walked in early twentieth-century Paris copied how American characters walked in Hollywood films. Using the example to explain that behind each change of collective behavior is an obscure social change (in this case, Hollywood cinema's transnational circulation), Mauss suggested that new bodily moves are revelatory of the new social and cultural phenomena beyond the individual faculties of the mind. Resonating with Mauss's idea, Chinese labor prescription pointed to the emergence of a new laboring body, rather than reinforcement of class consciousness, that blended revolution with reform of work.

Beginning in the mid-1950s, mass participation in China's hydraulic engineering married the reform of the labor habitus with the cause of industrializing the countryside beyond the factory proper. Like labor management, China's construction of hydraulic infrastructure was first prompted by the Soviet model, which stressed the leading role of the central government, continual and considerable financial investment, and rural service to the urban centers. Having gone through decades of wars, however, China immediately found itself short of technological and financial inputs to extend Soviet-style projects all over the country. In 1955, a farmland irrigation campaign was launched to promote the policy of "masses assisted by the state" (*min ban gong zhu*), a political mobilization of the people to undertake provincial and local hydraulic projects. In 1958, Liu Shaoqi, then vice chairman of the Chinese Communist Party, consolidated the primacy of the mass power and announced that the efforts to remake nature had "quickly gripped the imagination of the huge army of hundreds of millions of working people and have been transformed into an immense material force."[18] The laborers soon took center stage in the widespread mass hydraulic campaign wherein the theory of labor as a biological impulse was put into practice to generate bodily delight derived from construction.

In this context, the planning of the Ming Tombs Reservoir began in the winter of 1957 in Changping. Guided by Mao's slogan "Surpass Britain, Catch Up with the US" (*chaoying ganmei*), the construction work commenced without a thorough survey of Changping's geographical conditions. Because of its location near the capital, the reservoir was immediately made an exemplary project for mass participation. From January to May 1958, the number of builders grew substantially from about thirty thousand to fifty thousand. Despite administrative efforts to organize the laborers into two divisions respectively responsible for material supply and embankment, the constantly changing blueprint and local peasants' inexperience in hydraulic work slowed down the process. The circumstances were improved with the involvement of the People's Liberation Army (PLA), deployed from Beijing on May 3. At the same time, the Reservoir Command Center implemented the policy of "technical delegation" (*jishu xiafang*) to solicit problem-solving ideas from the dam builders across the construction site, all of which were conceptually embellished as "technological revolution" (*jishu geming*) in the official discourse when the dam was completed on July 1, 1958.[19]

In a different fashion engendered by the same policy, Red Flag Canal began with a series of smaller hydraulic projects within Henan Province from 1957 to 1959. Located in a landlocked area along the Taihang Mountains, Lin County of Henan was the site of 550 villages, more than 300 of which had been tormented by regular droughts that ingrained an environmental memory of water inaccessibility and poverty. During times of severe disasters, as the local cadres and villagers realized, small canals and reservoirs could barely provide sufficient water for agricultural production and life. In October 1959, the county committee proposed an ambitious plan to channel the Zhang River from neighboring Shanxi Province into their parched villages, which later culminated in Red Flag Canal, consisting of 350 tributary canals, 134 tunnels, and 150 bridges extending from north to south. In the aftermath of the nationwide famine caused by the Great Leap Forward, the canal builders started without heavy equipment deployed by the state. Digging a canal through the mountains, they had to make their bodies behave like bulldozers, cranes, and tractors in taming unruly nature. With no input of laborers from outside, construction depended primarily on villagers' time-honored craftmanship and lasted ten years, from 1960 to 1970.[20]

Both projects received considerable attention from cultural workers in theater, photography, music, literature, and cinema. The cultural discourse not only communicated the achievement of mass hydraulic endeavors across the nation but also consolidated the laboring body as the determining factor in China's infrastructural modernization. With the goal of turning representations into actions, corporeal infrastructure in Chinese revolutionary culture linked the materiality of the body with the materiality of water infrastructure and suggested the latter as a concrete extension of the former. As Mary Douglas points out, "The human body is always treated as an image of society and . . . there can be no natural way of considering the body that does not involve at the same time a social dimension."[21] Chinese cultural workers made sure not only to address the hydraulic infrastructure as imaginary symbols of socialist supremacy, but more ambitiously aimed for the correction, management, and discipline of people's bodies by naturalizing the intensive and even risky work of dam and canal building.

Politics Plus Techniques

On May 25, 1958, the Ming Tombs Reservoir became a media sensation across the country when Mao Zedong, Zhou Enlai, Liu Shaoqi, and Zhu De visited the construction site. A short newsreel entitled "Leaders Working with Us" (*Lingxiu yu women tong laodong*) was shot and widely screened to reinvigorate the Yan'an-style campaign that "blurred the distinction between Party leaders and the masses by emphasizing shared labor and sacrifice."[22] As the newsreel showed with its focus on the bodily presence of the national leaders, thought alone would not build the dam. People's commitment to dam construction must be translated into a variety of new ways of using the body. In turn, their manual improvisation and technical innovation would endow them with a utopian physicality that led them to transcend pain, fatigue, and other physiological limits. The collective work of dam building, to borrow Chenshu Zhou's observation of the film projectionists in the same period, called on the laborers to become "a mode of embodiment . . . where the strengthening of the mind was integrated with the training of the body."[23]

However, not all forms of labor were naturally compatible with the needs of mass hydraulic engineering. Brute strength only engendered frustration rather than a delightful sense of fulfillment. Entering the construction space often involved a process of adjusting and rediscovering one's body. Centering on infrastructural labor, the Reservoir Command Center edited and published *The Builders of the Ming Tombs Reservoir* (*Jianshe shisanling shuiku de renmen* 1958), a five-volume essay collection that documented and promoted the individual experiences of construction work. While covering a great number of laborers from different corners of the country, most of the essays rehearsed a narrative pattern that accounted for people's new movements and rhythms acquired during construction. In these biographical sketches, the universality of mass productivity was achieved through the self-remodeling of the physical body.

A young man named Ma Qingzhi, for instance, was nicknamed "Little Tiger" at the construction site for his sculptural physique. Born to a family of porters dating back to his grandfather's generation, he grew up carrying sacks and pushing wheelbarrows. Having managed to reinvent himself as a soldier two years earlier in the

PLA, Ma nevertheless found his "steel muscles and iron bones" built from childhood experience and military service inadequate in dam building. Like many other builders, he approached his "incompetence" head-on, adding loads of dirt and rocks on his shoulder pole to drive out soreness and other physical discomfort. On a stormy night, when the loudspeaker announced a middle-aged peasant Aunt Liu's vow to surpass her male comrades, Ma's blood boiled and drove him to excavate twenty-five cubic meters of dirt in one night. Having trained his shoulders and legs, he achieved "greater outcome, higher speed, better quality, and less cost" (*duo, kuai, hao, sheng*), the production principle common during the Great Leap Forward. Eventually, Ma was named model laborer for grasping how to use one basket as two baskets and take one leap that equaled two steps.[24]

The story of Little Tiger is one of the many examples that identify self-regeneration and corporeal malleability as the staple features of a model laborer. Echoing Ying Qian's insights on the cinema of the Great Leap Forward, the acceleration bespeaks the political demands of speed and sleeplessness as driving forces for the socialist builders to transcend clock time.[25] Yet the focus on time management leaves the qualitative change of infrastructural labor unaddressed. In the competition between the dam builders ran an impulse to surpass not just other laborers but oneself. Ma's disappointment in his initial performance and desire to be ever more productive suggest that the builder must be highly aware of his own body. After all, it was none other than Ma himself who continued to supervise his own physical efficacy. Though most of the essays in the collection sing the praises of laborers making outstanding contributions by breaking production records, what really defines them as role models is not merely the result of hyperproductivity but their voluntary enhancement of productivity. In other words, the figures in *The Builders of the Ming Tombs Reservoir* were meant to give life to the socialist prescription of labor as a natural necessity of the people. In this ideality, the dam builders were supposed to thrive on the spontaneity of labor, not perish for the outcome of construction. How to produce and maintain such spontaneity was the primary concern of Tian Han, who visited, joined, and closely observed the building of the reservoir.

In early May 1958, Tian Han returned to Beijing from a two-month writing retreat in the city's western suburb. Tremendously impassioned by the mass hydraulic project, he traveled from his Beijing home to the site of the Ming Tombs Reservoir in the northern outskirts and participated in the construction work on three separate nights from late May to early June.[26] It took Tian Han only seven days to finish the script of *The Caprice of the Ming Tombs Reservoir*. After his last "fight" at the construction site, as the military metaphor went, the ardent Tian Han met with Xiong Wei, the administrative assistant of Chinese Youth Art Theater, and Jin Shan, the actor and director who later adapted the drama into film. At the beginning of their meeting, Tian Han declared that this new drama was to "show the grandiose world-making endeavor with people's awakened labor under the leadership of the Party."[27] Casting the collective work as a manifest of the dam builders' craving for labor, Tian Han planned to inscribe "the strength and beauty," "the interiority and exteriority" of the heroic builders.[28] Administering people's skyrocketing passion and energy with a stage performance, as Tian Han would soon show, should allow the socialist laborers to emerge and flourish.

A theatrical example of the corporeal infrastructure aesthetic, *The Caprice of the Ming Tombs Reservoir* consists of thirteen acts, following a group of scientists, artists, and city cadres visiting and interviewing the mass laborers at the construction site. Within the tent of the Command Center, the drama begins with the visitors' discussion of the fifteenth-century Ming dynasty, when slaves were deployed to build the tomb for the emperor's burial. The subsequent nine acts take the audience on a tour of the dam area, where the visitors explore Changping County to see how individual laborers from different production brigades work and live. The final act concludes the drama with a science-fiction scene twenty years after the completion of the dam. On this historical continuum of past, present, and future, the drama juxtaposes and contrasts hydraulic construction in imperial history with the ongoing socialist period and its afterlife in the fantastical communist society. What connects the sweeping scope of time in one locale is the changing relationship between mass labor and the environment. In general, the drama reiterates the aesthetic convention of "prescriptive chronotope,"[29] first employed by the Chinese writer Lao She 老舍 (1899–1966) in his stage drama *Dragon Whisker Creek* (*Longxu gou*) in 1949. According to Yomi Braester, this aesthetic convention emphasizes the spatial transformation of a particular place before and after the founding of the PRC and presents the ideologically prescribed future as the ultimate form of the nation. While following this established paradigm, Tian Han's reservoir drama reverses the earlier human-space relationship by demonstrating that renewing oneself, especially through reforming the body, is the prerequisite of a new national environment. Dam building based on collective labor is thus evoked as a technology of self-engineering that promises agency and self-improvement to the masses.

Episodic conversations between visiting intellectuals from the city and the dam builders structure the first eight acts of the drama. For the intellectual characters—the biologist, the historian, the writers, the painter, and the musician—to interview the working people is not just to collect their experiences of dam construction as the ingredients for artistic creation, but more importantly to request the masses' education. In act 3, for example, the writer Lin Kun comes across Li Shixi, who has become a "star" laborer for having only one arm but being able to transport heavy loads of dirt using one wheelbarrow and two baskets. When trying to help Li push the wheelbarrow, Lin finds himself struggling to stabilize the weighty containers filled with dirt. Astonished by Li's extraordinary coordination of the body, the writer proclaims in an appreciative tone that it is the laborer's mind, straightened out by political thought, that enables him to overcome his inconvenient physical condition. Li's response, however, catches the writer off guard: "Thank you for your help. You may not know strength doesn't just come from politics but is also a technical concern. Here we call it 'politics plus techniques, strength with a hardworking mind.' None of them is dispensable. See you."[30] The model laborer then disappears swiftly from the interviewers' sight and leaves Lin in silence when the rest of the intellectual fellows burst into laughter.

Two perceptions of dam building labor clash in this brief encounter. For the writer Lin Kun, physical efficacy is a direct reflection of thought reshaped by ideological training. When revolutionary passion is smoothly transmitted from the mind to the body, the latter is conceived as nothing more than a terminal expression of political enlightenment. But for the laborer Li Shixi, the laboring body is not a passive receptacle awaiting ideological stimulation. Instead, it is an active player that acquires and invents problem-solving skills by and for itself. In practical terms, resolution generated by political consciousness does not guarantee the rapid progress of dam construction. With his straightforward rebuttal, Li pushes for the recognition that training the body is essential because it activates the dormant knowledge in the head, by which the agency of the mass laborers is developed and deployed to make self-improvement an instinctual reaction. Whereas Lin celebrates the intellectual root of revolution, Li counters his idea by suggesting that only by "doing" can "thinking" obtain its purposefulness.

Dramatizing these conflicting views of labor, Tian Han suggests that the mass hydraulic project must take the body as both the means and target of reform. Li Shixi's invocation of the popular idiom denies that the body is a sheer instrument of dam building. He acknowledges the importance of mental power derived from the renewal of thought, but since dam building in the end is a physical practice, it needs the builders to set their bodies in motion to cope with various challenging conditions. These challenges are sometimes environmental (storms are mentioned repeatedly in the essay collection and the drama), sometimes technological (shown by another model worker, Ren Lianhua, repairing broken trucks),[31] but more often come from the builders themselves—Li's preexisting disability recalls the "incompetence" that Ma Qingzhi discovered about himself on the first day of work. To be awakened as a socialist laborer, people are taught to view their bodily weakness and indolence as signs of inadequacy. As another student character, Xiao Yang, later asserts in act 9, "The shoulder is just a bag of cheap bones. The more we spoil them, the more trouble they cause."[32] In this act, where Xiao Yang proudly describes how she continuously struggles with bloody blisters from carrying shoulder poles, she defines pain and bleeding as defects the socialist laborer must discard. From the model laborer to the female student, Tian Han's dam-building characters assertively promulgate and embody the mechanism of hydraulic construction as perfection of the body: with self-scrutiny comes a heightened self-awareness, and with self-awareness comes the laborer's drive to engage ever more actively and even cre-atively with dam building in hopes of turning weakness into strength. In this mode, shoulder poles, wheelbarrows, and other vernacular implements are no longer con-struction equipment but become tools of body reform.

To illustrate the miraculous effects of dam building on the laborers, act 13 takes a great temporal leap into 1978, twenty years after the completion of the reser-voir. This futuristic sci-fi act brings a communist paradise by making references to new motor vehicles, home-use helicopters, and children's invention of smart calculators. Among the technological objects, the dam builders' bodies, which are no longer enslaved by the biological constraints of age and illness, stand out. Chen Peiyuan, a veteran of the Korean War, has visited the construction site with his intellectual fel-lows twenty years ago. Having participated in dam building, he now has become aston-ishingly young and fit. Reunited with Chen, the biologist Huang Zhongyun, another intellectual who had visited the reservoir without participating in labor, is confounded by his old pal's unnatural look. The gray-haired Huang asks the youthful Chen if he has taken any hormonal pills or dyed his hair. In reply, Chen claims:

> I didn't take medicine or use hair dye. It is Nature's Law that humans age and die. We can't change the law, but we don't have to subjugate ourselves to it. If we want to nurture younger successors, we will need to prolong our life span and draw lessons from our experience, so we can serve mankind. Didn't you see the new retirement policy? Eighty years old is just middle age now. People now retire when they are one hundred and ten.[33]

Gradually, Chen leads the conversation into a discussion of a series of China's devel-opmental plans, including a hydroelectric station in Taiwan and exploration of outer space. The excitement then prompts the characters into singing. In the chorus, the drama comes to an end with the characters imagining a tourist trip to the moon.

In this last act, Tian Han pivots China's future on bodies beyond biological finitude. Dam building as a project of reform has successfully produced the regen-erative body while leaving behind those who have failed to reform. With the con-trasting bodily images of those who have benefited from dam building and those who resist it and gradually grow weak, Tian Han not only imagines China's future as a dreamland that thrives on technological advancement but more vividly envis-ages it as a utopia where infrastructural work has given the laborers near immortality and uncorruptible corporeality—a transcendental power to defy not just clock time but biological time.

Re-creating the Construction Site

After seven days of writing the script, Tian Han immediately crafted a performance on stage to make the power of dam-building labor not only intelligible to the audi-ence's mind but also sensible to their bodies. On June 9, 1958, he convened a meeting with the producers and actors of Chinese Youth Art Theater to further clarify his ideas for the mise-en-scène. Emphasizing the aesthetic principles of his drama, the playwright pronounced:

The performance isn't confined within the four walls of the stage. Nor is it regulated by the unities [of action, time, and space]. Characters travel across the stage like running streams. All the labor teams walk among the audience from the stage's left, the middle, and the right when they announce their work progress. Besides the delivery of lines, there are also poems, lyrics, songs, clapper talks, and dance. . . . This is a comprehensive mixture of multiple art forms.[34]

The theatrical device of "breaking the fourth wall," wherein performers directly address the audience by acknowledging their presence as spectators, had been in common use in modernist theater since the early twentieth century. Extensively theorized and employed by the German playwright Bertolt Brecht (1898–1956), the idea was to awake the audience from indulging themselves in the fictive world by highlighting the separate spaces on and off stage. After having seen the Chinese opera star Mei Lanfang's performance in Moscow in 1935, Brecht famously praised the Peking Opera master's "awareness of being watched."[35] Such a deliberate (mis) reading of Mei's acting helped Brecht critique the European convention of the "unseen" audience and remove the illusion of staged reality to promote "the instructive theater."[36] But for Tian Han in 1958, to make an instructive drama that aimed at the spectatorial bodies rather than minds, raising consciousness of spatial separation was far from enough. To shape the audience not as distanced seers but engaged participants, he found a bolder inspiration from an old colleague, Xiong Foxi (1900–1965).

From 1932 to 1937, the dramatist Xiong Foxi organized dozens of drama troupes in Ding County of Hebei Province to implement his experiment in popularizing modern spoken drama, a cultural genre that had remained alien to the peasantry until Xiong's arrival. During four years' sojourn in the countryside, Xiong hosted workshops, revised scripts, and built theaters to incorporate the local peasants in understanding, appreciating, and even creating spoken drama based on their own life experiences. In *Crossing* (*Guodu*, 1935), a drama about peasants building a bridge to sell their goods across a river monopolized by a local ferry owner, Xiong built an open-air theater using trees, a mud wall, and the sky to create a natural ambience. During the performance, actors sat among the audience before making their entrance. Some peasants even mistook an actor as a real street vendor and dashed to buy a pack of cigarettes.[37] In the 1930s, Xiong treated the whole theater as the stage without the demarcation between the lighted space of performance and the dark space of the seats. Though terminated due to the outbreak of the Second Sino-Japanese War, Xiong's experiment tried to enlighten the Chinese peasantry with the modern ideas of class and oppression with the practice that he later described as "the integration of the audience and the performers" (*guanzhong yu yanyuan hunhe de xinshi yanchufa*).[38] His popularization attempt disintegrated the perceptual difference between drama and life as a theatrical precedent for rural mobilization.

Near the end of June 1958, Tian Han adopted Xiong's theatrical device for the premiere of *The Caprice of the Ming Tombs Reservoir* at the Sun Yat-sen Park Music Hall. Pushing the break of the fourth wall further, Tian Han distributed actions across the theater to enact an immersive interaction, in which "the spectators do not merely witness the situations . . . [but] are made to physically experience them."[39] In this imaginary participation in dam building, the performers' bodily presence next to the audience respatialized the theater as a virtual construction site wherein those who went there to watch the performance became those who were there to join the construction work. Spectatorial experience was made into a collective labor scene in the simulation of the construction space. At the same time, the geographical distance between the city and its far suburb was substantially shortened by a theatrical conduit that transported the Beijing audience to rural Changping. A review article acclaimed the premiere for "leading people into a vast world" and "making them feel they were actually there."[40] On July 2, two days after the dam had been announced completed, the troupe moved the drama to the reservoir site, where the artificial set was merged with the local natural view and the performers became indistinguishable from the dam builders on and off stage.[41]

Providing a theatrical version of corporeal infrastructure, *The Caprice* aimed to foster the ever-growing strength, power of endurance, and ability of self-improvement to awaken the universal productivity of the masses. Yet neither Tian Han nor his audiences foresaw the gruesome outcome of the Great Leap Forward in which they had joyfully engaged. Two years after the completion of the reservoir, famine swept the country as a grave life challenge to millions of the Chinese peasants. It was also during this time of disaster that the construction of Red Flag Canal began. Building a trunk almost a thousand miles long, villagers in Lin County not only struggled with the shortage of dietary nourishment but also regularly confronted the precipitous mountains that blocked the way for the Zhang River to flow into the Henan villages. In the shadow of famine, the cultural wave of broadening and emboldening the promise of an affluent communist China retreated together with the campaign. The reemphasis on "the authentic"—as opposed to "the romantic"—representation of infrastructural building made cultural workers seek images and sounds that would boost people's morale and reinforce the masses as the agents of technological advancement.

Meanwhile, starting in 1957, many young urbanites already journeyed to the rural area for remote industrialization that later culminated in the official start of "Going down to the Countryside" (*xiaxiang*) in the late 1960s.[42] When the educated youth confronted the wilderness, they also met peasants with traditional knowledge of farming but no advanced systems of enhancing production. The contrast led the youth to construe the rural habitual ways of agricultural production as the residues of the past that the socialist nation wanted to leave behind.[43] Peasants may not have had the knowledge to farm in a modern manner, but their experience in manual work became an inspirational source of infrastructural construction. As the reportage *Carols of Red Flag Canal* (*Hongqi qu song*, 1974) shows, some canal-building youngsters followed peasants' teaching and advice in stonemasonry and carpentry work.[44] When the documentary *Red Flag Canal* was produced in 1970, the cinematic rendering of corporeal infrastructure strengthened the imperative of hydraulic expansion. By screening a neatly organized space and standardized labor procedures, the film re-created old rural practices into rational techniques, thereby modifying the "backwardness" of peasant labor that did not fit the industrial vision.

Documenting from the Sky

Socialist documentary in China had never been plain reports without the filmmakers' artful touch. Since the first five years of the PRC, the Chinese film industry had adopted and adapted the Soviet theory of nonfiction film to disseminate revolutionary messages through carefully crafted audiovisual forms. Prominent in this mode of documenting the nation in making was the continual criticism and warning against visual patchworks made up of fragmentary snaps of lived experience. Deep-seated in this discourse, as Ying Qian discerns, was "a fundamental distrust of the visible world" that posited the unstudied facts as "superficial, messy, and full of contingencies that would confuse and mislead."[45] To make documentaries in New China was to unravel the observed world with cinematic aesthetics that countered unfiltered naturalistic, "objective" films. For many socialist cultural workers, reenactment became an acceptable method to imbue the images with the desired meanings.[46] After a brief period (1958–60) of combining on-site shooting with professional actors and fictive elements, documentary policy reverted to the rule of actuality when the famine took its toll on the Chinese population. At the first national conference of newsreel and documentary film in 1960, subtle but critical reflection on the hyperbolic trends of the Great Leap Forward culture led the officials in the Cultural Bureau to rephrase the guiding principle as pursuit of the real.[47] Yet offering didactic interpretations rather than bare illustrations of life remained paramount.

From 1960 to 1968, filmmakers from the Central Newsreel and Documentary Studio followed and recorded the project of Red Flag Canal. But after viewing a rough cut of the original reels, the Henan Province Committee discredited the film for failing to do justice to the massive scale of the canal and saw a strong need to recuperate the spectacular scenes of canal builders reorganizing the terrestrial surroundings with their makeshift creativity. Soon the committee's plan to remake the documentary led it to appoint Jiang Yunchuan (b. 1923), a veteran journalist who joined the communist film troupe during the party's retreat in Yan'an in 1942.[48]

Since the beginning of the Cultural Revolution in 1966, Jiang had been deprived of his title as the vice-editor in chief at the studio. After years away from the editing table, Jiang was summoned one afternoon in 1969 and told to produce a new documentary for the canal project that had just caught the attention of the state authority. Negotiating briefly with the propaganda division that supervised the studio, Jiang managed to retrieve his journalist certificate, put together a crew of five cinematographers, and then set off for Lin County. His task was to re-create the building process in an appealing fashion without fictional fabrication.[49]

Unlike Tian Han, who complied with forward-moving temporal order in his drama, Jiang employs a flashback structure to start the film with the canal system at its finish. It opens with a sequence that interweaves scenes of Henan's landscape, the rural bounty, and peasants' everyday life substantially improved after the installation of the canal. The beginning is a tracking shot that places the camera over the running water in the trunk canal, which was already in use when Jiang arrived in Henan. A series of aerial shots follows that offers an overview of the Taihang Mountains. The first three shots, showing no hint of human habitation, center on the outskirts of the region framed by the irregular curves of several mountain chains. Coming to a plain area, the camera then captures compounds of villages dispersed around a building resembling a water tower on the top of a hill. The human touch on nature immediately becomes prominent in the next shot, which exhibits several giant characters "The People's Commune Is Great" (*Renmin gongshe hao*) carved on a slope. The same visual emphasis is then repeated to display "Learn from Dazhai for Agriculture" (*Nongye xue Dazhai*), another development slogan inscribed next to the canal.[50] While staying in high altitude, the camera moves increasingly closer to the ground to underscore the canal system's material shape unfolding like an endless winding path. Leading the viewer to gaze at the provincial borderland like a painted scroll, the aerial sequence heightens the viewer's sensitivity to the canal as an edifice connecting and traversing large expanses of the rural space.

Since the twentieth century, the view from high above has served as a surveillance medium to scrutinize and control the space beneath an aircraft. In 1902, during the last decade of the Qing dynasty, European powers deployed helium balloons equipped with cameras to collect critical intelligence of Chinese cities, rivers, and infrastructures from the sky.[51] In the early 1930s, military navigation gave way to a quotidian hunger for Orientalist spectacles when a German pilot working for Eurasia Aviation Corporation took hundreds of aerial photos along his itinerary between China and Germany.[52] At the other end of the world in the same period, the US federal government started an economic restructuring that used aerial images to turn Midwestern farmers' rugged individual homesteads into an all-encompassing grid of productive fields. As Jason Weems argues, the verticality of the aerial vision "embodied the promise of modernization on a vast and systematic scale" and "dissolved traditional patterns of rural life into unrecognizable

Figures 1–4.

abstraction."[53] In the heyday of the New Deal, the rectilinear land of the rural Midwest compelled American farm owners to think of themselves as skillful, rational-thinking workers and managers whose agricultural production was conceptually placed in a nationwide production web built with intensive government intervention.[54]

Across the ideological divides, the opening sequence of *Red Flag Canal* employs the same visual technique to abstract and aestheticize rural China reshaped by the infrastructural system.[55] Seeing the canal from the sky takes the viewer beyond the everyday horizontal perception of the infrastructure (figs. 1–4). From the "empty" shots of the mountains and the village compounds, the airborne view shows the county's transformation from a barren virgin land to an energy zone whose scenic beauty is identified in its engineered, rather than natural, components. Against gravity, this aerial vantage point carries a unique power that endows the audience with a disembodied source of visuality to see the Lin County's environment in its totality. With the visual totality, the synoptic images strip agrarian life of its pastoral aura to rationalize the eyes of the audience so that they learn to perceive rural land not as an object of sightseeing but as the source of energy subject to extraction.

This message is further elaborated when the camera comes down to the ground (figs. 5–8). In the sequence following the aerial images, the transformative power of the infrastructural system becomes visible on an everyday level. In shots that offer visual proof of land regimentation, the canal bank, reservoir walls, and irrigation ditches present an array of straight, oval, and rectangular lines that frame the rural space into shapes of different sizes. Paralleling the material forms of the infrastructure are peasants tilling the field, studying newspaper articles, and shouldering water buckets in diagonal or horizontal lines. The abstraction recodifies the land to convey a strong sense of spatial order. The geometry-filled images are then put in drastic contrast to the memory of the old, disaster-ridden county where villagers had to travel long distances to fetch water and frequently wrestled with prolonged drought, symbolized by the cracked earth and withering vegetation. This transformation is encapsulated in an animation sequence that summarizes the film's opening. Showing a local map that returns the viewing eye to high altitude, the animation first shows a cartographic overview of the county and then sketches out the canal from its Shanxi origin branching out to its Henan terminals, a trajectory punctuated and complemented by numerous reservoirs, portal bridges, and hydroelectric stations. From the sky to the ground and then back to the sky, the opening of *Red Flag Canal* echoes the 1930s American visual regime in its application of aerial vision "as both instigator and foil for newly emergent conditions of modern agricultural production."[56] But using the elevated view to generate a new perception of the countryside was by no means the end goal of the documentary. While the images insinuate that the land is no longer formless and inhospitable, the visual pedagogy must also translate the order of space into the order of behavior to urge the laboring people to mirror the new shape of the land.

Building above the Ground
After the seven-minute opening, the film moves into its major segment, which focuses on portraying the people who spent ten years marching through the mountains, digging tunnels, building bridges, manufacturing explosives, and chipping stones to create the new socialist rural order through infrastructure construction. Different from the depiction of people's proclivity to adapt themselves to the physical discomfort of dam building, the canal film foregrounds how the mass builders navigate the hostile environment in which laboring bodies are presented as a phalanx of trailblazers in places that are the most unwelcoming to human presence. One mountain after another, the documentary develops the unending missions as a corporeal battle generalized in a slogan as "fearless of bitterness, fearless of death" (*yi bupa ku, er bupa si*).[57] Aestheticizing this slogan on screen, the audiovisual presentation of the infrastructural venture replaces the earthbound construction of dams with sequences of mountain quests in which the canal builders combat the uninhabitable space.

    In an uplifting music score featuring horns and strings, the image dissolves from the animated map into a long, high-angle shot of the peasant army marching underneath the slogan "Rearrange Lin County's Rivers and Mountains" (*chongxin anpai linxian heshan*) painted on a cliff. A series of images go on to emphasize the

Figures 5–8.

construction team en route. Medium shots and close-ups alternate to capture people carrying shovels, sewing machines, and medical kits and eventually settling down
in a cramped cave where the peasants participate in a collective reading session of
Mao's quotation books. As the music rests, the film brings in the construction scenes.
Two low-angle shots sweep the wind-eroded mountain walls and then cut to the depiction of Ren Yangcheng (b. 1927), a model laborer best known for his skills in clearing
mountain paths of rolling stone. A process sequence ensues to exhibit Ren's unique
approach: he hammers three or four stakes deep into the earth on the mountain top,
makes strong knots on his waist and chest with a thick long rope, rolls the other end of
the rope around the stakes, and slides down the cliff while wielding a stick to chase
down the loose rocks, bouncing on and off the rocky wall to balance his body (figs. 9–
10). Several low-angle shots then capture Ren and his fellow builders swinging and
walking in the air like hawks patrolling the sky. As the film goes on to demonstrate, this
technique is quickly learned and adopted when the builders use explosives to blast
their way into the mountain. The vertical composition of the image becomes principal
in many of the following sequences, in which the documentary offers more spectacular shots of male and female peasants lifting bricks and stones to build portal
bridges. The visual emphasis on height presents the technicality of labor as an eye-
catching stunt.

      This cinematic representation of canal construction is different from the the-
atrical rendering of dam building with its attentive gaze at infrastructural labor as an
artisanal process and forceful rhythm that makes labor not only visible but also audible. Visually, the documentary invites close observation of the builders' specific skill

Figures 9–10.

sets by codifying the process as a step-by-step series of operational actions. Here, Tian Han's dramatic focus on cultivating malleable strength, pain endurance, and self-regeneration is replaced with a sequential demonstration that emphasizes an observation of engineering techniques. Breaking the process down on the screen allows the viewer to see the rigor and creativity invested in the builders' manual work as technical actions, that is, as premeditated procedures oriented toward a productive goal. Integrating the illustration of labor discipline and the sensuous appeal from the use of the sky as a backdrop of labor, the canal documentary, as Salomé Aguilera Skvirsky observes of cinema's long history of representing labor, "promise [s] to transform a messy, chaotic, mystified modern world into a rational and conceptually masterable entity through training in visualization."[58] While the drama of the Ming Tombs Reservoir highlights that the socialist body emerges from confronting one's physical limits and corporeal vulnerability, the canal film eschews any digression, interruption, or failure the builders may have experienced to compose a smooth method of construction. The succession of actions creates a sense of order in the canal-building labor, resonating with the ways in which the aerial shots and geometric aesthetic give order to the rural space. Visualizing the construction as a combination of the physical expression of passion and a well-designed and carefully executed work process, the film presents the builders as inventors and shapers of order whose technical uses of the body turn labor order (the sequential steps) into spatial order (the geometric shapes of landscape).

Besides the visual spectacle of working at heights, the documentary also features prominently the sounds of construction. Like many other documentaries in the socialist period, *Red Flag Canal* involves no instances where the audience can hear the builders talk. In the absence of testaments from the people, socialist documentary employs voice-over commentary to frame and dictate the meanings of images. Without personalized articulation, such as the dialogue Tian Han deploys in his drama, what the audience encounters in the documentary is actions that visually verify the commentator's description, but rarely an embodied voice—people are only collectively audible in long shots that show them shouting "Long live Chairman Mao" in the celebratory scene of water rushing through the sluice. The result of such voiceless individuals is that the filmed subject is always being narrated rather than narrating themselves.

Having no voice except in slogan chanting, however, does not mean dead silence on the side of the filmed. Between the music tracks and the voice-over narration, Jiang inserts in multiple scenes an auditory stream of thunk-thunk-thunk, a diegetic sound coming from the canal builders pounding stakes with hammers. Whenever the sound appears, the loud, nondiegetic score is either put on pause or substantially turned down to direct the audience's full attention to the pounding alone. By amplifying and repeating this sound of construction, the documentary makes the canal builders "speak" with the steady rhythm manifesting their ideologically endowed strength. As Haun Saussy notes, "Rhythm is not the skeleton of language stripped of its content, but the enabling medium of content."[59] The film's treatment of the thunk-thunk-thunk exemplifies Saussy's conceptualization of rhythm, which functions as "a formatting of the receiving surface,"[60] that is, shaping the listener's habit to catch, recognize, and absorb the rhythm so that the message is conveyed directly to the auditory nerves without having to go through the register of a conscious mind.[61] Thus *Red Flag Canal*'s acoustic cues liberate the ear temporarily from the exhilarating music to induce and synchronize the audience's bodily reaction to the laborers' choreographed movements. While the aerial vision, geometric aesthetic, and the use of the cliff space aim to configure a visual instruction, the rhythm bypasses the mental processing of infrastructural work to intensify the labor training with an aural stimulus. Integrating the images and sound that make socialist infrastructural labor simultaneously observable and audible, the documentary portrays the mass laborers as a collective converter that, by effectively managing the bodies, turns nature into resource.

Conclusion: From Mobilization to Extraction

As an arena where laborers were remolded as organic apparatus for infrastructural projects, China's mass hydraulic engineering relied on cultural works to render the demand for universal productivity achievable. For the state to restructure the countryside with hydraulic edifices, the theatrical and cinematic versions of corporeal infrastructure merged the imperative of hydraulic advancement with the prescription of socialist labor to discipline mass physical energy and develop people's techniques of craftsmanship. From the late 1950s to the early 1970s, China's continual pursuit of water resources turned cultural works into a technopolitical device of human resource extraction that emphasized the representations' evocative power in translating policy on paper into embodied actions. While the socialist spectacles have now become widely accessible not only for Chinese people but also for global audiences on the internet, this highly aestheticized memory of hydraulic engineering also obscures those whose lived experience did not match the prescriptive visions of development.

In the case of the Ming Tombs Reservoir, when mass dam building evolved from a mobilization policy to a compulsory responsibility in many production brigades, the obsession with speed led many brigade leaders to dismiss builders' exhaustion as an unacceptable reaction. At the end of each day, the members of the same labor team would have to line up and support each other by the arm on their way back to the dormitory. Some could not return to work, and others fell ill for a long time.[62] In the case of Red Flag Canal, the official chronicles published in the 1990s often credit the local cadres for their wise leadership and commitment to national development, which has overshadowed the brutal incidents that occurred during the construction process. A landslide following an explosion in the early 1960s took nine lives in a storm of dirt and rocks. The survivors then dug up the corpses only to find they were already deformed and unrecognizable. None of these stories appeared in public representations of infrastructure until the recent revisit to the Mao years. As three of the women builders recalled in a 2015 documentary series, the backbreaking building work disrupted their menstrual cycles and left them unable to close their fingers unless they grabbed one hand tightly with the other.[63] While idealized infrastructural labor found its unpleasant counterparts in indelible body memory, the laborers also become embodied reminders of the muscles and bones that gave Chinese infrastructure material forms before the infrastructure could wield its power in social and economic transformation.

Yuan Gao is a PhD candidate in Chinese language and literature at Washington University in St. Louis. His research engages with the rising field of infrastructure studies to renew the knowledge of Chinese cultural production and infrastructural politics. He is completing his dissertation, "Corporeal Technology: Hydraulic Infrastructure and the Cultural Politics of Labor in China, 1952–1993." His next project examines the Burma Road and its representations in the transnational context of China, Southeast Asia, and the United States.

Notes

I wish to thank the editors of this special issue, especially Wesley Attewell for his patience and communication since the drafting of this article. Letty Chen, Zhao Ma, Jianqing Chen, Uluğ Kuzuoğlu, Flair Donglai Shi, and Renren Yang provided timely guidance and encouragement. Chang Xu, Miao Dou, Zijing Fan, and Kun Huang supported me with their friendship. The anonymous reviewers' comments and suggestions helped me develop an earlier version of this article. My gratitude goes to my grandma, who passed away while I was working on the article, who devoted her life to teaching at Yunnan Water Conservancy and Hydropower School, and who gave me her unconditional love from the beginning of my life.

1. See Nye, *American Technological Sublime*.
2. This term refers to a nineteenth-century idea, to "harmonize the movements of the body with those of the industrial machine" (Rabinbach, *Human Motor*, 2).
3. This does not mean that there were no cultural works for audiences' sentimental responses. Chinese artists such as Zhang Xuefu (1911–87) created paintings to depict infrastructure in its completion. Here I focus on the portrayal of construction rather than on the finished objects. For the paintings, see Ho, *Drawing from Life*, 129–57.

4. See Rubenstein, Robins, and Beal, "Infrastructuralism."

5. See Larkin, *Signal and Noise*.

6. Graham and Marvin, *Splintering Urbanism*, 19.

7. See Cupers and Meier, "Infrastructure between Statehood and Selfhood."

8. Richard White, in his history of the Columbia River, has shown that human laborers always played an indispensable role in exploiting the hydropower of the river. The old source of technology, the laboring body, coexisted with other ever-evolving technological apparatuses (*Organic Machine*).

9. Larkin, "Politics and Poetics of Infrastructure," 329.

10. Xu, *Laodong wenti*, 1.

11. Xu, *Laodong wenti*, 1.

12. Siegelbaum, "Making of Stakhanovites."

13. Zhonghua quanguo zonggonghui, *Laodong jinsai yu laodong taidu*, 7. My paraphrase of the Chinese translation of Stalin's speech.

14. Yan, *Shehui zhuyi zhidu xia de laodong*, 24.

15. See Gao, *Tan chuangzaoxing de laodong*.

16. See Gao, *Laodong chuangzao xingfu*.

17. Mauss, *Techniques, Technology, Civilization*, 80.

18. Liu, "Present Situation," 422.

19. Zhang, "Shisanling shuiku chubu yanjiu," 17–23.

20. See Linzhoushi hongqiquzhi bianzhuan weiyuanhui, *Hongqiqu zhi*.

21. Douglas, *Natural Symbols*, 78.

22. Pietz, *The Yellow River*, 196.

23. Zhou, *Cinema Off Screen*, 75.

24. Tao, "'Xiaolaohu'—Ma Qingzhi," in *Jianshe shisanling shuiku de renmen*, 1:74–81.

25. Qian, "When Taylorism Met Revolutionary Romanticism."

26. Dong, *Tian Han zhuan*, 737–819.

27. Li, *Tian Han chuangzuo ceji*, 119.

28. Li, *Tian Han chuangzuo ceji*, 119.

29. Braester, *Painting the City Red*, 28.

30. Tian, *Tian Han quanji*, 6:250.

31. Guan and Zhang, "Dishike hongxing—ji yidengjiang huodezhe Ren Lianhua tongzhi," in *Jianshe shisanling shuiku de renmen*, 1:82-88.

32. Tian, *Tian Han quanji*, 6:281.

33. Tian, *Tian Han quanji*, 6:321–22.

34. Li, *Tian Han chuangzuo ceji*, 127.

35. Brecht, *Brecht on Theater*, 92.

36. Brecht, *Brecht on Theater*, 71.

37. Xiong, *"Guodu" jiqi yanchu*, 15.

38. Xiong, *Xiju dazhonghua zhi shiyan*, 95.

39. Fischer-Lichte, *Transformative Power of Performance*, 40.

40. Fang, "Tan huaju 'Shisanling shuiku changxiangqu,'" 35.

41. There is no primary source that gives a detailed record of the performance at the construction site, except a short, general description by Li, *Tian Han chuangzuo ceji*, 129.

42. See Zhang, *Going to the Countryside*, 182–207.

43. See Schmalzer, *Red Revolution, Green Revolution*, 100–128.

44. Lin, *Hongqi qu song*, 43–54.

45. Qian, "Crossing the Same River Twice," 601.
46. Ding, "Xinwen jilu dianying jinnianlai de chengji he wenti," in *Xinwen jilu dianying chuangzuo wenti*, 19–34.
47. See Xia, Chen, et al., *Weile xinwen jilupian de gengda yuejin*; and Chen and Shi, *Dangdai zhongguo dianying xiajuan*, 2:3–39.
48. For more autobiographical information, see Jiang, *Guangying liuzhuan*, 25–109.
49. Li, *Shidai yingzhi*, 161–69.
50. Dazhai became a model farm from a poor, small production brigade in the late 1950s. It was promoted widely in the 1960s for its success stories of China's self-reliance after the Sino-Soviet split. See Meisner, "Dazhai."
51. For the first photo album with more than a dozen aerial snaps of China, see Officiers du Génie du Corps Expéditionnaire, *La Chine à terre et en ballon*.
52. Castell, *Xiyangjing*, 1–2.
53. Weems, *Barnstorming the Prairies*, x.
54. Weems, *Barnstorming the Prairies*, 45–125.
55. See Jiang's interviews in the 2015 documentary series Fan, *Dianyingyan kan Zhongguo II: Hongqiqu*.
56. Weems, *Barnstorming the Prairies*, xxv.
57. Shuili dianli bu zhengzhi bu xuanchuan chu, *Linxian hongqiqu*, 34–41.
58. Skvirsky, *Process Genre*, 56.
59. Saussy, *Ethnography of Rhythm*, 33.
60. Saussy, *Ethnography of Rhythm*, 158.
61. Before 1949, Chinese left-wing poets incorporated the rhythm of mass labor in their modern verses as part of the mobilization project. Their effort was to bridge the modern poetic sound with the sound of labor already familiar to the workers. The documentary use of labor sound was thus different from the pre-1949 literary experiment because it no longer represented the acoustic memory of toil but rather the supposedly genuine and spontaneous rhythm of the socialist labor. For analysis of the poetic rhythm of labor before 1949, see Kang, *Youshengde zuoyi*.
62. Zhang, "Shisanling shuiku chubu yanjiu," 35.
63. Fan, *Dianyingyan kan Zhongguo II, disanji: Hongqiqu*.

References

Braester, Yomi. *Painting the City Red: Chinese Cinema and the Urban Contract*. Durham, NC: Duke University Press, 2010.

Brecht, Bertolt. *Brecht on Theater: The Development of an Aesthetic*. Translated and edited by John Willet. New York: Hill and Wang, 1964.

Castell, Graf zu. *Xiyangjing: Yige deguo feixingyuan jingtou xia de zhongguo, 1933–1936* 西洋镜：一个德国飞行员镜头下的中国 1933-1936 (*Western Mirrors: China through the Lens of a German Pilot, 1933–1936*). Beijing: Taihai chubanshe, 2017.

Chen Huangmei and Shi Fangyu, eds. *Dangdai zhongguo dianying xiajuan* 当代中国电影下卷 (*China Today: Film*). Vol. 2. Beijing: Zhongguo shehui kexue chubanshe, 1989.

Cupers, Kenny, and Prita Meier. "Infrastructure between Statehood and Selfhood: The Trans-African Highway." *JSAH: Journal of the Society of Architectural Historians* 79, no. 1 (2020): 61–81.

Dong Jian. *Tian Han zhuan* 田汉传 (*Biography of Tian Han*). Beijing: Beijing shiyue wenyi chubanshe, 1996.

Douglas, Mary. *Natural Symbols: Explorations in Cosmology*. New York: Routledge, 1996.

Fan Qipeng, dir. *Dianyingyan kan Zhongguo II: Hongqiqu* 电影眼看中国II： 红旗渠 (*Seeing China through the Cinematic Eye II: Red Flag Canal*). China Central Television Documentary. YouTube, July 9, 2018. https://www.youtube.com/watch ?v=U2BSWmioYm8&t=580s.

Fang Chu. "Tan huaju 'Shisanling shuiku changxiangqu'" 談話劇《十三陵水庫暢想曲》(On the Drama "The Caprice of the Ming Tombs Reservoir"). *Xiju bao*, no. 13 (1958): 35.

Fischer-Lichte, Erika. *The Transformative Power of Performance: A New Aesthetic*. Translated by Saskya Iris Jain. New York: Routledge, 2008.

Gao Guang. *Tan chuangzaoxing de laodong* 談創造性的勞動 (*On Creative Labor*). Shanghai: Shanghai renmin chubanshe, 1956.

Gao Yefu. *Laodong chuangzao xingfu* 勞動創造幸福 (*Labor Creates Happiness*). Beijing: Zhongguo qingnian chubanshe, 1956.

Graham, Stephen, and Simon Marvin. *Splintering Urbanism: Networked Infrastructures, Technological Mobilities, and the Urban Condition*. New York: Routledge, 2001.

Ho, Christine I. *Drawing from Life: Sketching and Socialist Realism in the People's Republic of China*. Oakland: University of California Press, 2020.

Jiang Yunchuan. *Guangying liuzhuan: Jiang Yunchuan dianying zhilu* 光影流转：姜云川电影之路 (*Between Light and Shadow: Jiang Yunchuan's Film Paths*). Beijing: Zhongguo dianying chu ban she, 2019.

Kang Ling. *Youshengde zuoyi: Shigelangsong yu gemingwenyi de shentijishu* 有声的左翼： 诗歌 朗诵与革命文艺的身体技术 (*The Sound of the Left Wing: Poetry Reading and Body Techniques in Revolutionary Culture*). Shanghai: Shanghai wenyi chubanshe, 2020.

Larkin, Brian. *Signal and Noise: Media, Infrastructure, and Urban Culture in Nigeria*. Durham, NC: Duke University Press, 2008.

Larkin, Brian. "The Politics and Poetics of Infrastructure." *Annual Review of Anthropology*, no. 42 (2013): 327–43.

Li Yi, ed. *Shidai yingzhi: xinwen jilu dianying juan* 时代影志：新闻纪录电影卷 (*The Visual Chronicles of Time: The Documentary Cinema Volume*). Beijing: Zhongguo dianying chubanshe, 2018.

Li Zhiyan. *Tian Han chuangzuo ceji* 田汉创作侧记 (*Profiles of Tian Han's Creative Works*). Chengdu: Sichuan wenyi chubanshe, 1994.

Lin Feng. *Hongqi qu song* 红旗渠颂 (*Carols of Red Flag Canal*). Zhengzhou: Henan renmin chubanshe, 1974.

Linzhoushi hongqiquzhi bianzhuan weiyuanhui, eds. *Hongqiqu zhi* 红旗渠志 (*Chronicles of Red Flag Canal*). Zhengzhou: Sanlian shu dian, 1995.

Liu Shaoqi. "The Present Situation, the Party's General Line for Socialist Construction and Its Future Tasks, May 5, 1958." In *Communist China, 1955–1959: Policy Documents with Analysis*, edited by Center for International Affairs and the East Asian Research Center, 416–37. Cambridge, MA: Harvard University Press, 1962.

Mauss, Marcel. *Techniques, Technology, Civilization*. Translated and edited by Nathan Schlanger. New York: Durkheim Press, 2006.

Meisner, Mitch. "Dazhai: The Mass Line in Practice." *Modern China*, 4, no. 1 (1978): 27–62.

Nye, David E. *American Technological Sublime*. Cambridge, MA: MIT Press, 1994.

Officiers du Génie du Corps Expéditionnaire. *La Chine à terre et en ballon*. Paris: Berger-Levrault, 1902.

Pietz, David A. *The Yellow River: The Problem of Water in Modern China*. Cambridge, MA: Harvard University Press, 2015.

Qian, Ying. "Crossing the Same River Twice: Documentary Reenactment and the Founding of PRC Documentary Cinema." In *Oxford Handbook of Chinese Cinemas*, edited by Carlos Rojas and Eileen Cheng-yin Chow, 590–609. New York: Oxford University Press, 2013.

Qian, Ying. "When Taylorism Met Revolutionary Romanticism: Documentary Cinema in China's Great Leap Forward." In "Political Enchantments: Aesthetic Practices and the Chinese State," edited by Gloria Davies, Christian Sorace, and Haun Saussy. Special Issue, *Critical Inquiry* 46, no. 3 (2020): 578–604.

Rabinbach, Anson. *The Human Motor: Energy, Fatigue, and the Origins of Modernity*. New York: Basic Books, 1990.

Rubenstein, Michael, Bruce Robins, and Sophia Beal. "Infrastructuralism: An Introduction." *MFS: Modern Fiction Studies* 61, no. 4 (2015): 575–86.

Saussy, Haun. *The Ethnography of Rhythm: Orality and Its Technologies*. New York: Fordham University Press, 2016.

Schmalzer, Sigrid. *Red Revolution, Green Revolution: Scientific Farming in Socialist China*. Chicago: University of Chicago Press, 2016.

Shisanling shuiku zongzhihuibu, eds. *Jianshe Shisanling shuiku de renmen* 建設十三陵水庫的人們 (*The Builders of the Ming Tombs Reservoir*). 5 vols. Beijing: Zuojia chubanshe, 1958.

Shuili dianli bu zhengzhi bu xuanchuan chu, eds. *Linxian hongqi qu* 林县红旗渠 (*Red Flag Canal in Lin County*). Beijing: Shuili dianli chubanshe, 1973.

Siegelbaum, Lewis H. "The Making of Stakhanovites, 1935–36." *Russian History* 13, no. 2/3 (1986): 259–92.

Skvirsky, Salomé Aguilera. *The Process Genre: Cinema and the Aesthetic of Labor*. Durham, NC: Duke University Press, 2020.

Tian Han. *Tian Han quanji* 田汉全集 (*The Complete Works of Tian Han*). Vol. 6. Shijiazhuang: Huashan wenyi chubanshe, 1990.

Weems, Jason. *Barnstorming the Prairies: How Aerial Vision Shaped the Midwest*. Minneapolis: University of Minnesota Press, 2015.

White, Richard. *The Organic Machine: The Making of the Columbia River*. New York: Hill and Wang, 1995.

Xia Yan, Chen Huangmei, et al. *Weile xinwen jilupian de gengda yuejin* 為了新聞紀錄片的更大躍進 (*For the Greater Leap of Newsreel Documentary*). Beijing: Zhongguo dianying chubanshe, 1961.

Xiong Foxi. *"Guodu" jiqi yanchu* "過渡"及其演出 (*"Crossing" and Its Performances*). Shanghai: Zhengzhong shuju, 1937.

Xiong Foxi. *Xiju dazhonghua zhi shiyan* 戲劇大眾化之實驗 (*The Popularization Experiment of Drama*). Shanghai: Zhengzhong shuju, 1937.

Xu Xian. *Laodong wenti* 勞動問題 (*The Labor Problem*). Hong Kong: Shenghuo shu dian, 1949.

Yan Beiming. *Shehui zhuyi zhidu xia de laodong* 社會主義制度下的勞動 (*Labor in the Socialist System*). Beijing: Zhongguo qingnian chu ban she, 1956.

Zhang Naiyi. "Shisanling shuiku chubu yanjiu" 十三陵水库初步研究 (Preliminary Research on Ming Tombs Reservoir Project). Master's thesis, University of Science and Technology of China, 2018.

Zhang, Yu. *Going to the Countryside: The Rural in the Modern Chinese Cultural Imagination*. Ann Arbor: University of Michigan Press, 2020.

Zhonghua quanguo zonggonghui, eds. *Laodong jingsai yu xinde laodong taidu* 勞動競賽與新的勞
    動態度 (*Production Competition and the New Labor Attitude*). Beijing: Gong yun cong shu,
    1950.
Zhongyang xinwen jilu dianying zhipianchang, eds. *Xinwen jilu dianying chuangzuo wenti* 新聞
    紀錄電影創作問題 (*The Problems in Producing Newsreel Documentary*). Beijing: Zhongguo
    dianying chubanshe, 1958.
Zhou, Chenshu. *Cinema Off Screen: Moviegoing in Socialist China*. Oakland: University of
    California Press, 2021.

A Moonless Night

Solveig Qu Suess

When I began shooting a documentary recounting my mother's career as an optical engineer, the story was complicated by a nondisclosure agreement she signed with the Chinese state in 1987. Constructing a personal narrative, it would seem, required navigating a promise of confidentiality to a powerful state actor. Following its decade of political closure, my mother had been placed on one of the first international projects where Western designs of optical instruments were purchased by the Chinese state. She contributed to the production of instruments for seeing at a distance and at night, instruments defined as critical technology for development by the government. Desires by the company and state to hide this state-of-exception project had eclipsed the desires of my mother as she fell in love with a Western colleague on the project. My mother was expelled from China to Switzerland in 1987, as her decision to marry the Western colleague led to threats of state-directed disappearance, marked her as a traitor, and banned her from her workplace. The film project, *Little Grass*, navigates around this nondisclosure and subsequent absence of information, weaving together alternative genealogies of optics through our mother-daughter relationship and archival footage, exploring where tensions are held between memory and its images, belonging and statecraft, lens crafting, and transposition.

Radical History Review
Issue 147 (October 2023)   DOI 10.1215/01636545-10637190
© 2023 by Solveig Qu Suess

Figure 1. Still from *Little Grass*, HD. Image courtesy of Solveig Qu Suess.

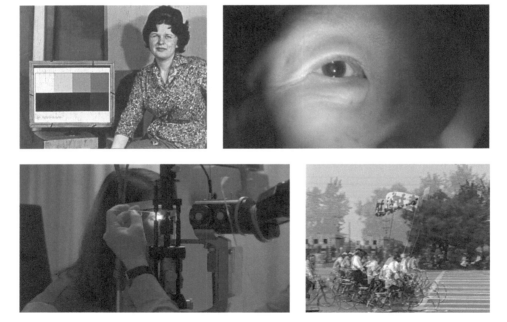

Figure 2 (upper left). *In Service of Progress*, Image-Film Zeiss Jena, 1964. Image courtesy of Zeiss Archives. Figures 3–5 (upper right, lower left and right). Stills from *Little Grass*. Images courtesy of Solveig Qu Suess.

My mother had always been private. But with me, each year I grew, she'd gift me her deepest secrets. "Like pieces of an onion, I am me, and they can go to hell." She'd tell me when I'd asked, what she'd say if they asked. In my eyes, she had always been more of an apple.

With the absence of accounts and records of this transaction as a key premise, the film explores how to narrate an event that cannot be narrated yet has registered its presence across time and space, including within my personal history. Starting from this space of absence, I ask: What does this void make present about the project, the optical instruments themselves, and more generally, about ways of seeing and ways of knowing? To begin piecing together a genealogy of the instruments my mother had worked on, I accessed the archives of other companies previously involved with optical trade in China during the 1980s, including those of Zeiss, a German manufacturer of optical systems. One of the largest and oldest optical manufacturers in the world, Zeiss is most famous for its production of lenses for glasses and medical instruments, and, even more so, for providing the lens on the Hasselblad camera that famously captured the Blue Marble image from Earth's orbit in 1972. The void located where the details for the optical instruments my mother had worked on should have been emphasizes how hidden and diffused infrastructures of optical systems are at the same time attached to a much larger complex, where forms of power continue to embed themselves in the historical development of network technologies.

> Power is never power in general, but always power of a particular kind: modalities of power such as authority, domination, seduction, manipulation or coercion have their own relational spatialities.
> —Andrew Sayer, "Seeking the Geographies of Power"

I typed the five-letter word *China* into the Zeiss corporate archival database, and the search yielded a whole genre of photos documenting official visits and optical demonstrations. These images often showed groups of delegates and diplomats holding precision optical devices, their fingers pointing out key features set to usher in the many engineered possibilities to come. Interspersed were supplementary photos, taken by the team of visiting representatives from Zeiss, of "day-to-day" life in China, including images of kids bundled up for the cold and an elderly man carrying containers of goods. Another image series featured a planetarium that had been gifted by Zeiss as a form of diplomacy with China in 1957. The building was the first large-scale planetarium of its kind in China and, for a short period, the only planetarium in Asia.[1] The company had installed these planetariums all over the world in places where important business relations were being nurtured. "Successfully performed in the service of knowledge transmission," this network of planetariums symbolically conjured images of the distant cosmos, a system to be mirrored by the new network of earthly relations that their instruments would bring forth.[2]

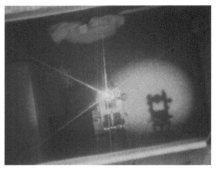

Figure 6 (upper left). Still from *Little Grass*. Image courtesy of Solveig Qu Suess. Figure 7 (upper right). *Facts*, Image-Film Zeiss Jena, 1980. Image courtesy of Zeiss Archives. Figure 8 (lower left). Delegation from the People's Republic of China, led by the minister for heavy machinery, visiting the Zeiss plant on October 9, 1953. Image courtesy of Zeiss Archives. Figure 9 (lower right). Trade fair for the Photonics industry, Munich, Germany, 2022. Image courtesy of Solveig Qu Suess.

The search results displayed photos originating from two main time sequences, one from the 1950s—the early days of the Chinese Communist Party—and the other lasting from the end of the 1970s into the 1980s. The Cultural Revolution (1966 to 1976) and its attendant social and economic turmoil sits in the gap between these two series. Following that decade, during which China, under the leadership of Mao Zedong, saw mass cultural-historical material destruction and the attempted purging of capitalist and traditional elements from Chinese society, leaders wanted to open China up to the global market. By the late 1970s, the then new prime minister Deng Xiaoping rerouted scientific and technological ambitions away from defense and toward the economy under the ambition of integrating China into the global market. Optical technology, specifically, was framed as a crucial way for China to "catch up" with the West. "During the beginning of the eighties, there was so much investment. They purchased the machines, the training, the people, their travels, hotel, everything was all included. We belonged to a state company, so this had been a huge investment."[3]

During the early 1980s, my mother was placed on one of the first international projects where Western designs of optical instruments were purchased by the Chinese state. Staff from different countries were flown in to install and train personnel to use and maintain the new machines. These new ways of seeing were only made possible by collaborating with countries that were not ideologically aligned with the Chinese state. Indeed, they were often labeled as Western imperialists, and the Chinese state publicly disavowed their presence and referred to them as occupying forces. Yet despite being nonaligned, the various participants were united under the modernist project of progress. As the term *modern* became equivalent to both economic development and the technology necessary to facilitate such development, the previously defined and often-criticized *capitalism* was folded into the more forward-looking *modernity*. Optical technologies, previously labeled as modern owing to their development by so-called Western imperialists, were stripped of the various political connotations of class analysis and the critique of the capitalist mode of production.[4] Optics, in other words, would serve to modernize the Chinese state.

My database queries revealed that many of the instruments from the 1970s and 1980s were machines that improved the precision of land measurement and increased the range of visibility, particularly in the infrared spectrum, beyond what had been visible to the human eye. Following the Korean War and because of ongoing threats from US interventions across Asia, China recognized that developing its capability to visualize space was as important for military advantage as it was for economic gain. The state's acquisition of Western designs and optical filters that amplified dim lighting conditions simply by enhancing reflections from the moon and stars allowed it to match foreign military equipment for seeing at night. New forms of optical media such as nine-band sensors or RMK-A aerial cameras allowed data to be scanned and translated into infrared photography, making visible not only the spectral signatures of minerals, petroleum, and coal resources but also of pollution from urban and oceanic topographies. What also crystallized from this deployment of new optical media were developments in methods to extract rare earth minerals, launching China into an industrial revolution. The visualizing of land and air coincided with broader geopolitical events, and the ability to see at night and into the earth from a distance was instrumental in bringing China into the global market, reshuffling much of the world's organizational logics.[5] These perceptual apparatuses purchased from the West mobilized light, both in its wave form and in how it interacts with objects of interest, in ways that unleashed both military and market infrastructures.

These moments of optical exchange engendered a shift to a different epistemological formation that allowed particular ways of seeing and, therefore, different ways of organizing life. "Vision," Donna Haraway notes, "is always a question of the power to see—and perhaps of the violence implicit in our visualizing practices. With whose blood were my eyes crafted?"[6] In posing this question, Haraway suggests that vision is always embodied, partial, and responsible for what is seen and how it is perceived. Imagining a capitalist future required an active reproduction of territories

Figure 10. Still from *Little Grass*. Image courtesy of Solveig Qu Suess.

for that future's realization, and it was through these precise optical instruments that reformatted environments, territories, landscapes, subjectivities, and social relations that such a future could be called forth.[7]

> There's a scene where my father holds the camera on a double rainbow, and my mother stands next to him. A general haze that frequently drowns the Swiss countryside town my father is from, where my mother still lives now. This must've been filmed right after they were married, in 1987. He zooms in and focuses long on the refraction of light, scattered through the valley's misty conditions, neatly arranging the range of visible colors. He holds it long, as if he was afraid of losing the moments to time. The scene was one of the few that I could find that gave hints to my parent's past fascination with optics.

In the making of *Little Grass*, placed alongside materials found through home movie archives and the archives of optical companies, appear many scenes composed of recorded time spent together with my mother in northwestern Switzerland. If the optical instruments had been tools for bringing sovereign power into new space-times of a globally connected world, they also became another medium for crossing times and spaces for me and my mother. I interrogate the fabrication of

Figures 11–12 (upper left and right). *In Service of Progress*, Image-Film Jena, 1964. Images courtesy of Zeiss Archives. Figure 13 (lower left). Booth with astronomical instruments. Carl Zeiss Jena took part in the Beijing exhibition, 1959. Image courtesy of Zeiss Archives. Figure 14 (lower right). Still from *Little Grass*. Image courtesy of Solveig Qu Suess.

optical instruments here not only to draw out the politics embedded in the times and spaces it enabled, but also in how this history mobilized particular exclusions. Many of the power relations that surround these narratives of progress were purposefully omitted—through state machinations like nondisclosure agreements. Yet they still found their way into the present through gaps within our lives, gaps that can show what was left out of the frame as much as what was being captured.

The film process has focused largely on how difficult it is to represent memory through film, which in this case includes the absence of any accounting of the main project that my mother worked on. Family footage shot after her arrival in Switzerland, as well as our present dreams, have become the archival knowledge for the production of images. Since it escapes materiality in many ways, we narrated *around* the classified project, about a variety of topics big and small. We spoke about love and her feelings when she met my father, a Swiss engineer, who was flown in to install the optical coating machines. We spoke about feelings of displacement, of pressures to assimilate, and our different relationships to home. In *Little Grass*, the politics of the nondisclosure agreement, which had served the desires of the Chinese military-industrial infrastructure, show up as forms of alienation, as protective coping mechanisms, as a constant negotiation of identities and knee-jerk reactions whose meanings we are only just collectively piecing together. The nondisclosure my mother signed, scales between the personal, to the nation-state and ideological, where following the threads of the personal, had started to reveal the other side of the scale and filled each other in.

    Little Grass, a documentary film by Solveig Qu Suess, is expected to be released by 2024.

Solveig Qu Suess works within the fields of documentary film, art, and research. Drawing links across time and distance, her films and writings look into the optics of an increasingly unpredictable world. Exploring questions of power and perception, the negotiation of bodies and environments, and image practices that escape the boundaries of their frame, she uses filmmaking as a means to research and connect registers of the intimate and geopolitical. She is currently a researcher at the Critical Media Lab, Basel, and a PhD candidate in urban studies at the University of Basel.

Notes

1.   Beijing Planetarium, "Cosmos Theater."
2.   Zeiss, "Planetarium Installations in Australasia," www.zeiss.com/planetariums/int/about -us/references/installations-in-australasia.html (accessed January 6, 2023).
3.   Xin Li, interview with author, June 20, 2022.
4.   Liu, *Information Fantasies*, 30.
5.   Bazdyrieva and Suess, "Future Forecast."
6.   Haraway, "Situated Knowledges," 585.
7.   Parikka, *Operational Images*, 46.

References

Bazydrieva, Asia, and Solveig Suess. "The Future Forecast." In "New Silk Roads." February 2020. *E-Flux Architecture*. https://www.e-flux.com/architecture/new-silk-roads/313108/the -future-forecast/.

Beijing Planetarium. "Cosmos Theater." *Beijing Planetarium*. https://www.bjp.org.cn/en/ (accessed January 6, 2023).

Haraway, Donna. "Situated Knowledges: The Science Question in Feminism and the Privilege of Partial Perspective." *Feminist Studies* 14, no. 3 (1988): 575–99.

Liu, Xiao. *Information Fantasies: Precarious Mediation in Postsocialist China.* Minneapolis: University of Minnesota Press, 2019.

Parikka, Jussi. *Operational Images: From the Visual to the Invisual.* Minneapolis: University of Minnesota Press, 2023.

Sayer, Andrew. "Seeking the Geographies of Power." *Economy and Society* 33, no. 2 (2004): 255–70.

Zeiss. "Planetarium Installations in Australasia." https://www.zeiss.com/planetariums/int/about -us/references/installations-in-australasia.html (accessed January 6, 2023).

CURATED SPACES provides a focus on visual culture in relation to social, historical or political subject matter.

Connecting the Countryside

Radio Network and the Infrastructure of the Masses in Socialist China

Yingchuan Yang

Some peasants in Shanghai, it was reported in 1966, wrote a poem in praise of the latest achievement brought by the Chinese socialist state. The poem reads:

An iron wire connecting thousands of families;
a loudspeaker hanging in every household.
Good people and good deeds are mentioned every day;
news and state policies are delivered to home.
Revolutionary songs and modern operas;
truly powerful in improving our thoughts.
Forecasting the weather and talking about sciences;
a bumper harvest is thanks to it too.[1]

This poem applauds the wired broadcasting (*youxian guangbo*) system, more commonly known as the radio network (*guangbo wang*), that was erected all across rural China beginning in the 1950s. In Shanghai, the radio network had reached 90 percent of all communes by 1962. By the time this poem was written, all ten counties and 196 communes in Shanghai had a broadcasting station, and more than 98 percent of brigades could listen to broadcast via the radio network.[2] The number of loudspeakers further increased to 381,500, or one for every two and a half households. In some brigades there was even one loudspeaker for each family. Such a

Radical History Review
Issue 147 (October 2023)   DOI 10.1215/01636545-10637204
© 2023 by MARHO: The Radical Historians' Organization, Inc.

massive broadcasting system required significant human resources; 445 full-time staff worked for the radio network.[3] On a national scale, China already possessed almost two thousand radio stations and six million loudspeakers in 1964, which means that more than 95 percent of all cities and counties had their own radio network.[4] Even though urbanites were picking up radio technology as a hobby the 1950s and 1960s, the radio set remained extremely rare in rural China. The radio network was the foremost and often the only way for most rural people to listen to broadcasts throughout the socialist period.

Although the radio network was an extensive infrastructure that played a key role in disseminating information in rural China, it has only received scattered scholarly attention. The early generation of political scientists such as Alan P. L. Liu was interested in studying how the socialist state used the broadcasting system in strengthening its legitimacy and integrating the nation.[5] More recently, Andrew F. Jones has characterized the radio network as a top-down information system that functioned to "modernize, reorganize, and regulate rural space and the temporal rhythms of rural life."[6] While this description outlines the purposes of the radio network, Jones fails to capture the complexity of radio networks as a diverse infrastructure that was under constant contestation and modification. An exclusive focus on the radio network's function has also yet to take into consideration how such a massive infrastructure was established and operated, leaving its technical aspects unexplored. A number of newer histories of radio in China have not avoided this pitfall either.[7]

This article investigates the establishment, operation, and maintenance of the radio network on an everyday basis by looking *at* the radio network rather than *through* it. It has always been assumed, not incorrectly, that the socialist state was eager to use technology to strengthen its rule, and in many cases was quite proficient in it, but little is known about how exactly the state built and maintained these technologies in the first place. This article thus examines one of the technological endeavors to govern China at the most local level. In doing so, it adds to the recently fecund field of grassroots history and offers fresh perspectives on socialist China through a technological lens.[8] A local and everyday perspective challenges the purported efficiency of the radio network, which was in reality used in many more ways in addition to indoctrination and regulation. Such multifaceted and unintended uses of the radio network were an unexpected result of how it was run on the ground.

By attending to the everyday, technical aspects of one of the most ambitious—yet at the same time one of the most neglected—infrastructure projects in modern Chinese history, this article complicates an area of scholarship commonly known as infrastructure studies. Although scholars have recently taken up infrastructure as an object of critical inquiry, infrastructure studies have been largely confined to capitalist experiences.[9] With a case study of socialist China, this article turns the spotlight onto the politics of infrastructure under socialism and thus destabilizes some of the basic assumptions behind infrastructure studies that customarily interrogate infrastructural development against the backdrop of liberal modernity. The radio network was certainly "a key technology of government" for the Chinese socialist state, but it did not precisely serve "to separate politics from nature, the technical from the political, and the human from the nonhuman."[10] Instead, one key premise of socialist infrastructure development was its attentiveness to the inherently political character of infrastructure. The recognition of its political capacities made the radio network both a mechanism of governance and a tool of inclusion, disciplining the populace through broadcasts while creating a sense of belonging for its builders and users as members of the socialist nation.

In this light, the radio network is indicative of what Brian Larkin calls the "totality of both technical and cultural systems," as its construction, maintenance, and utilization were never only about the development of radio technology per se.[11] In his work, Larkin charts how the colonial Nigerian state used radio to technologize and expose local spaces to outside information and forms of leisure.[12] In the same vein, the radio network was initially envisioned and implemented as an attempt to impose a new information order under Chinese socialism. However, this venture was soon curtailed and transformed by local conditions that frustrated a completely top-down intervention. The Central Broadcasting Bureau, the government agency in charge of the radio network, never had enough resources to carry out this grand plan on its own, so much of it was run not by state-dispatched personnel but rather by villagers who were recruited to be technicians, correspondents, and broadcasters. As an infrastructure that benefited from bottom-up support as much as top-down planning, the radio network uncovers the transformative potential of placing the people at the heart of infrastructure projects. The often-cited slogan "relying on the masses" (*yikao qunzhong*) was not only political rhetoric but also a concrete reality in socialist rural China, where radio networks managed to burgeon despite the perceived and real lack of capital, equipment, and expertise.

With a description of the radio network that flourished in rural, instead of urban, China, this article paints a more favorable picture of the socialist Chinese countryside in terms of infrastructure development, and it also expands our knowledge of the workings of the Chinese socialist state. The extant literature on modern China has privileged the more visible infrastructure projects such as railroads and the military-industrial complex, whereas we have been recently reminded that indispensable infrastructures of communication tend to be overlooked by both users and scholars.[13] The radio network, the most important telecommunications tool for most parts of the country, underpinned the socialist state by facilitating the transmission of information and amplifying state capacity. Conventionally, rural China under socialism is portrayed as being sidelined in industrial development and as merely the theater of land reform and agricultural collectivization.[14] Even though the socialist state pressured many highly skilled rural-based artisans into farming, rural broadcast workers at the same time acquired technological literacy to operate broadcast equipment and run the radio network.[15] Revealing how this fundamental infrastructure took off and functioned redirects our attention on the socialist state away from its institutional organizations and political campaigns to its infrastructural and material base.

Radio networks not only permitted the rural populace to contribute to the production and dissemination of information but also brought them together as members and, to an unprecedented extent, active builders of the new society. A central concept in communist political rhetoric, "the masses" (*qunzhong*) were hailed as the origin of legitimacy of the Chinese Communist Party. For this reason, who constituted the masses became the critical question in defining the prospect of Chinese socialism, and the masses had to be incessantly "made through revolutionary practices" based on the immediate, ever-shifting circumstances of the revolutionary enterprise.[16] Accordingly, the extant historiography usually understands the masses as a political and social category that was to be constantly molded and remolded by cultural formations and political campaigns.[17] While acknowledging the political implications that this label carried (and still carries), this article contends that the masses were also constructed as a technological category in socialist China. The socialist citizenry was defined by their involvement in state-led technology campaigns such as the radio network; in turn, as people strove to build and run their own radio networks, they spontaneously took part in assembling and buttressing the telecommunications system that was integral to the socialist state. An infrastructure of the masses, in other words, could only be made possible by the masses.

Primary sources for this article mostly come from Shanghai, and this is not only because the Shanghai Municipal Archives remains the most accessible repository of socialist-era documents in China, rendering the city the most feasible locale of study. More important, due to its economic power and political importance, Shanghai had the most successful radio network; in the neighboring affluent province of Jiangsu, the radio network reached 94 percent of all brigades only in 1977, compared to 98 percent in Shanghai in 1964.[18] The conditions in Shanghai in many ways encapsulated the ideals of the infrastructure, and Shanghai's experiences were often representative of the success and failure of the radio network on a national scale. It should be noted that most of the primary sources in this article were produced by the state and cannot be read as an "objective" reflection of the voices of the masses. Still, they contain invaluable information on the working conditions of local broadcasters and the challenges they faced. This article also uses autobiographical materials to look into the firsthand experiences of people who worked for the radio network.

Designing the Radio Network

The radio network was not a socialist invention, but it was first envisioned by the Nationalist government to tackle the spatial inequality in broadcasting in Republican China (1912–49). In 1937, the Kuomintang official Wu Baofeng (1899–1963) proposed to establish a nationwide radio network, taking as a model the system of chain broadcasting in the West, to alleviate the lack of broadcasting in remote areas, as there were more than thirty radio stations in Shanghai but none in Inner Mongolia, Tibet, Qinghai, or Xinjiang, which together constituted almost half of China's territory. The radio network that Wu had in mind would relay the central station's programs at certain times of the day and otherwise play local programs. The Nanjing government adopted Wu's plan to set up a national radio network of four layers: central, regional, provincial, and local. However, the grand plan was strangled by the impending Second Sino-Japanese War and saw virtually no development from 1937 to 1941. Despite a renewed state interest in the radio network in 1941 as part of the war-preparation effort, World War II and the subsequent Chinese Civil War extinguished any real hope. As the Nationalist government itself admitted in 1947, "Despite vigorous attempts to promote broadcasting, no general progress can be expected very soon."[19]

After the founding of the People's Republic of China in 1949, the General Administration of Press orchestrated the construction of a nationwide radio receiving network called the radio reception network (*guangbo shouyin wang*). Much like the Nationalist radio network, it was intended to address the imbalance of radio set ownership. There were approximately one million radios in China in 1949, but the majority were owned by upper- or middle-class families in large cities. Every layer of government above the county level, as well as schools, factories, and army units, was to have at least one radio monitor (*shouyinyuan*) whose job was to listen to the Central People's Broadcasting Station and the provincial broadcasting station and to pass on important information.[20] The position of radio monitor, too, could be traced back to Republican-era policies, when the Nationalist government dispatched radio monitors in rural areas to deliver information by "listening to news and propaganda broadcasts twice a day, transcribing and printing their content in new local newspapers, and posting the news items to wall papers (*bibao*) and blackboards in public areas."[21]

In this way, the early-1950s radio reception network was an infrastructure exclusively used for receiving information, as it was controlled by a small batch of dedicated staff who merely reproduced broadcasts. In contrast to the Nationalist government, which hired only 816 radio monitors in 1943, the nascent socialist state established almost 24,000 radio reception stations and sent out more than 20,000 radio monitors across China by 1952.[22] For many people in the countryside, this was the first time they heard a radio or received information from the broadcast (through the radio monitor). Indeed, the radio set was an extreme rarity in rural China throughout the socialist period. As seen in two pictures taken by the photojournalist Li Zhensheng (1940–2020) in Acheng County near the northern city of Harbin in 1964, after an alleged landlord was denounced, his family's personal belongings were confiscated and publicly displayed in the county as testimony to their luxurious lifestyle and "bourgeois status." Central to this exhibition was a radio receiver.[23] In more remote areas, such as the Inner Mongolia steppe, local villages did not even have electricity before 1966, let alone radios or other home appliances.[24] Hence, the radio reception network became an important means for people in rural China to acquire up-to-date information, but it was still considerably limited in its accessibility. Even in the relatively wealthy province of Zhejiang, it was common for a few hundred peasants from several villages to listen to one single radio together.[25]

In 1952, the Jiutai County broadcasting station in Jilin discovered by chance the possibility of amplifying the radio reception network through the extant telephone network by connecting the county's central broadcasting studio directly to the telephone network. Then the loudspeakers would be able to receive radio signals from the landline just like telephones. This telephone-based model was much more convenient for listeners, who did not have to gather together at a radio set, and local broadcasters in the county could curate the programs to be played on the air. This prototype radio network was such a novelty that peasants from nearby counties traveled to Jiutai County in droves just to hear it. This technological model was soon popularized across the nation at the county level.[26] In Jilin, it played twice a day for a total of four hours.[27] Still, this system had several shortcomings. Because they shared the same network, telephone and broadcast could not be used concurrently, and the broadcasting station usually had to compromise by running for no more than four hours a day. Also, since the power supply for the entire system in a county only came from the telephone line, the number of loudspeakers this system could support was limited to a few hundred.[28] For less developed areas where even the telephone was unavailable, this setup was not possible at all.

The most commonly used type of radio network did not appear until the third National Working Conference on Broadcasting was held in Beijing in 1955, during which Mao Zedong (1893–1976) demanded the development of rural radio networks. He proposed building the radio network within seven years, so that every village in China would be able to listen to broadcasts via the wired system.[29] The next year, the Central Broadcasting Bureau came up with a more concrete plan according to which the wired broadcasting system would be available in every commune within five to twelve years, depending on local circumstances.[30]

To accomplish this, the rural radio network took up both a new political organization and a new infrastructural form. Politically, it was made a priority for the local governments. Technologically, it was no longer ancillary to the telephone but now enjoyed an independent infrastructure, as each radio network began to run on dedicated poles, wires, and speakers. A typical rural radio network is, technically speaking, a rather simple system: the county-level broadcasting station wirelessly receives the Central People's Broadcasting Station in Beijing as well as the provincial broadcasting station, serving as the center of broadcast in the county. It is then connected to local broadcast studios (*guangbo zhan*), which are connected to numerous speakers through wires. The local broadcast studio is the most important node in this system since it both receives broadcasts from the county-level station and sends broadcast signals to the loudspeakers. Broadcast workers at the local broadcast studio are responsible for maintaining the infrastructure under their jurisdiction. Depending on local conditions, the radio network could be founded at the county, commune, or even brigade level (especially in densely populated and rich regions such as Shanghai).

Although it was not exactly a marvel of technology, the radio network required significant resources to be constructed, as each locale with a radio network needed its own sets of wires, poles, and loudspeakers. In his discussions with the Central Broadcasting Bureau in 1956, Liu Shaoqi (1898–1969), then vice president of China, weighed in with more detailed instructions on how to actualize the radio network, in which he was mostly concerned with the feasibility of building such an extensive infrastructure in the countryside. Liu suggested that the standards should not be set too high: for the wooden poles that support the wires, it would be fine as long as "they do not fall." From the beginning, the radio network was designed to be as affordable for the state as possible. Liu also forbade the broadcasting stations from collecting a listening fee.[31] Despite not having to pay a fee, the rural populace was meant to finance the infrastructure that they would be using. As Liu said, "If the masses want [the radio network], then let [the state] do it; if they don't then hold it until later. If they want it, then we extend the wires to their commune, and they pay for the power lines they use, buy their own loudspeakers, and the commune finds the wooden poles on its own. They can also help themselves with setting up the wires."[32] While Liu seemed to give people the freedom of choice, he simultaneously shifted the financial burden to the masses and made it easier for the local governments to support the radio network with relatively few resources. Liu's directive also marked the first appearance of the overarching principle of "relying on the masses," as he stated that "the development of the radio network mostly relies on the masses."[33] The masses were envisioned as an inherent part of the radio network from its inception, and subsequently they would be involved in all aspects of the infrastructure.

The financial contribution from the masses was integral to the radio network, and it was later developed into the model of "three-in-one" (*san jiehe*), that is, joint financing by the state, the community (the local commune, production brigade, or production team), and the masses. In this scheme, the state was only responsible for basic infrastructures such as electricity and roads. Except in poor regions where direct state support was provided, it was the local community and the listeners themselves that primarily funded most radio networks. As Mei Yi (1914–2003), then vice director of the Central Broadcasting Bureau, explicitly pointed out in 1964, "In setting up the wires, materials from and labor of the masses should be used as much as possible." Moreover, as a principle, the listeners had to purchase their own speakers. Of course, Mei also acknowledged the regional variations in China and let the local authorities determine the appropriate charge plan depending on local situations.[34]

The "three-in-one" configuration made the radio network economically feasible. According to a 1958 budget sheet, the entire radio network system in Shanghai would cost around 3.6 million yuan, of which the masses themselves would have to pay 700,000 yuan in the form of speakers. Then, there were two possible ways for the municipal government and the local communes and production brigades to divide the remaining 2.9 million. In the first scenario, the communes and brigades would spend 2.6 million, so the municipal government would need to contribute only about 330,000 yuan. Alternatively, even if the municipal government could be more generous and pay 1.6 million, the communes and brigades would still have to hand over 1.3 million.[35] Either way, the radio network in Shanghai was mostly funded by the local communities and the radio listeners themselves rather than the municipal government. Likewise, in 1956, the Beijing municipal government paid around 122,000 yuan toward the annual construction and maintenance budget of the radio network, whereas the local communities were responsible for the remaining 185,000 yuan.[36] In other regions, mass support for building the radio network came in numerous ways, often in the form of underpaid or even uncompensated labor. In rural Shaanxi, local laborers were mobilized to lodge and feed the technicians and broadcasters.[37] Peasants in Anhui were called up to volunteer on the construction site.[38]

Although Liu Shaoqi forestalled the collection of a listening fee in 1956, the radio network did not remain free forever, at least in Shanghai. In 1960, people in Qingpu County were already paying for the infrastructure, and their payments made it possible for the radio network in Qingpu to be financially self-sufficient and even have an occasional surplus.[39] Four years later, the Shanghai Broadcasting Bureau reported that half of the communes in the city were turning in a fee, and it was pushing the local broadcast stations to accelerate the progress in charging listeners. Each speaker (usually used by a single household) carried a fee of 0.2 to 0.3 yuan every month.[40] This charge was modest, considering that the average annual income per capita in rural Shanghai in 1958 was around 133 yuan, so most families would be able to afford it.[41]

Building the Radio Network with Amateur Technicians
Central to an infrastructure are always those "who manage, maintain, and extend" it.[42] Nevertheless, current scholarship pays virtually no attention to the "broadcast workers" (*guangbo gongzuozhe*) who built and maintained the radio network in socialist China. During the fifth National Working Conference on Broadcasting in May 1958, the Central Broadcasting Bureau formalized Liu Shaoqi's earlier call to depend on mass contribution for the radio network into the principle of "relying on

the masses."[43] As Zhou Xinwu (1916–2000), another vice director of the Central Broadcasting Bureau (together with Mei Yi), told fellow broadcast cadres in 1958, the key to a successful broadcast network was to "make broadcast work the masses' own job."[44] This guideline of "relying on the masses" both stemmed from the socialist ideology of garnering political support from the people and manifested the pragmatic reality of running such an extensive infrastructure with limited financial and human resources.[45] As a result, the majority of rural broadcast workers were not dispatched by the state but rather recruited from the masses. A total of 448 people were working for the radio network in suburban Shanghai in 1960, whereas only 86 of them had state employee status (*bianzhi*), a requisite for job security, pension, and other benefits; the remainder were students or peasants.[46]

Rural people worked for the radio network in different capacities. Many procured knowledge of radio technology and served as amateur (*yeyu*) technicians. In Shanghai, according to the most common type of arrangement, a brigade hired a dedicated technician to be in charge of maintaining broadcast equipment, and the brigade was responsible for their salary. In another scenario, a commune would have a few people oversee everything in the commune on an ad hoc basis known as "half worker, half peasant" (*yi gong yi nong*). They farmed as usual but maintained the broadcast equipment when necessary. Moreover, there was an abundance of volunteers who would fix minor problems. In contrast, professional technicians on the state employee payroll served mostly in managerial and supervisory roles by providing training to amateur technicians. They also managed the more technologically complex parts of the radio network such as the electrical grid.[47]

Given that so many of these newly minted broadcast workers were recruited from the masses, it was necessary to offer them germane training in radio technology. The most readily available resource was the print media. Whether they were on the state employee payroll or not, all broadcast workers had access to a range of materials that helped them become proficient technicians. The center of knowledge production in radio network technology was Shanghai. Comprehensive treatises on the radio network, such as *Rural Wired Radio Network Technology* and *Common Knowledge of Rural Wired Broadcasting*, were published in Shanghai in subsequent years.[48]

These technical publications on the radio network largely catered to lay readers, featuring easily comprehensible guides on radio technology. *Common Knowledge of Rural Wired Broadcasting*, first published in 1966 and revised in 1971, is an A-to-Z guide covering virtually all aspects of radio network in an accessible manner for rural technicians with little or no background in relevant subjects. It contains generously illustrated instructions on how to set up wires, choose and install loudspeakers, and common troubleshooting tips. Later, this book would be translated into Uyghur and published in Xinjiang.[49]

Many other technical guides were printed in the form of magazines, pamphlets, and posters. The popular national technical magazine *Radio* (*Wuxiandian*) published detailed instructions on installing, designing, modifying, and assembling parts and devices for the radio network using conveniently available, sometimes homemade, raw materials. In the first issue of 1960, for instance, *Radio* carried detailed instructions for repurposing a dry battery radio set into a radio receiver for a commune broadcasting station.[50] Another guide detailed how to set up an uninterruptible power supply following the principle of "walking on two legs" (*liangtiao tui zoulu*), referring to the combination of standard approaches (using a transformer) and improvisational ones (putting ethanol in gasoline generators).[51] *Convenient Loudspeaker*, a short manual of only sixteen pages published by the Youth and Children Publishing House, told how to make a loudspeaker with such straightforward instructions and accessible raw materials that even kids could give it a shot.[52]

The coexistence of native, mass, and practice-oriented techniques (known as *tu*) and imported, elite, and theory-based ones (known as *yang*) was central to the socialist science system.[53] Although radio technology had a foreign origin, the actual installation, operation, and maintenance of the radio network often had to rely on *tu* methods, given the lack of cutting-edge equipment and properly trained personnel to operate them. The absence of *yang* technology notwithstanding, a highly technological infrastructure such as the radio network could only function smoothly with the assistance of *tu* technology that was comprehensible and accessible to the technologically untrained masses. It was often with these makeshift devices that local broadcasters overcame the lack of proper ready-made broadcasting equipment. Peng Zhijian, the only broadcaster on a small farm in Hainan, learned how to repair balanced armature speakers, a kind of rudimentary speaker, with used parts. She was thus able to install extra speakers on the farm's radio network.[54] In another case, the radio network on a nonelectrified farm could run for six hours a day with "electricity generated by a tractor."[55]

Despite the lack of professionals and experts, the radio network went through constant technological improvements throughout the socialist period, and these innovations were often initiated at the grassroots level by county-level broadcasting stations and factories. The largest investment for the infrastructure was in the poles and wires, which together accounted for 60 percent of the total budget; they also happened to be the most delicate part of the whole system and required regular maintenance.[56] Initially, wooden poles were used, but they were vulnerable to moisture, wind, and worms. In 1962, Qingpu County in Shanghai switched to cement poles.[57] The following year, the Yuhang County broadcasting station managed to manufacture a type of cement pole as cheap as wooden ones but ten times as durable. This technology was soon popularized, and many broadcasting stations founded their subsidiary cement pole factory.[58] By 1972, almost twenty thousand cement poles had been erected across Shanghai, manufactured by local factories.[59] For the wires, the Rongcheng County broadcasting station in Shandong invented an oil coating technology in the mid-1970s that could extend the life of iron wires for up to five years. Two coastal county stations in Guangdong, where the climate is exceptionally humid, also experimented with burying wires underground.[60]

In his study of statistics in the early People's Republic of China, Arunabh Ghosh posits that a "variety of stratagems . . . were employed" to deal with its incapacity in the statistical system due to limited resources.[61] By the same token, even though the radio network had a shortage of professional staff, the state solved the problem by training the users of the radio network to become technicians. In contrast to the statistical system, the radio network required less specialized knowledge and expertise, so people with little formal training could more easily become well-versed in radio technology and learn to be proficient broadcasters, thanks to widely available printed materials on radio technology. Having mastered the relevant technology, some of the amateur technicians at the local level then became involved in mass innovation in technology, bringing about technological advancements that were actualized with unusual materials and unconventional means.

Running the Radio Network as Correspondents and Broadcasters

Apart from installing and maintaining the radio network, the masses both received broadcasts and participated in creating its content, since a key part of "relying on the masses" was to recruit them as correspondents (*tongxunyuan*) for the radio network. While the consumers and the producers of propaganda often overlapped in radio broadcasting, the radio network in socialist China stood out by encouraging listeners to get involved in running the infrastructure.[62] The role of correspondent had a distinctively socialist genealogy that began with workers and peasants being encouraged to write for newspapers in the 1920s Soviet Union, to improve both their literacy levels and political participation.[63] The Chinese Communist Party similarly invited workers and peasants to contribute to its newspaper *Liberation Daily* in its revolutionary base of Yan'an in the 1940s.[64] The radio network adopted and expanded this scheme. Instead of an educational opportunity, however, the hiring of broadcast correspondents was meant to alleviate the lack of dedicated broadcast workers. A group of correspondents was formed in each county, and the broadcasting stations actively engaged with them through meetings, interviews, letters, and the distribution of broadcast programs. It was estimated that the correspondents submitted fifteen to thirty articles daily to the county broadcasting stations, and the county stations' self-made programs mostly depended on their contributions.[65]

In 1958, the Shanghai Broadcasting Bureau published an internal journal, *Shanghai Broadcast*, for correspondents and broadcast workers to connect with each other and receive information on running the radio network. *Shanghai Broadcast*, similar to the radio network itself, was organized in a decentralized manner. Each commune would have to form a "communication group" of three to five people chosen from the broadcast workers, and each county would appoint an editor to coordinate all the commune-level communication groups.[66] *Shanghai Broadcast* solicited submissions from its readers, asking for news and experiences of the local radio networks. Instead of a dedicated editorial staff, *Shanghai Broadcast* was run by the editors from the counties with submissions from local broadcast workers who dabbled in the role of correspondents. The local broadcasters were responsible for editing and publishing the journal, and, in that capacity, would also shape the operation of the rural network itself.[67]

In 1964, the Fengxian County broadcasting station ran a program that was dedicated to the poor and lower-middle peasants (*pinxiazhongnong*) and committed to propagate "good people and good deeds" (*haoren haoshi*) from this class category. In the past decade, it was the local cadres who filled the airwaves. Following the Four Cleanups movement in 1963, class struggle ascended to be the central political agenda, so the broadcasters were compelled to turn the poor and lower-middle peasants into the new protagonists for rural broadcasting.[68] Broadcasters and correspondents followed them closely to tell stories that illustrated their moral superiority, such as how two poor peasants slept in the fields to help the seeds sprout with their body temperature. It was claimed that, having heard this tale, other people in the commune also chose to sleep in the fields to assist agricultural production.[69]

The Propaganda Department routinely held meetings for the county broadcasting station staff, during which the municipal government passed on the latest work plan and solicited feedback from the rank-and-file broadcast workers. From these meeting minutes, we are able to get a sense of the challenges they faced. The local broadcast workers often complained about the lack of substantial state support. Chen Weibao, the Shanghai County broadcasting station chief, bemoaned that his station only had one full-time editor. In Jiading County, six out of the seven staff members suffered from various chronic diseases. As some lamented, "[The state] used us a lot but helped and educated us very little."[70] While all broadcast workers, as a part of the propaganda system, were regularly monitored by the socialist state, a tight fiscal budget limited the purview of actual state support, either financial or material, and left the burden to the broadcast workers on the ground.

When additional material support by the state was hard to come by, the local populace sometimes stepped in to help on an ad hoc basis. In Shaanxi, elementary and middle school students were recruited to teach literacy to peasant broadcasters.[71] In another example in Hebei, Jia Zhangwang (b. 1954) returned to his home village to be a farmer upon graduating from high school in 1972, when universities were suspended during the Cultural Revolution. When his commune was digging a small canal in 1976, he was recruited by the commune broadcast station to contribute as a casual correspondent and broadcaster because he was familiar with the situation on the construction site. Over the period of one week, Jia read eighteen articles to his fellow villagers. He returned to his agricultural job once the canal was finished.[72]

Relying on the masses to run the radio network was certainly not the only time the socialist state tapped local human resources to sustain its infrastructure projects. To fight soil erosion in rural Shaanxi, for instance, the local populace was ordered to prioritize water and soil conservation over agricultural production, triggering a wide outcry and public resistance.[73] In contrast, rural residents welcomed mass participation in the radio network, because the network cooperated with and often counted on the peasants as part of the infrastructure, and in turn was much more successful in bringing concrete, positive changes to the countryside. Unlike in certain projects of developing science and technology that extracted lay knowledge, radio network users were valued not for their know-how in radio technology or experience in broadcasting—they had none—but for their familiarity with local circumstances and eagerness to make their own stories heard, making them excellent agents in operating the radio network and bringing about attractive and effective broadcast materials.[74]

The Socialist Soundscape

For the socialist state, the radio network was first and foremost a propaganda tool; as Alan P. L. Liu astutely summarized, the content of broadcast always adhered to "the immediate and dominant task of the nation in each period."[75] In 1972, it was estimated that 36 percent of programs aired by the Baoshan County radio station were political propaganda, especially in the national campaign to criticize revisionism and rectify work style (*pi xiu zhengfeng*) launched that year targeting Lin Biao (1907–71) and Chen Boda (1904–89).[76] Poor and lower-middle peasants were brought into the studio to "speak bitterness" (*suku*), publicly recounting their woes to fuel outrage against the party's foes.[77] When Mao Zedong called on the nation to study philosophy, the radio networks in Shanghai designed a series of programs, with local examples drawn from Baoshan County, to explicate the meanings of philosophy, an otherwise arcane and distant term for the peasants. One such example was how a team of poor and lower-middle peasants, by studying dialectical materialism, especially Mao's own concept of "one divides into two" (*yi fen wei er*), overcame pessimism brought by bad weather to ensure a bumper harvest.[78] Even in the late 1970s, an American scholar observed that "political messages are heard daily by almost everyone" through the local radio network in a commune near Guangzhou.[79]

Besides political propaganda, cultural programs were a central feature of the rural radio network. Rural residents in Shanghai were particularly fond of Shanghai opera, Yue opera, Wuxi opera, and Pudong musicals. Some peasants even installed an extra loudspeaker at home at their own expense to better listen to these operas.[80] While scholars have examined the rise of a new socialist sonic culture, rural China remained a stronghold for traditional local operas at least in the 1960s, as there was little evidence that they were bent for propaganda purposes.[81] In fact, it was expressly noted that local operas were warmly received for their "local characteristics, with tone and content familiar to the masses." Revolutionary popular music was welcomed as well, such as "Socialism Is Good" ("Shehuizhuyi hao") and "Mount Erlang" ("Erlang shan").[82] Later in the Cultural Revolution, quotation songs adapted from *Quotations of Chairman Mao* would replace those earlier songs as the only tunes of revolution.[83]

Through the correspondents or by writing to the broadcasting station, listeners could provide input on the broadcast programs, and they repeatedly demanded more content tailored to the rural audience. One peasant from Xianghe County in Hebei wondered, "I think there should be more crosstalk shows [*xiangsheng*] on rural life, why can't I hear any?" Another, from Yi County, requested more traditional operas that promoted friendship between commune members and caring for the elderly.[84] Radio programs became a centerpiece of rural cultural life, which was shaped by the listeners themselves.

The radio network was utilized to disseminate useful information and knowledge "for the purposes of promoting economic development . . . and cultivating [the] citizenry."[85] In Shanghai, the weather forecast was said to have an accuracy of 90 percent, and everyone, cadres and peasants alike, would quietly listen to it. A peasant reported, "We used to look up at the sky every morning to tell the weather, but the weather changes constantly and this method is not reliable. Now by listening to the broadcast every morning, we know if it will rain."[86] In the event of extreme weather, the radio network was more efficient than wireless broadcasting in sending out a warning. When an imminent rapid increase in temperature was announced through the radio network, the Zhenbei Brigade in Jiading County was able to ventilate its greenhouses on time to protect the mushrooms.[87] The National Earthquake Bureau also teamed up with the Central Broadcasting Bureau to use the radio network to teach earthquake prediction and preparedness.[88]

Information on agricultural production, such as pest control and farming techniques, was in high demand as well, and broadcasters relayed programs apposite to local needs. When Songjiang County had a labor shortage in transplanting rice seedlings, the county radio station encouraged women to participate in agricultural production and taught them farming skills. Within a short time, 52,800 women, almost 60 percent of all women in Songjiang County, participated in rice transplanting.[89] In 1964, Nanhui County first experimented with intercropping wheat with rice, and the agricultural scientist Wang Baoyuan was invited to teach intercropping through the radio network; as a result the county managed to intercrop over 80,000 *mu* of land.[90]

With the omnipresence of radio broadcasts, daily life in rural China was technologized and vocalized. Meng Shengguo, who grew up on a remote state farm in southern Hainan, reported that as soon as the loudspeakers started to play energizing marching songs in the morning, everyone would wake up and start a day of working. Soothing tunes at noon meant that people could go back home to eat and take a nap, to be awoken again by light music. In the evening, the end of broadcasting concluded the day and the farm fell into silence and dropped off to sleep.[91] Here, two broadcasting schedules from Kuandian County in Liaoning and Guyuan County in Ningxia are representative of the typical programs of local radio networks outside Shanghai.[92]

Kuandian County Broadcasting Station Program Schedule, 1955[93]
First Broadcasting (5:55–7:00)

5:55	Opening song and program preview
6:00	Relay of *Cultural Programs* from the Central People's Broadcasting Station
6:15	Cultural programs
6:30	Relay of news and newspapers summary from the Central People's Broadcasting Station
7:00	End of broadcast

Second Broadcasting (11:55–13:00)

11:55	Opening song and program preview
12:00	Local news
12:20	Cultural programs
12:30	Relay of *News* from the Liaoning People's Broadcasting Station
12:45	Relay of *Cultural Programs* from the Central People's Broadcasting Station
13:00	End of broadcast

Third Broadcasting (17:55–20:30)

17:55	Opening song and program preview
18:00	Relay of *News* from the Central People's Broadcasting Station
18:15	Cultural programs (Mondays, Saturdays, and Sundays) Technology lectures (Tuesdays and Thursdays) Life consultant (Wednesdays and Fridays)
18:30	Relay of *Cultural Programs* from the Central People's Broadcasting Station
19:00	Relay of local programs across Liaoning from the Liaoning People's Broadcasting Station
19:20	Local news
19:40	Local weather forecast
19:45	Relay of *Cultural Programs* from the Central People's Broadcasting Station
20:00	Relay of local programs across China from the Central People's Broadcasting Station
20:30	End of broadcast

Guyuan County Broadcasting Station Program Schedule, 1968[94]
First Broadcasting (6:40–8:00)

6:40	Opening quotation songs
7:00	Relay of news and newspapers summary from the Central People's Broadcasting Station
7:30	Local programs on the Cultural Revolution
8:00	End of broadcast

Second Broadcasting (12:25–13:30)

12:25	Opening song and program preview
12:30	Relay of news and cultural programs from the Central People's Broadcasting Station
13:30	End of broadcast

Third Broadcasting (18:20–21:00)

18:20	Opening song and program preview
18:25	Quotation songs and local revolutionary cultural programs
18:35	Local programs on the Cultural Revolution
19:00	Relay of Cultural Revolution programs from the Central People's Broadcasting Station
19:30	Relay of Cultural Revolution programs from the Ningxia People's Broadcasting Station
20:00	Relay of news, cultural programs, and songs from the Central People's Broadcasting Station
21:00	End of broadcast

As in colonial Nigeria, the radio network was designed as a public technology. However, in contrast to the Nigerian case, in which the colonial state intended to bind the local populace "into wider national and imperial circuits" through radio, the radio network in the socialist Chinese countryside adapted to the extant agricultural rhythm of life.[95] Its programs were scheduled according to everyday rural cycles and tailored to the needs and preferences of peasants. As mentioned above in Meng's narrative, the radio network was interwoven with the specific farm, where everyone ate, worked, and slept with one accord. With its operation adapted to local circumstances, the radio network and the soundscape it shaped were fundamentally tied to local rather than national life.

While all the local radio networks were supposed to relay programs from the Central People's Broadcasting Station as well as the provincial broadcasting station, the actual broadcasting process was operated by broadcasters on the ground and was largely unsupervised. As a result, much of the content of broadcasts was determined at the county, or sometimes the commune, level. Local cadres could often make use of the radio network at will. Zhang Jinfeng, a writer from rural Shandong, recalls that the broadcast would sometimes be cut off by the commune broadcaster to make announcements. Even the village head could seize the radio network to give a speech. In order to make people less annoyed at his truncating the broadcast, he usually played songs and Lü opera before addressing the villagers.[96]

Because the radio network was often in the hands of local broadcasters, the quality of the broadcasts was inconsistent. When people were working in the field, the Qiyi Commune in Shanghai County played the song "Hot Blood" ("Rexue ge"), which includes the following lyrics: "Who wants to be a slave? Who wants to be a horse or cow?" This unfortunate choice of music hurt the peasants' morale. When giving speeches on the radio, municipal cadres usually spoke in Mandarin, and the locals, who only understood Shanghainese, did not bother to listen at all. Mistakes also happened, as many broadcasters were poorly trained, one of whom spoke of Algeria (*Aerjiliya*) as if it were two countries (Aer *ji* Liya).[97]

Occasionally, the radio network could become downright antirevolutionary. When the Fengxian County broadcasting station was relaying the Shanghai People's Broadcasting Station in May 1973, voices from the Taiwanese station Voice of Free China, on a similar frequency as the Chinese one, mixed in with the broadcast.[98] More often, the radio network malfunctioned because of human error. In August 1974, Li Zaiyun, the Party Committee secretary of Beizhuang Brigade in Liantang Commune in Qingpu County, decided to use the radio network to mobilize the villagers in preparation for a typhoon. While adjusting the equipment, Li accidentally tuned the radio receiver to a Taiwanese station that alleged that peasants lacked food and clothes in mainland China and instigated a rebellion. Instead of immediately turning it off, Li kept the radio network playing for about ten minutes, making the Taiwanese propaganda heard through more than two hundred loudspeakers in the brigade. Li and other local cadres tried to cover it up until a worker named Shen

Ruiyun reported this scandal to the county level. When Qingpu County launched an investigation into this issue, it was further discovered that the Liantang Commune regularly cut off broadcasting from the Qingpu County broadcasting station to play its own programs. In the Silian Brigade, almost anyone could make use of the brigade radio network to make an announcement.[99] Three years later, in 1977, the broadcaster in the Zhaotun Commune, also in Qingpu County, played a propaganda tape of the Cultural Revolution, which had ended almost one year earlier.[100]

The actual content of broadcasting from the radio network was never uniform; rather, each county, town, village, and even the individual broadcaster had a say in what sounds came out of their loudspeakers. Accordingly, the socialist Chinese soundscape was not only peppered with quotation songs and political slogans but also contained local opera, useful information, and, occasionally and by accident, the relay of foreign radio stations. Even if the radio network was created by central directive to mitigate the shortage of propaganda workers and amplify state capacity, its management was localized and its programs vernacular. In meetings, the Central Broadcasting Bureau repeatedly urged local broadcast stations and broadcast workers to improve the quality of propaganda.[101] Yet the unsatisfactory conditions of radio propaganda were an inevitable result of its decentralized nature. As propaganda became a highly technical and local activity, the results on the ground could be variable and unreliable owing to local broadcasters' incompetence or negligence, undermining the grand goal of promoting the state's revolutionary enterprise.

Conclusion

How was such a massive infrastructure accomplished with so little? This article contends that mass participation in infrastructure development underpinned the success of the radio network even with relatively little state support. Accordingly, it sees the radio network not as an infrastructure of control or indenture, but rather as a mechanism that redressed the underdevelopment in rural China, of course not without its limits or problems. This new infrastructure was spearheaded by the state, but it was only made possible by rural people themselves, as the radio network was a largely grassroots, bottom-up endeavor that was funded and operated at the local level. Monetary contribution came from the local communities and even individual listeners, and most programs were locally made by broadcasters in the county or even the commune. In this way, broadcasters both benefited from a state-sponsored infrastructure project and contributed to the project itself as members of the socialist citizenry. It was only with the power of the masses that the radio network was constructed, and this in turn defined who the masses were in socialist China.

To be sure, the socialist Chinese radio network was not the only instance in which infrastructures were intimately intertwined with the formation of political subjectivities. In postapartheid South Africa, for instance, everyday infrastructures such as the prepaid water meter are "the location where citizenship is fashioned through a variety of measures."[102] Unlike a colonial social order (or the neoliberal one, which inherited much of its racism from colonialism), which exploits infrastructures to *exclude* certain groups of people from citizenship, however, the socialist Chinese state staged a politics of *inclusion* by subsuming the rural populace into the technological and sonic realm of the radio network. The slogan of "relying on the masses" is hardly seen in other infrastructure development projects, in China or elsewhere, because infrastructures are usually too massive to be singlehandedly managed by nonstate actors. In this sense, the contribution by mass broadcast workers to the radio network draws intriguing parallels to what AbdouMaliq Simone calls "people as infrastructure," by which he refers to the phenomenon that people's activities weave together social fabrics and lubricate city life in Johannesburg.[103] On the one hand, the Chinese radio network shared the same bottom-up characteristics and was undoubtedly shored up by rural residents, who did things that the state was unable to do; on the other hand, the radio network represents a unique model of infrastructure both as the result of a strategic decision by the state to "outsource" its operation to the masses and, as the article has detailed, by serving fundamentally different purposes from infrastructures in the (neo)liberal world.

While some scholars have regarded the foremost purpose of the radio network as "the fostering of imagined communities in *national* terms," by looking at *local* specificities this article firmly rejects the view that the radio network always functioned in the interests of national integration.[104] More frequently, what people heard from the radio network had little to do with the grand ambition of revolution. Actual broadcast programs consisted of both state-sanctioned, nonpolitical content, such as local operas and scientific and technical knowledge, and transmission of foreign radio stations that were never supposed to be on the air. The failure to adhere to official policies in broadcasting, quite ironically yet somehow unsurprisingly, originated in the state's inability to offer more substantial support to the radio network; it had no alternative but to rely on the masses to operate the infrastructure. As the masses occupied the stage of broadcasting in rural China, they mostly played what they liked and needed and sometimes made mistakes in their broadcasts. By pointing to a historical moment when the masses were put at the center of an infrastructure project, this article suggests that perhaps the best way to realize "the urgent political project of reclaiming infrastructure from militaries, markets, and empires" is to have infrastructures run by the users themselves.[105]

After the conclusion of the Cultural Revolution in 1976, the state steadily reduced its already little support for the radio network. In 1977, the Shanghai People's Broadcasting Station submitted a report calling for more funding for the rural radio network.[106] However, it appeared that the municipal government turned a deaf ear to this report, as a largely identical report was submitted again in the next year.[107] The second report was obviously brushed aside as well. Soon the broadcasting system had problems retaining local broadcast workers. In 1979 an urgent report to the municipal government stated that broadcasters in Chongming County had directly petitioned (*shangfang*) the Shanghai Broadcasting Bureau. This was in large part a historical problem: in a 1963 directive, the Central Broadcasting Bureau made no mention of broadcast workers outside the state payroll system regarding their welfare.[108] The issue became increasingly pressing in the late 1970s, since many rural broadcast workers had already worked for the rural radio network for more than two decades and were approaching retirement, but they were still poorly paid and had not acquired state employee status.[109] Two years later, in 1981, the municipal government finally agreed with reluctance to admit some of them into the state employee system on the basis of their seniority, but the unlucky ones who did not get the chance would have to be "properly treated" by each town or commune.[110]

The next year, the Shanghai Bureau of Finance complained that the rural radio network was costing the municipal government too much, and such financial losses were blamed on "leftist influences," a postsocialist euphemism for socialist ideology. The proposed solution was to abandon all state support for the radio network.[111] Even though this extreme measure was not realized owing to fierce opposition from the Broadcasting Bureau, it can be safely assumed that any additional resources for the radio network would be out of the question thereafter.[112] The conditions of radio networks in other parts of China gradually deteriorated too, and attempts at revitalization proved to be fruitless. In Jiangxi, even the official records acknowledge that, since the mid-1980s, "a series of actions to revive [the radio network] have been taken, but the recovery is difficult and slow."[113] In 2000, the party's official newspaper, *People's Daily*, reported that, out of more than two hundred thousand loudspeakers in Taikang County in Henan, almost none were functional.[114]

The withdrawal of state support was coupled with the rise of new media technologies, making the rural radio network essentially derelict. Television had reached more than 92 percent of the Chinese population by 2000.[115] A younger generation of rural women have adopted the mobile phone as their entry point to the urban-centered contemporary Chinese society.[116] That being said, the demise of the rural radio network should not be viewed simply as the triumph of new technologies but must be understood against the backdrop of the shift in political economy in rural China. Under the postsocialist regime, state policies subjugate collectivized agricultural production to the privatization and marketization of the countryside. In contrast to the collective experience of listening to the radio network, the more privatized technologies of televisions and mobile phones are now more consonant with the "decollectivized rural social life."[117] If the socialist sensitivity toward the mass-based nature of infrastructure helped construct a national radio network that both served and was supported by the masses, it was swiftly sundered in the postsocialist period, when infrastructure has been redefined as the foremost component of productive forces and as basically neutral across different social systems. Hence the radio network went into decline as soon as the countryside was no longer a productive site under state capitalism. With the disappearance of the socialist countryside, where the masses were brought together in using and operating the radio network, "an iron wire connecting thousands of families" has been cut off.

Yingchuan Yang is a PhD candidate at Columbia University. His dissertation, "Revolution on the Air: Radio and the Mass Technology of Chinese Socialism," offers a new narrative of modern Chinese history with an emphasis on previously ignored actors and through a technological lens. He received his BA in history from University of California, Los Angeles.

Notes

I am grateful to Eugenia Lean, who directs the dissertation on which this article is based, for her penetrating insights and unwavering support. A shorter version has been presented at an Association for Asian Studies Emerging Fields in Asian Studies Workshop on "Technology in Asia," for which I especially thank Joseph S. Alter, Aleksandra Kobiljski, and Aparajith Ramnath. I have also benefitted from the feedback from the editors of the issue and the reviewers. Nicole Elizabeth Barnes and Benjamin Kindler provided incisive comments on an early draft. Tiffany Yang sharpened the presentation.
1.   Shanghai Municipal Archives (hereafter cited as SMA), B92-2-1029, 3.
2.   The commune system of agricultural collectivization was first introduced in 1958; under it the rural area was divided into three administrative levels: commune, production brigade, and production team. It was formally abolished in 1981.
3.   SMA B92-2-1029, 1–2.
4.   The first two statistics are from Liu, *Radio Broadcasting*, 120; the third is from *Renmin ribao*, "Fazhan nongcun guangbo wang."
5.   Liu, *Radio Broadcasting*; Liu, *Communications and National Integration*, 118–29.
6.   Jones, *Circuit Listening*, 60.
7.   Wang, "Listening to the State"; Alekna, "Reunified through Radio," 227–93; J. Li, "Revolutionary Echoes."
8.   For a definition of grassroots history in the socialist Chinese context, see Brown and Johnson, "Introduction," 4–5.
9.   For example, see Larkin, "Politics and Poetics of Infrastructure." In this review essay, only 3 out of the more than 120 entries in the bibliography are on socialist countries.
10.   Appel, Anand, and Gupta, "Promise of Infrastructure," 4–5.
11.   Larkin, *Signal and Noise*, 6.
12.   Larkin, *Signal and Noise*, 48–72.
13.   For railroads, see Köll, *Railroads*; for the military-industrial complex, see Meyskens, *Mao's Third Front*. Nicole Starosielski underscores the importance of the undersea cable network in *Undersea Network*, especially 3–10.
14.   For example, see DeMare, *Land Wars*; and Hershatter, *Gender of Memory*.
15.   For the narrative of deskilling, see Eyferth, *Eating Rice from Bamboo Roots*.
16.   Lin, "Mass Line," 123.
17.   This is true for both Chinese and Western scholarship. See, respectively, Li Lifeng, "'Qunzhong' de miankong"; and Xiao, *Revolutionary Waves*.
18.   Jiangsu sheng difangzhi bianzuan weiyuanhui, *Jiangsu sheng zhi*, 196.

19. This paragraph is largely based on Li Yu, *Zhongguo guangbo xiandaixing liubian*, 165–69.

20. Zhao, *Zhongguo guangbo dianshi tong shi*, 178–80.

21. Alekna, "Reunified through Radio," 112, see also 132–42.

22. The numbers come from Li Yu, *Zhongguo guangbo xiandaixing liubian*, 168; and Zhao, *Zhongguo guangbo dianshi tong shi*, 179.

23. Li Zhensheng, *Red-Color News Soldier*, 53–54.

24. Wei, "Nanwang de jiyi," 117–18.

25. *Dangdai Zhongguo de guangbo dianshi*, 1:353–54.

26. *Dangdai Zhongguo de guangbo dianshi*, 1:35, 354–57.

27. Jilin sheng difangzhi bianzuan weiyuanhui, *Jilin sheng zhi*, 206–8.

28. *Dangdai Zhongguo de guangbo dianshi*, 2:201–2.

29. *Zhongguo de youxian guangbo*, 1.

30. *Dangdai Zhongguo de guangbo dianshi*, 1:35.

31. *Zhongguo de youxian guangbo*, 2–4.

32. *Zhongguo de youxian guangbo*, 2–4.

33. *Zhongguo de youxian guangbo*, 2–4.

34. *Zhongguo de youxian guangbo*, 166–70.

35. SMA B92-2-403, 12–13. It is not clear which financial plan was adopted.

36. Beijing Municipal Archives 088-001-00737, 198–99.

37. Sha and Zhang, "Zuowei 'xin meiti,'" 126.

38. Anhui sheng difangzhi bianzuan weiyuanhui, *Anhui sheng zhi*, 124.

39. SMA B92-2-696, 11.

40. SMA A22-1-792, 62–63.

41. Shanghai shi tongji ju, *Xin Shanghai sishi nian*, 398.

42. Appel, Anand, and Gupta, "Promise of Infrastructure," 13.

43. SMA B92-1-287, 30–36.

44. *Zhongguo de youxian guangbo*, 150.

45. For a more thorough discussion of the Communist Party's "mass line" policy, see Lin, "Mass Line."

46. SMA B92-2-696, 6–12.

47. SMA B92-2-1029, 7–8.

48. Chen, *Nongcun youxian guangbo wang jishu*; Fan, *Nongcun youxian guangbo changshi*.

49. *Xinjiang tong zhi*, 243.

50. Zhejiang sheng Fuyang guangbo zhan, "Tu yang bing ju."

51. *Wuxiandian*, "Guanche 'liangtiao tui zoulu.'"

52. Xu Guomin, *Jianbian kuoyinji*.

53. Schmalzer, *Red Revolution, Green Revolution*, 34–38.

54. Peng, "Wo de nongchang guangboyuan riji," 82–83.

55. Nathan, *Chinese Democracy*, 163.

56. *Dangdai Zhongguo de guangbo dianshi*, 2:203–4.

57. *Shanghai guangbo dianshi zhi*, 557.

58. *Dangdai Zhongguo de guangbo dianshi*, 2:204–5.

59. *Shanghai guangbo dianshi zhi*, 159–60.

60. *Dangdai Zhongguo de guangbo dianshi*, 2:205.

61. Ghosh, *Making It Count*, 180.

62. For the case of radio propaganda in Angola, see Moorman, *Powerful Frequencies*, 49–71. I thank Amanda Lanzillo for this reference.

63. Lenoe, *Closer to the Masses*, 32.

64. Li Haibo, "'Xini geming.'"

65. SMA B92-2-1029, 8–9.

66. SMA B92-2-499, 7, 13, 17–18; see also SMA B92-2-407, 11–13.

67. SMA B92-2-499, 30–31.

68. The Four Cleanups (to cleanse politics, economy, organization, and ideology) was a movement launched by Mao Zedong to intensify class struggle as a prelude to the Cultural Revolution.

69. SMA B92-2-1029, 25–28.

70. SMA A22-1-792, 56–58.

71. Sha and Zhang, "Zuowei 'xin meiti,'" 126.

72. Jia, *Guangkuo tiandi*, 176–77.

73. Muscolino, "Contradictions of Conservation."

74. For an example of the state extraction of local knowledge, see Schmalzer, *Red Revolution, Green Revolution*.

75. Liu, *Communications and National Integration*, 124.

76. The campaign was to denounce Lin Biao, who was once designated as the successor of Mao but died during his escape to the Soviet Union, and Chen Boda, a former secretary of Mao and a close associate of Lin.

77. Speaking bitterness had become a routine procedure of political campaigns at this point; see Javed, *Righteous Revolutionaries*, 73–77, 170–74.

78. SMA B285-2-79, 25–27. For "one divides into two," see Tian, *Chinese Dialectics*, 155.

79. Bennett, *Huadong*, 57.

80. SMA B92-2-696, 8.

81. Relevant scholarship on the new socialist sonic culture includes Huang, "Listening to Films"; and Mittler, *Continuous Revolution*, 33–127.

82. SMA B92-2-696, 8.

83. Jones, *Circuit Listening*, 71–74; Mittler, *Continuous Revolution*, 208–9.

84. Xu Zhiwei, "'Shiqi nian' shiqi," 51–52.

85. Culp, *Power of Print*, 244.

86. SMA B92-2-696, 8.

87. SMA B92-2-1029, 41.

88. *Zhongguo de youxian guangbo*, 95–96.

89. SMA B92-2-696, 8.

90. SMA B92-2-1029, 20. One *mu* is 0.0667 hectare.

91. Meng, "Nanbin nongchang yi jiu," 18–19.

92. According to interviews conducted in the 1980s, this kind of thrice-daily broadcast was the most common pattern across the nation. Nathan, *Chinese Democracy*, 163.

93. *Liaoning sheng zhi*, 164.

94. *Ningxia tong zhi*, 831.

95. Larkin, *Signal and Noise*, 56. It should be noted that this is also different from the situation in contemporary Nigeria, where it is not important to actually comprehend the messages broadcast through loudspeakers; see Larkin, "Techniques of Inattention."

96. Zhang, "Laba, geyao," 174.

97. SMA A22-2-797, 75–76.

98. SMA B285-2-66, 2–3.

99. The incident and follow-up investigation are both recorded in SMA B285-2-178, 5–7.

100. SMA B282-2-567, 1–2.

101. *Zhongguo de youxian guangbo*, 192–93.
102. Von Schnitzler, *Democracy's Infrastructure*, 27.
103. Simone, "People as Infrastructure."
104. The quote is from Coderre, *Newborn Socialist Things*, 37. As I suggest above, this emphasis on the (intended) purposes of radio in socialist China largely builds on and follows the research agendas of political scientists during the Cold War and should be seriously complicated by historical scholarship.
105. Attewell, Mitchell-Eaton, and Nisa, "Political Lives of Infrastructure."
106. SMA B285-2-585, 1–5.
107. SMA B285-2-707, 1–2.
108. *Zhongguo de youxian guangbo*, 93.
109. SMA B285-2-928, 1–3.
110. SMA B285-2-1320, 1–4.
111. SMA B127-6-402, 41–46.
112. SMA B127-6-402, 55–56.
113. *Jiangxi sheng guangbo dianshi zhi*, 34–35.
114. Li Funong, "Taikang nongcun."
115. Zhu and Berry, "Introduction," 3.
116. Wallis, *Technomobility in China*.
117. Day, *Peasant in Postsocialist China*, 5.

References

Alekna, John Norman, Jr. "Reunified through Radio: Media, Technology, and Politics in Modern China, 1923–1958." PhD diss., Princeton University, 2020.

Anhui sheng difangzhi bianzuan weiyuanhui, ed. *Anhui sheng zhi: guangbo dianshi zhi*. Beijing: Fangzhi chubanshe, 1997.

Appel, Hannah, Nikhil Anand, and Akhil Gupta. "Temporality, Politics, and the Promise of Infrastructure." In *The Promise of Infrastructure*, edited by Nikhil Anand, Akhil Gupta, and Hannah Appel, 1–38. Durham, NC: Duke University Press, 2018.

Attewell, Wesley, Emily Mitchell-Eaton, and Richard Nisa. "The Political Lives of Infrastructure: A Call for Proposals from the *Radical History Review*." H-Atlantic, January 14, 2022. https://networks.h-net.org/node/16821/discussions/9538975/political-lives-infrastructure-call-proposals-radical-history.

Bennett, Gordon. *Huadong: The Story of a Chinese People's Commune*. Boulder, CO: Westview Press, 1978.

Brown, Jeremy, and Matthew D. Johnson. "Introduction." In *Maoism at the Grassroots: Everyday Life in China's Era of High Socialism*, edited by Jeremy Brown and Matthew D. Johnson, 1–15. Cambridge, MA: Harvard University Press, 2015.

Chen Tiangui. *Nongcun youxian guangbo wang jishu*. Shanghai: Shanghai kexue jishu chubanshe, 1965.

Coderre, Laurence. *Newborn Socialist Things: Materiality in Maoist China*. Durham, NC: Duke University Press, 2021.

Culp, Robert. *The Power of Print in Modern China: Intellectuals and Industrial Publishing from the End of Empire to Maoist State Socialism*. New York: Columbia University Press, 2019.

Dangdai Zhongguo de guangbo dianshi. 2 vols. Beijing: Zhongguo shehui kexue chubanshe, 1987.

Day, Alexander F. *The Peasant in Postsocialist China: History, Politics, and Capitalism*. Cambridge: Cambridge University Press, 2013.

DeMare, Brian. *Land Wars: The Story of China's Agrarian Revolution*. Stanford, CA: Stanford University Press, 2019.

Eyferth, Jacob. *Eating Rice from Bamboo Roots: The Social History of a Community of Handicraft Papermakers in Rural Sichuan, 1920–2000*. Cambridge, MA: Harvard University Asia Center, 2009.

Fan Dunxing, ed. *Nongcun youxian guangbo changshi*. 2nd ed. Shanghai: Shanghai renmin chubanshe, 1971.

Ghosh, Arunabh. *Making It Count: Statistics and Statecraft in the Early People's Republic of China*. Princeton, NJ: Princeton University Press, 2020.

Hershatter, Gail. *The Gender of Memory: Rural Women and China's Collective Past*. Berkeley: University of California Press, 2011.

Huang, Nicole. "Listening to Films: Politics of the Auditory in 1970s China." *Journal of Chinese Cinemas* 7, no. 3 (2013): 187–206.

Javed, Jeffery A. *Righteous Revolutionaries: Morality, Mobilization, and Violence in the Making of the Chinese State*. Ann Arbor: University of Michigan Press, 2022.

Jia Zhangwang. *Guangkuo tiandi: wo de hui xiang zhiqing huiyilu*. Beijing: Renmin chubanshe, 2018.

Jiangsu sheng difangzhi bianzuan weiyuanhui, ed. *Jiangsu sheng zhi: guangbo dianshi zhi*. Nanjing: Jiangsu guji chubanshe, 2000.

Jiangxi sheng guangbo dianshi zhi. Beijing: Fangzhi chubanshe, 1999.

Jilin sheng difangzhi bianzuan weiyuanhui, ed. *Jilin sheng zhi: xinwen shiye zhi; guangbo dianshi zhi*. Changchun: Jilin renmin chubanshe, 1991.

Jones, Andrew F. *Circuit Listening: Chinese Popular Music in the Global 1960s*. Minneapolis: University of Minnesota Press, 2020.

Köll, Elisabeth. *Railroads and the Transformation of China*. Cambridge, MA: Harvard University Press, 2019.

Larkin, Brian. "The Politics and Poetics of Infrastructure." *Annual Review of Anthropology* 42, no. 1 (2013): 327–43.

Larkin, Brian. *Signal and Noise: Media, Infrastructure, and Urban Culture in Nigeria*. Durham, NC: Duke University Press, 2008.

Larkin, Brian. "Techniques of Inattention: The Mediality of Loudspeakers in Nigeria." *Anthropological Quarterly* 87, no. 4 (2014): 989–1015.

Lenoe, Matthew. *Closer to the Masses: Stalinist Culture, Social Revolution, and Soviet Newspapers*. Cambridge, MA: Harvard University Press, 2004.

Li Funong. "Taikang nongcun: youxian guangbo wu shengyin." *Renmin ribao*, January 23, 2000.

Li Haibo. "'Xini geming': Yan'an shiqi tongxunyuan yundong de dongyuan jishu fenxi." *Chuban faxing yanjiu* no. 4 (2019): 100–5.

Li, Jie. "Revolutionary Echoes: Radios and Loudspeakers in the Mao Era." *Twentieth-Century China* 45, no. 1 (2020): 25–45.

Li Lifeng. "'Qunzhong' de miankong: jiyu jindai Zhongguo qingjing de gainian shi kaocha." In *Xin shixue: 20 shiji Zhongguo geming de zai quanshi*, edited by Wang Qisheng, 31–57. Beijing: Zhonghua shuju, 2013.

Li Yu. *Zhongguo guangbo xiandaixing liubian: guomin zhengfu guangbo yanjiu (1928–1949 nian)*. Beijing: Zhongguo chuanmei daxue chubanshe, 2017.

Li Zhensheng. *Red-Color News Soldier: A Chinese Photographer's Odyssey through the Cultural Revolution*. London: Phaidon, 2003.

Liaoning sheng zhi: guangbo dianshi zhi. Shenyang: Liaoning kexue jishu chubanshe, 1998.

Lin Chun. "Mass Line." In *Afterlives of Chinese Communism: Political Concepts from Mao to Xi*, edited by Christian Sorace, Ivan Franceschini, and Nicholas Loubere, 121–26. Canberra: Australian National University Press, 2019.

Liu, Alan P. L. *Communications and National Integration in Communist China*. Berkeley: University of California Press, 1971.

Liu, Alan P. L. *Radio Broadcasting in Communist China*. Cambridge, MA: Center for International Studies, Massachusetts Institute of Technology, 1964.

Meng Shengguo. "Nanbin nongchang yi jiu." *Ye cheng*, no. 8 (2008): 18–19.

Meyskens, Covell F. *Mao's Third Front: The Militarization of Cold War China*. Cambridge: Cambridge University Press, 2020.

Mittler, Barbara. *A Continuous Revolution: Making Sense of Cultural Revolution Culture*. Cambridge, MA: Harvard University Asia Center, 2013.

Moorman, Marissa J. *Powerful Frequencies: Radio, State Power, and the Cold War in Angola, 1931–2002*. Athens: Ohio University Press, 2019.

Muscolino, Micah S. "The Contradictions of Conservation: Fighting Erosion in Mao-Era China, 1953–66." *Environmental History* 25, no. 2 (2020): 237–62.

Nathan, Andrew J. *Chinese Democracy*. New York: Knopf, 1985.

Ningxia tong zhi: wenhua juan. Beijing: Fangzhi chubanshe, 2009.

Peng Zhijian. "Wo de nongchang guangboyuan riji." In *Zhiqing zai Hainan: shiliao xuan ji*, edited by Li Zhuquan, 3:79–85. Haikou: Nanfang chubanshe, 2019.

Renmin ribao. "Fazhan nongcun guangbo wang dali xuanchuan xin sixiang." November 21, 1964.

Schmalzer, Sigrid. *Red Revolution, Green Revolution: Scientific Farming in Socialist China*. Chicago: University of Chicago Press, 2016.

Sha Yao and Zhang Siyu. "Zuowei 'xin meiti' de nongcun guangbo: shehui zhili yu qunzhong luxian." *Guoji xinwen jie* 43, no. 1 (2021): 120–37.

Shanghai guangbo dianshi zhi. Shanghai: Shanghai shehui kexueyuan chubanshe, 1999.

Shanghai shi tongji ju, ed. *Xin Shanghai sishi nian*. Beijing: Zhongguo tongji chubanshe, 1989.

Simone, AbdouMaliq. "People as Infrastructure: Intersecting Fragments in Johannesburg." *Public Culture* 16, no. 3 (2004): 407–29.

Starosielski, Nicole. *The Undersea Network*. Durham, NC: Duke University Press, 2015.

Tian, Chenshan. *Chinese Dialectics: From Yijing to Marxism*. Lanham, MD: Lexington Books, 2005.

von Schnitzler, Antina. *Democracy's Infrastructure: Techno-Politics and Protest after Apartheid*. Princeton, NJ: Princeton University Press, 2016.

Wallis, Cara. *Technomobility in China: Young Migrant Women and Mobile Phones*. New York: New York University Press, 2013.

Wang, Yu. "Listening to the State: Radio and the Technopolitics of Sound in Mao's China." PhD diss., University of Toronto, 2019.

Wei Yuqin. "Nanwang de jiyi." In *Sai wai chun hua: yi jiu liu wu nian Tianjin shi shou pi fu Nei Menggu zhiqing chadui wushi zhounian jinian*, edited by Zhang Bingquan and Yu Deyuan, 116–21. Tianjin: Tianjin renmin chubanshe, 2015.

Wuxiandian. "Guanche 'liangtiao tui zoulu' de fangzhen jiejue gongshe guangbo zhan de dianyuan wenti." January 1960, 13–14.

Xiao, Tie. *Revolutionary Waves: The Crowd in Modern China*. Cambridge, MA: Harvard University Asia Center, 2017.

Xinjiang tong zhi: guangbo dianshi zhi. Urumqi: Xinjiang renmin chubanshe, 1995.

Xu Guomin, ed. *Jianbian kuoyinji*. Shanghai: Shaonian ertong chubanshe, 1959.

Xu Zhiwei. "'Shiqi nian' shiqi nongcun guangbo wang de jianli ji qi dui nongcun wenyi shengtai de chongsu." *Wenyi lilun yu piping* no. 6 (2020): 41–55.

Zhang Jinfeng. "Laba, geyao." *Xibu* no. 5 (2019): 173–78.

Zhao Yuming, ed. *Zhongguo guangbo dianshi tong shi*. New ed. Beijing: Beijing guangbo yingshi chubanshe, 2014.

Zhejiang sheng Fuyang guangbo zhan. "Tu yang bing ju, she she you guangbo: yong gaizhuang de gan dian shouyinji jianli gongshe guangbo zhan." *Wuxiandian*, January 1960, 10–12.

Zhongguo de youxian guangbo. Beijing: Beijing guangbo xueyuan chubanshe, 1988.

Zhu, Ying, and Chris Berry. "Introduction." In *TV China*, edited by Ying Zhu and Chris Berry, 1–11. Bloomington: Indiana University Press, 2009.

Bound Passages

Aviation, Deportation, and the Settler Carceral Transpacific

Jason Tuấn Vũ

On March 15, 2021, thirty-three Vietnamese refugees were deported from the United States on a charter plane from Dallas Fort Worth International Airport.[1] Decades earlier, these refugees had come to the United States after the Vietnam War, but with scarce support during their resettlement, they were served criminal convictions before attaining citizenship status, resulting in the loss of their permanent residency status.[2] As some of the first deportations to take place during the Biden presidency, this event signaled not only the administration's blatant disregard for its own promises of immigration reform but also its horrid indifference toward Southeast Asian American organizers who initiated a nationwide campaign calling for the immediate release of those in US Immigration and Customs Enforcement (ICE) custody.

While mourning this defeat, I remember scrolling aimlessly on social media, hoping against hope to find some news of a last-minute flight cancellation. Instead, I found a tweet from the immigration activist Thomas Cartwright, who shared live updates about the deportation flight as it made its way to Hà Nội's Nội Bài International Airport.[3] Before arriving in Vietnam, the flight was scheduled for two layovers—one at the Daniel K. Inouye International Airport (HNL) in Hawaiʻi and another at the Antonio B. Won Pat International Airport (GUM) in Guåhan.[4] These stops were supposed to be minor details in the tragic arc of these deportations, and

Radical History Review
Issue 147 (October 2023)   DOI 10.1215/01636545-10637218
© 2023 by MARHO: The Radical Historians' Organization, Inc.

yet I could not help but wonder what it meant for these refugees to pass through Hawaiʻi and Guåhan, sites of US colonial occupation that continues to this day. What did it mean to pass through these spaces of settler military power in the Pacific, which were crucial in the United States' imperial war in Southeast Asia? And what are we to make of these layovers, given their enmeshment in the carceral logics that bring about the ongoing criminalization of migrants and refugees in the United States?

Amid expectations of smooth and efficient transportation across vast distances, layovers are typically considered a marginal and bothersome aspect of aerial transportation, disrupting visions of speedy and direct flows under global capitalism and calling to mind "the fragilities and unintended consequences of circulatory systems that are often understood as unified and coherent."[5] Yet, despite their vexing nature, layovers are also vital to the logistical apparatus that makes up the infrastructure of modern-day aviation, providing crucial rest periods for flight crews and opportunities to refuel and switch planes. Layovers, in this sense, are not meaningless events but essential parts of air travel as we know it.

Just as the layover sustains global air travel, so too do Hawaiʻi and Guåhan serve as vital junction points in the rise and maintenance of the US's "imperial archipelago" in the Pacific.[6] Rather than viewing these layovers as incidental to the deportations themselves, this article focuses on them as critical moments through which to understand the related yet distinct processes of Indigenous dispossession and Southeast Asian refugee deportation. I argue that the layovers during the March 2021 deportation flight reveal Hawaiʻi and Guåhan as palimpsests of colonial occupation that are, in turn, used to bolster the further transit of global US empire. In doing so, I am interested in charting a critical transpacific geography that links the settler-colonial and carceral dimensions of US empire to the issue of Southeast Asian deportation, a convergence I term *settler carcerality*.

Settler carcerality refers to the manifold ways in which settler logics of elimination and replacement are deeply intertwined with carceral technologies of discipline and enclosure. These entanglements constitute a symbiotic relationship in which settler colonialism and carcerality work to mutually reproduce, reinforce, and refine one another across time and space, namely through the dispossession of marginalized subjects across the world. Settler colonialism remains foundational to our contemporary global order as a structure of ongoing Native genocide, namely through its "fundamental continuity" in "the exigencies of managing surplus populations."[7] At the same time, carcerality serves as an assemblage of punitive and exclusionary technologies that reinforce settler authority over colonized lands and peoples,[8] primarily by disrupting Indigenous lifeways and regulating the movement of labor, capital, and—in the case of the March 2021 deportation flight—criminalized subjects. Accounting for both sides of this circulatory relationship, settler carcerality points to the overlapping production of forced (im)mobilities that are essential to the form and function of contemporary settler states such as the United States.

Considering the specificities of colonization in Hawaiʻi and Guåhan, it is also necessary to discuss the military's key role in producing the conditions necessary for settler carcerality to take shape in both sites. Drawing from the context of Hawaiʻi, Juliet Nebolon proposes the term settler militarism to highlight the ways that "settler colonialism and militarization have simultaneously perpetuated, legitimated, and concealed one another."[9] Tiara Naʻputi extends this concept further to understand the material and discursive construction of Guåhan as a "militarized island ['territory']" of US empire.[10] Even as some populations do not permanently resettle on the islands but only pass through en route to other locations, the very act of these transits is underpinned by the permanence of settler-military infrastructures, including the repurposed terminals and runways that facilitate civilian air travel across the Pacific.[11] Building on settler militarism, settler carcerality thus highlights the ways that settler-colonial authority is secured through the formal institution of the military as well as everyday forms of violence. Such actions not only result in the enclosure of Indigenous lands and the displacement of racialized subjects but also blur the divisions often imagined between civilian and military domains.[12]

At first glance, US aerial infrastructure appears to be an unlikely site from which to interrogate settler carcerality as it operates across the Pacific. Relative to other modes of transportation, air travel is often understood as a fast and efficient method of transit across vast distances, uninhibited by common issues such as traffic jams and collisions. Yet the histories of HNL and GUM reveal aerial mobility in the Pacific as fundamentally built on multiple levels of violence committed against Indigenous peoples and other racialized populations. Put another way, the built infrastructures of aviation in Hawaiʻi and Guåhan are not only reminders of the colonial histories of these islands but also active sites where such violence continues to reverberate in altered forms.

With this in mind, I now turn to the layovers of the March 2021 deportation flight to Vietnam, approaching them as ephemeral nexus points that underscore the enduring layers of settler colonial dispossession and imperial displacement across the Pacific. Drawing from Yến Lê Espiritu's method of *critical juxtaposing*, I read across seemingly unrelated government reports, newspaper articles, and oral histories to "illuminate what would otherwise not be visible about the contours, contents, and afterlives of war and empire."[13] In particular, I connect the histories of HNL and GUM to their eventual deployment as layover sites in the March 2021 deportation flight, allowing for further elaboration of settler carcerality as a framework for bringing together differential forms of violence committed against colonized and racialized populations. These violences, I argue, are deeply shaped by related carceral logics that enable both the enclosure of Native lands and the forced (im)mobilization of racialized migrants and refugees. To conclude, I return to the March 2021 deportation flight by way of refugees' shared experiences aboard the plane. In doing so, I aim to reiterate settler carcerality as a framework for connecting struggles across seemingly discrete projects of imperial violence and dispossession.

Figure 1. US troops board a Pan American flight from Saigon, Vietnam, to Honolulu, Hawai'i. Pan American World Airways/ Annual Report (1966), ASM0341, box 2, folder 31, Special Collections, University of Miami Libraries, Coral Gables, Florida. Courtesy of Special Collections, University of Miami Libraries.

"Crossroads of the Pacific"

In 1966, Pan American World Airways (Pan Am) released an annual report detailing its various initiatives over the last fiscal year. Among these activities, Pan Am featured an image of American soldiers boarding a flight from Saigon to Honolulu (fig. 1). As the troops in this illustration board their flight, one soldier turns away from the plane with a wide smile, signaling his joyful anticipation of leaving South Vietnam, a site of escalating warfare. Indeed, for this soldier, and many like him, the opportunity to escape the battlefield for a sunny resort getaway was more than welcome.

The troops in this image represent some of the 194,000 American servicemen that year alone who were granted week-long vacations from Vietnam after months of fighting on the battlefield. With the help of Pan Am airplanes and personnel, approximately eight hundred troops left Saigon each day as part of the company's Rest and Recuperation (R&R) program with the US military. During this time, American GIs were allowed to travel to different resort areas across the Pacific, with Honolulu being especially popular for engaged and married soldiers.[14] General William Westmoreland, then acting as the commander of US forces in Vietnam, gave high praise to these R&R operations, referring to them as "an outstanding contribution to the morale and welfare of the United States Armed Forces in the Republic of Vietnam."[15]

Honolulu's role as a site of reunion for military families during the Vietnam War stands in stark contrast to its more recent use as a staging site for the separation of Southeast Asian refugee families via deportation. Such a tragedy highlights the nature of US empire in differentially deploying its infrastructural power to sustain lives it deems worthy while violating those it does not. HNL manifests this contradiction physically as the site where both military family reunions and refugee family separations have taken place. While highlighting this juxtaposition, however, it is also important to recognize that the March 2021 deportations were not the first displacements to occur at the site of HNL. Rather, to understand the extent to which the foundational infrastructures of US empire are rooted in both past and present forms of violence, we must trace HNL's existence to the United States' colonial occupation of Hawai'i—a history that goes back to the 1893 overthrow of the Hawaiian Kingdom.

HNL is built in the *ahupua'a* of Moanalua, a traditional land division known for its many fishponds and wetlands, which have sustained generations of Kānaka Maoli (Native Hawaiians) living in the area. Along with its abundance in natural resources, Moanalua is also rich in *wahi pana*, storied places of deep historical and spiritual significance to Native Hawaiian culture. For instance, one *mo'olelo* (story) tells of how King Kamehameha I rested in Moanalua after the Battle of Nu'unau in 1795, a decisive moment in the king's campaign to unify the Hawaiian islands under his rule.[16] As Kamehameha's descendent, Princess Bernice Pauahi Pākī Bishop eventually inherited Moanalua before passing it on in 1884 to Samuel Mills Damon, a white businessman whom Bishop had considered a friend.[17] Damon, however, went on to betray the Hawaiian monarchy in 1893, conspiring with other leaders of the settler-led coup to dethrone Queen Lili'uokalani.[18]

As a key member of the newly established settler society, Damon quickly moved to secure political and economic dominance in Hawai'i, suing the territorial government for exclusive fishing rights in Moanalua. The US Supreme Court ruled in Damon's favor, allowing him to take full ownership of Moanalua in 1904 and convert it for his own profit.[19] With local fishponds and marshlands destroyed by Damon's land development projects, many Kānaka Maoli in Moanalua were effectively displaced from their homes and forced to find other means of survival.[20] Through this radical transformation of Moanalua and the forced removal of its Native inhabitants, the stage was set for HNL's construction.

Upon Damon's death in 1924, his estate came under the management of trustees, who sold a significant portion of it to the Territory of Hawai'i. Consisting of nearly nine hundred acres of land and water, the acquired area was intended for use as the site of Hawai'i's first commercial airport, then known as John Rodgers Airport.[21] This endeavor was both expensive and labor intensive, with thousands of dollars poured into funding the construction of runways, buildings, and other infrastructure necessary for receiving flights into the airport. Given the massive resource demands of this airport construction project paired with additional public work projects, the Territorial Government of Hawai'i soon had to seek cost-cutting measures to make up for its dwindling funds. By the 1930s, it found an answer in converting the territory's prison population into a source of cheap labor.

According to a 1932 report by US Attorney General William D. Mitchell, 227 of the nearly 400 prisoners incarcerated in Oahu Prison were employed on public works projects that included airport construction.[22] Of the 227 prison laborers, 31 were specifically stationed at John Rodgers Airport, where their tasks ranged from clearing excess foliage to general runway maintenance. Inmates at the airport were also responsible for blasting and grading coral from the nearby seashores to produce ample construction material for runway construction and expansion. Records kept by the territorial government of Hawai'i show that prisoners contributed nearly a quarter of the coral used in runway construction from 1930 to 1931 alone.[23] Indeed, prison labor was deemed so valuable that, in a 1932 meeting, the Territorial Aeronautical Commission of Hawai'i noted its continued efforts to convince the High Sheriff of Hawai'i to send more prisoners for airport construction.[24]

Tracing the history of the criminal legal system in Hawai'i, Sally Engle Merry notes the ways that racialized immigrant communities were disproportionately criminalized by white settlers in the early years of US annexation. Viewed as threats to the social order, Chinese, Japanese, and Filipino workers found themselves subject "to special levels of surveillance and control," resulting in their incarceration and conscription into prison labor.[25] Connecting Merry's work to the history of HNL, it becomes clear that the use of prison labor in the airport's construction was a carceral process of racialized exploitation, one that occurred on lands stolen through settler logics of ownership and enclosure. Indeed, the very fact that HNL's construction took place on stolen Hawaiian lands highlights the enmeshment of settler-colonial and carceral logics in the history of its construction. The airport thus serves as a material representation of settler carcerality, a palimpsestic space built on the overlapping violences of Native dispossession and racialized incarceration.

Alongside settler proprietorship and prison labor, the US military also played a significant role in using and expanding HNL during World War II. After the 1941 attack on Pearl Harbor, US Armed Forces took control of all air bases in Hawai'i and converted them for use in the war effort. As a result, vast amounts of US military capital began to flow into the development of HNL, which was then called Naval Air Station (NAS) Honolulu. In the span of a few years, military officers began construction of four additional runways to facilitate the transit of military aircraft, a massive project requiring over ten million tons of coral to be dredged from surrounding seashores.[26] As a result of these renovations, NAS Honolulu became a crucial site for US air operations during World War II, with most military combat planes crossing the Pacific by way of the air base. By the end of the war, NAS Honolulu had become one of the largest airports in the United States, with a total area of 4,019.476 acres.[27]

In 1946, the US military returned NAS Honolulu to the Territory of Hawai'i, which renamed it Honolulu Airport the following year.[28] Despite its transfer to civil authorities, the militarized infrastructure left behind at HNL made it a central hub for all transpacific flights coming from the continental United States. While shifting to mainly commercial flights, HNL continued receiving military air transports because of its proximity to Hickam Air Force Base. In fact, out of all the United States' civilian airports, HNL received the greatest number of military aircraft, even during official peacetime.[29] In this way, despite its shift from military to territorial control, HNL remained deeply entangled with the military, both through its repurposed aviation technologies and the ongoing transit of US military personnel.

By 1951, HNL, now officially named Honolulu International Airport, was the third busiest airport in the United States, with plans underway for its expansion. During this time, the Hawai'i Aeronautics Commission (HAC) determined that major improvements would be necessary for HNL to keep pace with advancements in jet plane technology. These developments, detailed in the HNL Master Plan of 1951, emphasized the importance of acquiring more land for the construction of runways and terminals to accommodate greater air traffic.[30] Instead of serving military interests, however, the primary motivator for this wave of HNL's expansion was the growing presence of tourists on the islands from the 1950s onward. This shift toward tourism is evident in some of the key projects implemented by the HAC, including the expansion of HNL's overseas terminal as well as the construction of lei stands to welcome visitors to Honolulu.[31] Along with HNL's multi-million-dollar construction projects, these initiatives served to reinforce Hawai'i's imagined status as a tourist paradise, all while obscuring the enduring violence that underlay its production.[32]

Here, the perspectives of Kanaka Maoli scholars and activists help expose the consequences of HNL's construction and expansion on Hawai'i's natural environment. In her seminal book *From a Native Daughter*, Haunani-Kay Trask outlines the harm done to Native Hawaiian life and culture as a result of US colonialism. Of the many injustices she describes, Trask specifically denounces HNL as the site "where jet fuel from commercial, military, and private planes creates an eternal pall in the still hot air."[33] While noting the convergence of various actors invested in HNL's operation, Trask also uses the powerful image of an "eternal pall" to emphasize the deadly rates of pollution emitted by air travel.

S. Joe Estores and Ty P. Kāwika Tengan similarly note the environmental consequences of HNL's Reef Runway, a twelve-thousand-foot runway completed in 1977 that remains one of the airport's most well-known landmarks. As part of this project, over nineteen million cubic yards of coral were dredged from the sea and used as construction material for the runway, with some coming from Estores's home of 'Āhua Point. In his *mo'olelo*, Estores notes dramatic changes in the environmental conditions of 'Āhua Point before and after the Reef Runway's construction:

'Āhua Point lies beneath concrete and is no longer shown on maps. Mamala Bay is altered by the Reef Runway. The shoreline is no longer a habitat for the fish, crustaceans, or sea and land birds. The Pueo, the owl, is silent, no longer there. The great flocks of beautiful pheasants, kolea (plovers), 'iwa (frigate bird), bright red Cardinals, and albatross are no more. The once-great patches of mangroves full of Samoan crabs are gone. The salt works and marshes have been bulldozed over. Stewards of this land are no longer present.[34]

Among the grave ecological consequences that Estores describes, he includes the displacement of "stewards of this land," highlighting the role that the violation of

Indigenous sovereignty has had on the well-being of the natural environment. Indeed, at the time of the Reef Runway's construction, environmental activist groups such as Life of the Land tried to challenge the project in court given its predicted ecological consequences. However, in *Life of the Land v. Brinegar* (1973), the US Supreme Court upheld lower court rulings that permitted the Reef Runway's construction, citing scientific reports put forth by the US Department of Transportation.[35] As a result, the destruction of Hawai'i was allowed to continue, all for the sake of developing US aviation infrastructure in the Pacific.

Hawai'i continues to be a major tourist destination with millions of visitors flying in through HNL. Even in the midst of the COVID-19 pandemic, many have continued to come to Hawai'i on vacation, contributing to the islands' disproportionately high infection rates as well as straining the population's already strained resources.[36] The history of HNL reminds us that this trespass is not new; rather, it is situated within more than a century of settler carceral violence. And while militarism and tourism remain key reasons for air travel to and from Hawai'i, the layover of the March 2021 deportation flight reveals the ability of US empire to reconfigure its settler-military infrastructures to serve different imperial projects, including the carceral transit of refugees.

In 2010, the Office of Hawaiian Affairs reported on the disproportionately high rate of Kānaka Maoli incarcerated at the Saguaro Correctional Center in Arizona. Situating off-island captivity within the longer history of settler colonialism in Hawai'i, the report denounced these removals as "one of the most offensive and traumatic ways of alienating a Native Hawaiian person from the land [of Hawai'i]" and separating them from their families.[37] Given Hawai'i's colonial status as a US state, the removal of criminalized Native Hawaiians from Hawai'i is not technically a form of deportation. Nevertheless, their experiences resonate with those of deported Southeast Asian refugees, whose lives have likewise been torn apart by the carceral violence of US empire. The aerial routes taken by both groups alludes to as much; eleven years before the March 2021 deportation flight stopped at HNL, a group of 150 Hawaiian inmates flew out to Arizona from the very same airport.[38] Bound together by related yet distinct forms of imperial violence, these dual passages serve to illustrate the material realities of settler carcerality, the function and formation of US global empire through mutually reinforced structures of settler colonialism and carcerality.

Despite the immensity of racial-colonial violence that the United States has perpetrated in Hawai'i, the presence of insurgency remains evident in the ongoing anticolonial struggle enacted by Kanaka Maoli activists who continue to tell their stories against the genocidal elimination of their people.[39] While Hawai'i remains a key site of struggle against the US settler state, resistance extends to other sites as well. I now turn to Guåhan to chart another space shaped by the violences of settler carcerality.

Figure 2. CHamoru Nation protesters climb the fence of Naval Air Station Agana. Photo: Joyce Tainter. Joyce Tainter and Laura Jean Sablan, "CHamoru Nation Storms NAS," *Guam Tribune*, August 15, 1992.

Members of the Chamoru Nation Traditional Council climb over the locked gate at NAS, Agana yesterday to the waiting military security guards.   Photo by JOYCE TAINTER

"They're Fencing Us In!"

On August 14, 1992, members of the anti-imperialist organization Nasion CHamoru staged a protest against US aerial operations based in Guåhan. As they gathered in front of NAS Agana, their leader Angel Santos issued a statement that criticized the US military's exploitation of Guåhan. The gathered protesters then stormed the fences around the air base (fig. 2), prompting a confrontation with naval officers and police that resulted in the arrest of four Nasion CHamoru members, including Santos himself. In a final act of defiance as he was taken away by police, Santos denounced the military's ongoing occupation of his homeland in the following words: "They're not fencing themselves in, they're fencing us in, and when you look at defense around these military installations, we're inside the place, they're outside."[40]

Here, Santos exposes the enclosure of physical space as a strategy for reinforcing US colonialism in Guåhan through the restriction of CHamoru life and movement. Reminiscent of Laurel Mei-Singh's analysis of fencing as carceral infrastructure in Hawai'i, Santos's insight reveals the role of carceral technologies in transforming Guåhan's landscape into one of the most heavily militarized sites in the world—hence its reputation as the "Tip of the Spear" for American military presence in the Pacific.[41] Given this broader context, it is clear that Nasion CHamoru's protest was not just about NAS Agana but rather the entire infrastructure of settler colonialism imposed on the island.[42]

I begin with this story of protest to acknowledge the long history of CHamoru resistance against US empire while also underlining the significance of NAS Agana as a key site in this struggle. Despite its formal closure in March 1995, the air base continues as part of GUM, which took NAS Agana's place after its transfer to civilian authorities.[43] As the island's primary international airport, GUM serves as both a vital node of transpacific air travel and a site connecting Guåhan and the outside world. To think of GUM solely in terms of its infrastructural utility, however, is to obscure the violent processes of colonization through which the airport came to be in the first place. Challenging this erasure, I route GUM's history through CHamoru relations to the stolen lands on which it was built and the many lives that continue to be displaced because of it.

GUM resides on the land of Tiyan, meaning "stomach" in the CHamoru language. As with other villages, Tiyan's name alludes to the creation story of Fu'una and Puntan, sibling gods whose self-sacrifice created CHamorus and the islands they inhabit. In this story, Fu'una fashions Puntan's body into the different parts of the world, with Tiyan corresponding to his stomach.[44] It is through this act of creation, Craig Santos Perez argues, that CHamorus have held "the land itself as an ancestor" for generations.[45] Alongside this spiritual significance, the name Tiyan is also fitting given the region's historic role as an agricultural hub for the central villages of Guåhan, primarily through the growth of corn.[46] In 1521, however, CHamoru life became threatened by the arrival of the Spanish empire, which brought death and disease to the island before claiming it as theirs in 1564. About a century later, Spain declared the island a formal colony and began to forcibly reorganize CHamoru society, relocating many into large villages and pressuring conversion to Christianity.[47] These efforts served to alienate CHamorus from their Indigenous ties to the land, but Tiyan nevertheless remained an important agricultural center that sustained generations of CHamoru villagers.[48]

In 1898, the United States received Guåhan as a spoil of the Spanish-American War and proceeded to place the island under direct military rule, with one governor holding all political authority on the island. Despite CHamoru protests and the creation of an advisory Guam Congress in 1917, the governor held near-unlimited authority as he pursued the US military's goal of turning Guåhan into a "coaling station for U.S. naval vessels" headed to Asia.[49] Here, we see that in the US imperial imaginary, Guåhan was already constructed as no more than a stopover point to facilitate military transits across the Pacific. Not only did this foreshadow the island's eventual role in the March 2021 deportation flight but it also supplanted the Indigenous infrastructures long present on the island. Nonetheless, CHamorus continued to adapt to their colonial situation, with many at this time moving closer to Tiyan and establishing nearby villages such as Tamuning and Barrigada.[50]

World War II marked yet another devastating moment for Guåhan as Japanese forces came to occupy the island in December 1941. Initially, the Japanese military focused on extracting labor and resources from Guåhan to sustain its imperial war machine, all while suppressing CHamoru dissent through brutal acts of violence and torture.[51] By 1943, Guåhan's role shifted to the construction of defense infrastructure in preparation for impending US attacks.[52] One major project at this time was the construction of Guamu Dai Ni (Guam No. 2), an airfield in Tiyan meant to facilitate Japanese aerial combat against US forces. In an interview with *Pacific Daily News*, Eduardo Camacho shared his experience of being forced to work on the airfield as a fifteen-year-old boy, noting the long hours of work "without any compensation, without any break, without any food except one handful of rice and a red seed."[53] Indeed, these harsh conditions are representative of the experiences of many CHamoru laborers at this time, as well as Korean and Okinawan prisoners who were brought to the island to serve as an additional workforce.[54] Moreover, the process of clearing and leveling the land to make runways brought about ecological devastation that left the once lively landscape of Tiyan a barren and desolate shell of its former self.[55]

Upon the US victory in the Battle of Guam, the island returned to its status as an American colonial possession. This restoration is officially commemorated in Guåhan as "Liberation Day," when US forces successfully routed its Japanese occupiers and reestablished control of the island. In many ways, however, this pivotal moment in World War II simply represented a transition from one imperial power to another, with much of the same colonial infrastructure still intact. In fact, rather than dismantling Guamu Dai Ni and restoring Tiyan to its rightful CHamoru inhabitants, the US military renamed the base Agana Airfield and used it as a staging site for attacks on Japanese shipping containers and airfields in the Volcano and Bonin Islands.[56] Even after Japan surrendered in 1945, the base remained under US control, transferring from the US Armed Forces to the Navy, which subsequently renamed it NAS Agana.[57]

Beyond maintaining the already-present wartime infrastructures, the postwar moment also marked Guåhan's total transformation into "a modern military fortress" essential for "defending US global interests in the Asia-Pacific region."[58] With much of the island coming under US military ownership and vast amounts of capital being invested into further base development, the militarization of Guåhan only intensified as the island became a strategic location for counterinsurgency efforts across the Pacific. For instance, during the Vietnam War, Guåhan became a principal staging site for aerial bombardments in the region.[59] Although primarily originating from Andersen Air Force Base (AFB) during the war, US aerial operations also relied on militarized infrastructure that spanned the entire island.[60] Albeit less prominent than Andersen AFB, NAS Agana served as home for several units such as the US Navy's Heavy Photographic Squadron (VAP-61), which assisted in aerial bombardment missions including Operation Rolling Thunder through the use of photoreconnaissance technology.[61] Far from being peripheral to the US war effort, NAS Agana served as an important militarized site during the Vietnam War.

Situating NAS Agana within the longer history of CHamoru dispossession, I argue that the airfield represents a prime example of settler militarism in Guåhan, both through its illegitimate presence on stolen Native land as well as its role in bolstering US military power as a launching site for imperial warfare within and beyond the island. The air base also made permanent the displacement of many CHamorus who once inhabited Tiyan but were unable to return after the military took ownership. In this way, the US military participated in the settler-colonial dispossession of Indigenous people in Guåhan, monopolizing the island's resources and displacing CHamorus from their homes. To this settler-military connection, I add the necessity of attending to the various ways that carceral technologies have contributed to the subjugation of CHamorus and the maintenance of settler-colonial authority in Guåhan, including forced colonial labor and the enclosure of vast areas of land.

Although NAS Agana no longer operates as a US air base, it remains a vital part of GUM, which originated in 1962 when the US military lifted its ban on civilian air travel to and from the island.[62] Within a few years, GUM had its first international air terminal and began welcoming tourists in 1967. From then, the number of civilian flights to Guåhan gradually increased, necessitating the airport's continuing development and expansion. Under the Guam Airport Authority (GAA), plans were underway to improve the airport in 1978, including the construction of yet another international air terminal that was completed in 1982. By 1989, GUM had also constructed a multi-million-dollar industrial park as well as its own access road to allow for easier transportation to and from the airport.[63]

Even as GUM developed to accommodate growing tourism on the island, it still depended on NAS Agana's runways to facilitate incoming and outgoing civilian flights. In 1993, however, the Defense Base Realignment and Closure Commission issued a report that recommended closing NAS Agana and transferring its land to GUM. According to the report, the base's closure was a matter of cost efficiency for the military as Andersen AFB had the extra capacity necessary to accommodate all remaining naval personnel and equipment formerly stationed at NAS Agana.[64] Far from civilian air travel supplanting US military interests, then, the transfer of NAS Agana to GUM highlights the symbiotic relationship between tourism and militarism that perpetuates the US's settler-colonial presence in Guåhan.

April 1, 1995, marks the first day that GUM was fully operational as a civilian airport with the completion of NAS Agana's closure. Since then, the tourism industry in Guåhan has only grown stronger, becoming a significant part of the island's economy. In a 2016 report published by the Guam Visitors Bureau, Guåhan was receiving more than a million tourists annually, all of whom had to go through GUM for their trips.[65] These visitors, the report claimed, were responsible for generating thousands of jobs as well as billions of dollars in revenue for local communities throughout Guåhan. With figures like these, the bureau had no trouble in celebrating tourism as "the top economic contributor to Guam's economy."[66]

What these numbers do not show, however, is the material and psychological damage to Guåhan caused by tourism through the displacement of CHamorus, the commodification of their culture, and the exploitation of the island's natural resources. Keith Camacho links the history of tourism's development in Guåhan to Euro-

American colonial discourses that "feminized the Chamorro people as hospitable natives and Guam as a fertile paradise," making the island a seemingly paradisiacal site that welcomes all visitors.[67] Christine Taitano DeLisle further adds to this critique by noting the ways that the US military and Guåhan's tourism industry "invoke indigenous Chamorro culture" to legitimize the existence of their settler-colonial regime on the island.[68] This validation of US presence in Guåhan directly contributes to the island's ongoing environmental degradation, with increasing demand for luxury resorts and ocean excursions that inflict long-lasting harm on the island's coral reefs.[69] Here, it is important to note that these touristic endeavors do not supplant the force of military authority in Guåhan but rather work in tandem with it to ensure that the interests of US empire are maintained on the island. In this process of Indigenous dispossession, GUM has served as a key hub for the very transits that have reinforced Guåhan's status as an American colonial paradise.

Returning to the 1992 protest at NAS Agana, what this uprising makes abundantly clear are the ways that Indigenous CHamorus have continued to resist their elimination through various forms of dissent. From protests demanding an end to Guåhan's militarization to educational programs teaching CHamoru youth the stories of their people, Indigenous calls for decolonization are manifested on multiple fronts while also being rooted in a common desire to protect their ancestral lands.[70] In the context of Tiyan, this struggle is apparent in the as-of-yet unresolved conflict between Tiyan's original inhabitants, their descendants, and GUM. With the airport now occupying the lands that some three thousand Indigenous CHamorus once called home, former landowners and their descendants have called for reparations to be made for their losses. As recently as 2015, the CHamoru activist Vincente "Benny" Crawford filed a lawsuit demanding compensation for the loss of his ancestral lands.[71] These efforts, however, have met significant resistance from the United States, with Crawford's case being dismissed two years after it was filed and other reparation initiatives similarly scrapped or severely delayed.[72] Yet, despite so much pushback, ongoing CHamoru struggles for justice in Tiyan and Guåhan highlight the deep ancestral connection the people hold as the Indigenous stewards of the land—a relationship that refuses the violence of displacement and dispossession.

Existing at the intersection of military and civilian usage, GUM's development into an international airport brings together multiple histories that span the Spanish, Japanese, and American empires. Focusing on Tiyan, I have revealed the ways that Guåhan's status as a US settler colony has been reinforced not only through militarism and tourism but also by the deployment of carceral technologies that work to confine CHamoru life and mobility. In turn, these restricted spaces transform the island into a stopping point for multiple imperial transits, including military stopovers, touristic excursions, and more recently, the deportation of thirty-three Vietnamese refugees. To conclude, I now return to the tragic story of these deported refugees and reflect on the meaning of their passage through HNL and GUM.

Conclusion: Connecting Flights, Connecting Struggles

Among those deported on the March 2021 flight to Vietnam was Tien Pham, a Vietnamese refugee who came to California as a child with his family in 1996.[73] Convicted of attempted murder in 2000, Pham was sentenced to twenty-eight years in prison before receiving parole in June 2020. Upon his release, however, Pham was picked up by ICE at the very last minute and kept in custody until his deportation. Recalling his encounter with the other deportees on the plane to Vietnam, Pham notes the deep sense of sadness that permeated the cabin: "They were really lost. . . . They have families and businesses and properties they are leaving."[74] Along with those on the flight, Pham's experience reveals the far-reaching consequences of deportation, not only for those deported but also for the families and communities they were forced to leave behind. For a population that survived years of warfare in their homeland, these separations were an all-too-familiar act of American cruelty that remains unresolved. Indeed, along with the physical and emotional toll of ICE detention, many deported refugees struggle to adapt to their new lives, and experience many difficulties finding steady employment and obtaining official government documents.[75]

Situated within the ongoing crisis of Southeast Asian refugee deportation, the layovers of the March 2021 flight to Vietnam may appear minor details in a dire history that impacts so many lives. Yet, by highlighting the violent histories that underlie the creation of these layover sites, I have attempted to shed light on the related forms of imperial violence that brought about the conditions for these deportations to take place. Though the deportations originate outside the settler-colonial contexts of Hawai'i and Guåhan, I found something eerily resonant between Pham's story and the histories of the construction of both islands' airports, namely the violent strategies that resulted in the displacement of Indigenous and refugee communities and the disruption of their lifeways.

Grounding my argument in the history of transpacific aviation infrastructure, I have tried to articulate the relations between different imperial projects through the concept of *settler carcerality*, which highlights settler colonialism and carcerality as mutually reinforcing systems that work together to subjugate Native and racialized populations. Following the histories of HNL and GUM, I have traced the converging forms of racial-colonial violence that have contributed to each airport's creation. Starting with the dispossession of Indigenous lands, I have noted the ways that both airports developed through forms of coerced and carceral labor that likewise resulted in the devastation of local ecologies. These destructive processes, in turn, facilitated the further waging of US warfare throughout Asia and the Pacific, with the Vietnam War being a prime example.

Here, the importance of settler militarism as a framework for understanding US colonialism in Hawai'i and Guåhan is evidently clear; and while settler carcerality does draw on this concept, it is important to note that they are not entirely equivalent. Indeed, even as the US military deploys incarceration and surveillance in the management of settler-colonial spaces, these carceral logics also exceed the formal institution of the military, enacting violent forms of enclosure against marginalized subjects even in the apparent absence of military involvement.[76] Settler carcerality thus may be applied to a wider range of contexts than just the militarized space of the Pacific, contributing to a more expansive articulation of the US carceral state as it operates both within and beyond its imagined borders.

With this conceptual distinction in mind, I nonetheless argue that the histories of Kanaka Maoli and CHamoru dispossession behind HNL and GUM not only share similarities with the experiences of Vietnamese refugees but also serve as the conditions of possibility for the latter group's further displacement through deportation. Conversely, the US's ability to use these airports as parts of its carceral immigration enforcement system works to further naturalize the authority of the settler state over these subjugated islands. Settler carcerality is thus my attempt to think through this symbiotic relationship between settler colonialism and carcerality that connects seemingly distinct projects of imperial violence across time and space. Through settler carcerality, I do not intend to suggest mere one-to-one equivalences between Indigenous and refugee subjects that fail to account for the vexed triangulation of both groups vis-à-vis the settler state.[77] Instead, I have attempted to demonstrate how settler colonialism and carcerality are interconnected in ways that prove to be mutually reinforcing.

While recognizing the circuits of imperial violence that link Kānaka Maoli, CHamorus, and Vietnamese refugee experiences, I also want to emphasize another common thread that intersects with each group—that of resistance. Against conditions of exclusion and abandonment at the hands of US empire, each community has organized and demanded justice in different ways, from the restoration of stolen lands to the reunification of families broken apart by US immigration policies. Although these struggles are often seen as distinct from one another, I posit settler carcerality as a framework through which we can understand them as interconnected. In this way, my hope is that Indigenous resistance against the settler state and abolitionist struggles against the carceral state might be joined more closely against their common foe, pointing toward unrealized futurities where neither structure of oppression remains. For if our passages through oppression are bound together by layered histories and overlapping routes, so too must our work toward liberation be intimately linked.

Jason Tuấn Vũ is a PhD student in the Department of American Studies and Ethnicity at the University of Southern California. His research traces the intersections of Indigeneity, race, and empire across Asia and the Pacific through the history of US aerial warfare in Southeast Asia and its various afterlives.

Notes

This essay has benefited immensely from the critical engagement of many people throughout its various stages of development. In particular, I would like to express my deep gratitude to Thu-Hương Nguyễn-Võ, Evyn Lê Espiritu Gandhi, Việt Thanh Nguyễn, Adrian De Leon, Jackie Wang, Heidi Amin-Hong, Erin Suzuki, Ann Ngọc Trần, and the three anonymous reviewers for their crucial feedback. I would also like to thank the editorial team for this special issue of *Radical History Review*, especially Wesley Attewell for his constant guidance throughout the publication process. All faults are my own.

1. Levin, "Deported by Biden."
2. For more on the issue of Southeast Asian refugee deportation, see Southeast Asian Resource Action Center, "Devastating Impact of Deportation."
3. Cartwright, "We @WitnessBorder sourced the non-public flight info as scheduled now. Omni Air charter is scheduled to leave Dallas Monday night at 7:45 local time. It will stop in Honolulu and Guam before arriving in Hanoi at 11:30 AM on 17 March. If not stopped by @RepLowenthal @vietriseOC."
4. In addition to their listed names, HNL and GUM are known as Honolulu International Airport and Guam International Airport. These abbreviations are the official codes for each airport. When not quoting from another source, I default to the Indigenous spellings of Hawaiʻi, Kānaka Maoli, Guåhan, and CHamoru.
5. Chua et al., "Introduction: Turbulent Circulation," 2.
6. Thompson, *Imperial Archipelago*.
7. Lloyd and Wolfe, "Settler Colonial Logics," 111.
8. Mei-Singh, "Carceral Conservationism," 713.
9. Nebolon, "'Life Given Straight from the Heart,'" 25.
10. Naʻputi, "Archipelagic Rhetoric," 10.
11. See Gandhi, *Archipelago of Resettlement*, 136.
12. Loyd and Mountz, *Boats, Borders, and Bases*.
13. Espiritu, *Body Counts*, 180–81.
14. Chandler, "R&R in Vietnam," 36–38.
15. Pan American World Airways/Annual Report (1966), ASM0341, box 2, folder 31, Special Collections, University of Miami Libraries, Coral Gables, Florida.
16. Desha, *Kamehameha and His Warrior Kekūhaupiʻo*.
17. Pukui, Elbert, and Mookini, *Place Names of Hawaii*.
18. Liliuokalani, *Hawaii's Story by Hawaii's Queen*.
19. Damon v. Hawaii, 194 U.S. 154 (1904).
20. Downey, "The Sun Is Setting."
21. "John Rodgers Airport," Hawaii Aviation: An Archive of Historic Photos and Facts, Hawaii Department of Transportation, Honolulu (hereafter cited as Hawaii Aviation), https://aviation.hawaii.gov/airfields-airports/oahu/john-rodgers-airport/ (accessed November 9, 2021).
22. US Department of Justice, Office of the Attorney General, *Law Enforcement in the Territory of Hawaii*.
23. "John Rodgers Airport."
24. Meeting Minutes of the Hawaiian Territorial Aeronautical Commission (January 6, 1932), Hawaii Aviation, https://aviation.hawaii.gov/wp-content/uploads/2015/04/TAC-1932-01-06.pdf.
25. Merry, *Colonizing Hawaiʻi*, 189.

26. "John Rodgers Airport."

27. Kee, "Master Plan for the Honolulu International Airport," February 1951, Hawaii Aviation, https://aviation.hawaii.gov/wp-content/uploads/2015/03/Master-Plan-HNL-1951.pdf.

28. "Quarterly Summary of U.S. Naval Air Facility, Honolulu, Territory of Hawaii, 1 October 1945 to 31 March 1947," 1947, Hawaii Aviation, https://aviation.hawaii.gov/wp-content/uploads/2015/03/US-Naval-Air-Station-Honolulu-1947.pdf.

29. "HNL 1950s," Hawaii Aviation, https://aviation.hawaii.gov/airfields-airports/oahu/honolulu-international-airport/hnl-1950s/ (accessed November 9, 2021).

30. Kee, "Master Plan for the Honolulu International Airport."

31. Meeting Minutes of the Hawaiian Aeronautics Commission (March 13, 1952), Hawaii Aviation, https://aviation.hawaii.gov/wp-content/uploads/2015/04/HAC-1952-03-13.pdf.

32. For more on the intersection of militarism and tourism in Hawai'i, see Gonzalez, *Securing Paradise*.

33. Trask, *From a Native Daughter*, 19.

34. Estores and Tengan, "Sources of Sustainment," 81–82.

35. Life of the Land v. Brinegar, 414 U.S. 1054 (1973).

36. Bella, "Hawaii Governor Says."

37. Office of Hawaiian Affairs, *Disparate Treatment of Native Hawaiians*, 24.

38. Segal, "Captive Audience."

39. For more on Kanaka Maoli resistance, see Goodyear-Ka'ōpua, Hussey, and Wright, *Nation Rising*.

40. Tainter and Sablan, "CHamoru Nation Storms NAS."

41. Mei-Singh, "Carceral Conservationism."

42. Na'puti and Bevacqua, "Militarization and Resistance from Guåhan," 843.

43. Guam International Airport Authority, "Timeline."

44. Hattori, "Folktale."

45. Perez, "Chamorro Creation Story," 10.

46. Cruz, "Tiyan."

47. See Hezel, "From Conversion to Conquest"; and Hezel and Driver, "From Conquest to Colonisation."

48. Cruz, "Reshaping of Tiyan."

49. Hattori, "Guardians of Our Soil," 187.

50. Cruz, "Reshaping of Tiyan."

51. Na'puti and Bevacqua, "Militarization and Resistance from Guåhan," 843.

52. Higuchi, *Japanese Administration of Guam*, 118–19.

53. Limtiaco, "Eduardo G. Camacho."

54. Rogers, *Destiny's Landfall*, 152–69.

55. Cruz, "Tiyan."

56. US Office of Air Force History, *Air Force Combat Units of World War II*, 53–54.

57. US Department of the Navy, *Former Naval Air Station Agana*.

58. Na'puti and Bevacqua, "Militarization and Resistance from Guåhan," 843.

59. Espiritu, *Body Counts*, 28–38.

60. Lutz, "US Military Bases on Guam," 8.

61. Roberts, *Dictionary of American Naval Aviation*, 309–13.

62. Guam International Airport Authority, "From a Hut and Seaplanes."

63. Guam International Airport Authority, "Timeline."

64. US Defense Base Realignment and Closure Commission, *Report to the President*.
65. Tourism Economics, *The Economic Impact of Tourism on Guam*.
66. Guam Visitors Bureau, "About Guam Visitors Bureau."
67. Camacho, "Enframing I Taotao Tano'," vi.
68. DeLisle, "Destination Chamorro Culture," 563.
69. US Department of Commerce, National Oceanic and Atmospheric Administration, *Coral Reef Condition: A Status Report for Guam*.
70. Na'puti and Bevacqua, "Militarization and Resistance from Guåhan."
71. Cruz, "Reshaping of Tiyan."
72. Cruz, "Reshaping of Tiyan."
73. "Deported by Biden."
74. Castaneda, "O.C. Organizers Protest."
75. Pearson, "No Job, No Money."
76. Nebolon, "Settler-Military Camps."
77. Gandhi, *Archipelago of Resettlement*.

References

Bella, Timothy. "Hawaii Governor Says 'Now Is Not the Time' for Tourists to Visit While Covid-19 Crushes Hospitals." *Washington Post*, August 24, 2021. https://www.washingtonpost.com /nation/2021/08/24/hawaii-travel-covid-hospitals-ige/.

Camacho, Keith Lujan. "Enframing I Taotao Tano': Colonialism, Militarism, and Tourism in Twentieth Century Guam." Master's thesis, University of Hawai'i at Manoa, 1998.

Cartwright, Thomas (@thcartwright). "We @WitnessBorder sourced the non-public flight info as scheduled now. Omni Air charter is scheduled to leave Dallas Monday night at 7:45 local time. It will stop in Honolulu and Guam before arriving in Hanoi at 11:30 AM on 17 March. If not stopped by @RepLowenthal @vietriseOC." Twitter, March 14, 2021, 6:59 p.m. https://mobile.twitter.com/thcartwright/status/1371279967523323905.

Castaneda, Vera "O.C. Organizers Protest Biden Administration's Deportation of Vietnamese Refugees." *Los Angeles Times*, March 18, 2021. https://www.latimes.com/california/story /2021-03-18/orange-county-organizers-urge-halt-to-deportation-of-vietnamese-refugees.

Chandler, Jerome G. "R&R in Vietnam: Shelter from the Storm." *VFW Magazine*, March 2018.

Chua, Charmaine, Martin Danyluk, Deborah Cowen, and Laleh Khalili. "Introduction: Turbulent Circulation: Building a Critical Engagement with Logistics." *Environment and Planning D: Society and Space* 36, no. 4 (2018): 1–12.

Cruz, Manny. "Reshaping of Tiyan Leads to Decades of Battles for Compensation." *Pacific Daily News*, October 21, 2018. https://www.guampdn.com/news/culture/reshaping-of-tiyan -leads-to-decades-of-battles-for-compensation/article_cf40fbbf-0c68-5237-891d -64c8770e7493.html.

Cruz, Manny. "Tiyan: From Agriculture to Roadway Nightmare." *Pacific Daily News*, September 23, 2018. https://www.guampdn.com/news/culture/tiyan-from-agriculture-to -roadway-nightmare/article_cbaac5d0-444e-5176-8aba-9627378813e0.html.

DeLisle, Christine Taitano. "Destination Chamorro Culture: Notes on Realignment, Rebranding, and Post-9/11 Militourism in Guam." *American Quarterly* 68, no. 3 (2016): 563–72.

Desha, Stephen. *Kamehameha and His Warrior Kekūhaupi'o*. Translated by Frances N. Frazier. Honolulu: Kamehameha Schools Press, 2000.

Downey, Kirstin. "The Sun Is Setting on One of Hawaii's Last Legacy Estates." *Honolulu Civil Beat*, October 4, 2019. https://www.civilbeat.org/2019/10/the-sun-is-setting-on-one-of -hawaiis-last-historic-estat es/.

Espiritu, Yến Lê. *Body Counts: The Vietnam War and Militarized Refuge(es)*. Oakland: University of California Press, 2014.

Estores, S. Joe, and Ty P. Kāwika Tengan. "Sources of Sustainment: Fort Kamehameha and 'Ahua Point." In *Detours: A Decolonial Guide to Hawai'i*, edited by Hōkūlani K. Aikau and Vernadette Vicuña Gonzalez, 77–85. Durham, NC: Duke University Press, 2019.

Gandhi, Evyn Lê Espiritu. *Archipelago of Resettlement: Vietnamese Refugee Settlers and Decolonization across Guam and Israel-Palestine*. Oakland: University of California Press, 2022.

Gonzalez, Vernadette Vicuña. *Securing Paradise: Tourism and Militarism in Hawai'i and the Philippines*. Durham, NC: Duke University Press, 2013.

Goodyear-Ka'ōpua, Noelani, Ikaika Hussey, and Erin Kahunawaika'ala Wright, eds. *A Nation Rising: Hawaiian Movements for Life, Land, and Sovereignty*. Durham, NC: Duke University Press, 2014.

Guam International Airport Authority. "From a Hut and Seaplanes to an International Hub and Jet Planes Celebrate Airport Week 2011." A. B. Won Pat International Airport Authority, Guam, January 14, 2011. https://web.archive.org/web/20131219125049/http://www .guamairport.com/public-information/2022.

Guam International Airport Authority. "Timeline." A. B. Won Pat International Airport Authority, Guam. https://www.guamairport.com/corporate/about-our-airport/timeline (December 8, 2021).

Guam Visitors Bureau. "About Guam Visitors Bureau." Guam Tourism. https://www.visitguam .com/listing/guam-visitors-bureau/2462/ (accessed December 8, 2021).

Hattori, Anne Perez. "Folktale: Puntan and Fu'una; Gods of Creation." Guampedia, last modified May 31, 2022. http://www.guampedia.com/puntan-and-fuuna-gods-of-creation.

Hattori, Anne Perez. "Guardians of Our Soil: Indigenous Responses to Post-World War II Military Land Appropriation on Guam." In *Farms, Firms, and Runways: Perspectives on U.S. Military Bases in the Western Pacific*, edited by L. Eve Armetrout Ma, 186–202. Chicago: Imprint Publications, 2001.

Hezel, Francis X. "From Conversion to Conquest: The Early Spanish Mission in the Marianas." *Journal of Pacific History* 17, no. 3 (1982): 115–37.

Hezel, Francis X., and Marjorie C. Driver. "From Conquest to Colonisation: Spain in the Mariana Islands, 1690–1740." *Journal of Pacific History* 23, no. 2 (1988): 137–55.

Higuchi, Wakako. *The Japanese Administration of Guam, 1941–1944: A Study of Occupation and Integration Policies, with Japanese Oral Histories*. Jefferson, NC: McFarland and Company, 2013.

Levin, Sam. "Deported by Biden: A Vietnamese Refugee Separated from His Family after Decades in US." *Guardian*, May 3, 2021. https://www.theguardian.com/us-news/2021/may /03/biden-deportations-vietnamese-refugee-california-ice.

Lili'uokalani. *Hawaii's Story by Hawaii's Queen*. Boston: Lee and Shepard, 1898.

Limtiaco, Steve. "Eduardo G. Camacho Forced to Build Airstrip during Japanese Occupation." *Pacific Daily News*, October 14, 2018. https://www.guampdn.com/news/culture/eduardo-g -camacho-forced-to-build-airstrip-during-japanese-occupation/article_f41530d2-83a5 -579d-8a0a-cf293cfd4178.html.

Lloyd, David, and Patrick Wolfe. "Settler Colonial Logics and the Neoliberal Regime." *Settler Colonial Studies* 6, no. 2 (2015): 109–18. https://doi.org/10.1080/2201473x.2015.1035361.

Loyd, Jenna M., and Alison Mountz. *Boats, Borders, and Bases: Race, the Cold War, and the Rise of Migration Detention in the United States.* Oakland: University of California Press, 2018.

Lutz, Catherine. "US Military Bases on Guam in Global Perspective." *Asia-Pacific Journal* 8, no. 30 (2010): 1–16.

Mei-Singh, Laurel. "Carceral Conservationism: Contested Landscapes and Technologies of Dispossession at Ka'ena Point, Hawai'i." *American Quarterly* 68, no. 3 (2016): 695–721.

Merry, Sally Engle. *Colonizing Hawai'i: The Cultural Power of Law.* Princeton, NJ: Princeton University Press, 2000.

Na'puti, Tiara R. "Archipelagic Rhetoric: Remapping the Marianas and Challenging Militarization from 'A Stirring Place.'" *Communication and Critical/Cultural Studies* 16, no. 1 (2019): 4–25. https://doi.org/10.1080/14791420.2019.1572905.

Na'puti, Tiara R., and Michael Lujan Bevacqua. "Militarization and Resistance from Guåhan: Protecting and Defending Pågat." *American Quarterly* 67, no. 3 (2015): 837–58.

Nebolon, Juliet. "'Life Given Straight from the Heart': Settler Militarism, Biopolitics, and Public Health in Hawai'i during World War II." *American Quarterly* 69, no. 1 (2017): 23–45.

Nebolon, Juliet. "Settler-Military Camps: Internment and Prisoner of War Camps across the Pacific Islands during World War II." *Journal of Asian American Studies* 24, no. 2 (2021): 299–335.

Office of Hawaiian Affairs. *The Disparate Treatment of Native Hawaiians in the Criminal Justice System.* Honolulu: Office of Hawaiian Affairs, 2010. https://190f32x2yl33s804xzaogf14-wpengine.netdna-ssl.com/wpcontent/uploads/2015/01/native-hawaiians-criminal-justice-system.pdf.

Pearson, James. "'No Job, No Money': Life in Vietnam for Immigrants Deported by the U.S." *Reuters*, April 19, 2018. https://www.reuters.com/article/us-usa-vietnam-deportees/no-job-no-money-life-in-vietnam-for-immigrants-deported-by-u-s-idUSKBN1HR08E.

Perez, Craig Santos. "The Chamorro Creation Story, Guam Land Struggles, and Contemporary Poetry." *English Language Notes* 58, no. 1 (2020): 9–20. https://doi.org/10.1215/00138282-8237377.

Pukui, Mary Kawena, Samuel H. Elbert, and Esther T. Mookini. *Place Names of Hawaii.* Honolulu: University of Hawai'i Press, 1981.

Roberts, Michael D. *Dictionary of American Naval Aviation Squadrons.* Vol. 2. Washington, DC: Naval Historical Center, 2000.

Rogers, Robert F. *Destiny's Landfall: A History of Guam.* Honolulu: University of Hawai'i Press, 2011.

Segal, Dave. "Captive Audience." *Honolulu Star-Advertiser*, October 3, 2010. https://www.staradvertiser.com/2010/10/03/business/captive-audience/.

Southeast Asian Resource Action Center. "The Devastating Impact of Deportation on Southeast Asian Americans." Southeast Asian Resource Action Center, April 18, 2018. https://www.searac.org/wp-content/uploads/2018/04/The-Devastating-Impact-of-Deportation-on-Southeast-Asian-Americans-1.pdf.

Tainter, Joyce, and Laura Jean Sablan. "CHamoru Nation Storms NAS." *Guam Tribune*, August 15, 1992.

Thompson, Lanny. *Imperial Archipelago: Representation and Rule in the Insular Territories under U.S. Dominion after 1898.* Honolulu: University of Hawai'i Press, 2010.

Tourism Economics. *The Economic Impact of Tourism on Guam.* Tumon, GU: Guam Visitors Bureau, 2016.

Trask, Haunani-Kay. *From a Native Daughter: Colonialism and Sovereignty in Hawai'i*. 2nd ed. Honolulu: University of Hawai'i Press, 1999.

US Defense Base Relocation and Closure Commission. *Report to the President*. Washington DC: Government Printing Office, 1993.

US Department of Commerce, National Oceanic and Atmospheric Administration. Rep. *Coral Reef Condition: A Status Report for Guam*. Washington DC: Government Printing Office, 2018.

U.S. Department of Justice, Office of the Attorney General. *Law Enforcement in the Territory of Hawaii: Letter from the Attorney General Transmitting, in Response to Senate Resolution no. 134, Certain Information Relative to Law Enforcement in the Territory of Hawaii*. Washington, DC: Government Printing Office, 1932. http://moses.law.umn.edu /darrow/documents/Richardson%20Report.pdf.

US Department of the Navy. *Former Naval Air Station Agana*. Base Relocation and Closure. Project Management Office. https://www.bracpmo.navy.mil/BRAC-Bases/Other-West /Former-Naval-Air-Station-Agana/ (accessed December 9, 2021).

US Office of Air Force History. *Air Force Combat Units of World War II*. Edited by Maurer Maurer. Edison, NJ: Chartwell Books, 1994.

Uneven Mobilities

Infrastructural Imaginaries on the Hope–Princeton Highway

Desiree Valadares

An inaugural brochure advertising the Hope–Princeton Highway in interior British Columbia (BC) is conspicuously cinematic (fig. 1). It was designed for the official opening ceremony of this route on November 2, 1949. A diagonal orange film strip features a sequence of sepia-toned vignettes of the newly built highway set against a yellow background. These images are carefully assembled with snapshots of the road from its West Coast seaport (labeled "Vancouver") into the interior of the province and beyond (labeled "To the Okanagan Valley and Kootenays"). In the foreground, three interlocking embossed frames emphasize exceptional panoramic views of the Cascade Mountains and recreational attractions along this sinuous route.

The poster also prominently features text in varied font styles and colors for effect. The top left of the brochure reads, "British Columbia *Presents*." The lower right of the poster announces the name of the new highway and its grand opening: "*The* Hope–Princeton *Highway*, NOVEMBER 2, 1949." The overall graphic quality of this banner simulates a movie poster with the province represented as a film studio, the highway as the main attraction, and the date as its official release. The addition of the BC shield or armorial banner, an element of the province's visual heritage, authorizes or legitimates this highway as a provincial possession.

Radical History Review
Issue 147 (October 2023)   DOI 10.1215/01636545-10637232
© 2023 by MARHO: The Radical Historians' Organization, Inc.

Figure 1. The British Columbia Government Travel Bureau's (BCGTB) The Hope–Princeton Highway Inaugural Brochure, featuring a filmstrip and scenic vignettes. Courtesy of Royal BC Museum Archives.

A close reading of this poster for the Hope–Princeton Highway reveals how state or provincial efforts mobilized cinematic tropes for this newly opened $12 million route.[1] The creation of an imaginative geography reflected the preconceptions, desires, and tastes of several BC agencies that worked together to craft a highly aesthetic experience along this scenic corridor.[2] The inaugural opening event and associated promotional materials staged a new spatial imaginary for this long-anticipated route that connected BC's Lower Mainland to the Southern Interior.[3] In its symbolic form, the Hope–Princeton Highway reflected ideals of progress and aspirations of mobility.

The construction and promotion of this seemingly ordinary highway in Canada's westernmost province, known today as BC Highway 3 or the Crowsnest Highway, is an important story. Following this route reveals how state-crafted narratives distort labor history and land dispossession along roads and highways. Historical and contemporary efforts to narrate entangled colonial and carceral histories along such linear routes, spanning multiple jurisdictions, are especially challenging. For one, subversive or political claims to infrastructural space must compete with mainstream beliefs authorized by tourism promotion, selective commemoration, and scenic byway designations. This article considers multiple competing social and cultural imaginations of this multiscalar regional route and the tangled, contingent, and conflicted public histories that it produces. I ask: Who imagines infrastructure? What does a radical infrastructural imaginary entail? And how might such a radical imaginary be brought about through a study of labor and land?

This article critically examines how notions such as the "freedom of the road" are unequally and unevenly applied. The article positions the route as a technology of postwar mobility that reflected the centralizing ambitions of the Canadian state. Its construction relied on the forced labor of incarcerated Japanese men, whose internment was authorized under the doctrine of military necessity. While military necessity is recognized as a fundamental principle in international humanitarian law, it is striking that the same language was cited in justifying the building of the provincial highway and the wartime incarceration of individuals of Japanese descent in both western Canada and the United States. In this instance, the ability to safe-guard national interests through the doctrine of military necessity exacerbated inequalities between Canada's populations. As a connectivity project, the Hope–Princeton Highway was constructed in tandem with the Alaska Highway in northern BC, Yukon, and Alaska, in addition to other routes in interior BC.[4] The Hope–Princeton Highway thus fortified a national infrastructure premised on wartime coastal defense, Asian exclusion, and forced labor on the Canadian West Coast.

This article focuses on the Hope–Princeton Highway through the lens of uneven mobilities. Bringing together insights from infrastructure studies, mobility studies, and settler colonial studies, uneven mobilities is a concept that highlights uneven distribution of accessibility. Using this concept, I provide insight into polit-ical actors, namely the incarcerated forced laborers of Japanese descent whose unjust confinement and forced labor on this infrastructural route remained unac-knowledged until recently. The article relies on a range of archival sources that engage the visual culture of the highway and the subtle linkages between an imag-ined scenic landscape and an imagined multicultural Canada. This article also nar-rates this highway route by constructing pictorial and landscape relationships of colonialism and carcerality, linking them to uneven mobilities and economic devel-opment through the ubiquitous highway road sign—a contemporary initiative to mark and interpret sites of historical and cultural importance along this and other BC routes. The article then explores the infrastructural politics of this route at the scale of the body to expose moments of rest and resistance. This article advances a tentative theory of uneven mobilities by centering so-called road disturbances through acts of resistance such as rest, play, and work stoppages.

Interrupting the Circuitry of Capital
Differential mobilities are produced at various scales by a range of inequitable social relations and infrastructural realities. Research at the macroscale tends toward issues of global migration and material flows, border governance, and travel, while

studies at the regional scale of mobility infrastructure consider transportation, urban planning, and design.[5] Studies of uneven mobility at the microscale of the body and embodied subjectivity, and the ways in which gendered, racialized, classed, sexualized, able-bodied, citizen, and colonized subjectivities are constituted through uneven capacities to be (im)mobile. Addressing the injustices of unequal or differential mobilities requires that one develop a deeper understanding of not only uneven access to infrastructure but also bodily implications of differential mobilities, and liminal events or temporalities of stopping, going, passing, pausing, and waiting.

This article draws inspiration from the scholar Shiri Pasternak, who conceptualizes infrastructure routes through her notion of the "circuitry of capital," which envisions highways as "preserves of settler jurisdiction."[6] The circuit of capital is a conceptual tool first advanced by Marx to analyze the process of capitalist accumulation, its requirements, and potential contradictions. It is founded on consideration of the characteristic motion or metamorphoses experienced by capital value as it seeks self-expansion through the exploitation of wage labor. Pasternak, however, uses this term to consider how Indigenous peoples interrupt commodity flows by asserting jurisdiction and sovereignty over their lands and resources in places that form "choke points" to the circulation of capital. She notes that "the awesome potential of Indigenous peoples to 'shut down' the country through disruption to transport corridors was demonstrated by the Idle No More movement."[7] Similarly, Charmaine Chua and Deborah Cowen, in their studies of logistics, position "disruptions" as moments that reveal the vulnerability of commodity flows and the speed and integrity with which circulatory systems of supply chain capitalism are expected to function.[8] In particular, Cowen's focus on the body of the worker and its role in disruption offers a way to conceptualize everyday resistance and refusal to what she terms a "seamless logistics system."[9] This article also considers interruptions, disruptions, and choke points (or "road disturbances" as they are named in the archive) along the Hope–Princeton Highway to reveal how these everyday acts forge a powerful counternarrative to normative histories of highway routes premised on progress, mobility, and connectivity. For the purposes of this article, disruption to circulation or the act of (im)mobility takes a more materially grounded approach to expose the interplay between colonial and carceral logics.

I expand on the concept of uneven mobilities, commonly used in mobility justice and accessibility discourses, and reorient it to address the mobile enactments of Asian racialization in the making of what the scholar Nisha Toomey deems the "nexus of (im)mobility."[10] I argue that a mobilities paradigm offers new ways to think through the relationships among movements of racialized and Indigenous people, as these groups have historically relied on counter and subversive mobilities to resist, overturn, challenge, and escape traditional regimes of movement. Scholars such as Mimi Sheller, in her research on mobility justice, argue that mobilities research focuses not simply on movement but rather on "the power of discourses, practices and infrastructures of mobility in creating the effects of both movement and stasis."[11] In addition, Genevieve Carpio's 2019 book on the intersection of mobility, labor, and race and Carpio, Natchee Blu Barnd, and Laura Barraclough's concepts of "settler anchoring and mobility sovereignty" inform this article, connecting it to broader debates in critical ethnic and Indigenous studies.[12] Scholars of Asian North American studies, namely Iyko Day and Manu Karuka, Vernadette Gonzalez, Mona Oikawa, and Laura Ishiguro, actively consider the overlap between settler colonialism, Indigenous land dispossession, and racial capitalism in their respective studies.[13]

Two main sections of this article address the Hope–Princeton Highway through the framework of uneven mobilities. First, "Route Making" considers twinned histories of scenic designations alongside acts of rest, resistance, and immobility in the context of forced labor at the scale of the body; second, "Route Marking" studies contemporary efforts to erect historical highway markers to address histories of coerced labor and incarceration histories in the contemporary moment. Ultimately, the article advocates for a more nuanced understanding of the politics of uneven mobility in commemorative initiatives.

Route Making

Staging the Scenic

The route of the Hope–Princeton Highway, when it first opened to the public in 1949, was neither intrinsically scenic nor particularly interesting. Authorities found the route unappealing and dull, with long stretches of dense forests that obscured views. To make this route more interesting to motorists, pullouts and overlooks were carved into the mountains. These viewpoints provided motorists with a "thrilling travelogue of mountain peaks and scenic vistas" (fig. 2).[14]

Prior to the completion of the route, a major partnership was forged between the BC Division of Highways (today the Ministry of Highways and Infrastructure) and the Parks Division of the BC Forest Service. These two provincial agencies worked together to manage landscape experiences for motoring tourists along BC highways. The agencies collectively proposed the creation of E. C. Manning Park, a provincial park along the Hope–Princeton route, as a backdrop that would provide both scenic vistas and recreational opportunities. After World War II, additional government agencies were created to manage the travel boom. Travel by private automobile was a critical factor in the postwar growth of North American tourism. The British Columbia Government Travel Bureau (BCGTB) and the Department of Recreation and Conservation collaborated to curate family-friendly roadside experiences along highway corridors. These included historical attractions and roadside amenities that capitalized on myth, rumor, and legend. Public or local history was represented through souvenir sales, historical reenactments, and historic sites and markers as part of a larger campaign called "History on the Highways" (fig. 3).

Scenic Hope-Princeton Highway at 25 Mile Point

Figure 2. Vintage Hope–Princeton Highway postcard touting the "scenic" quality of the newly opened route at the 25-mile point.

This 1950s brochure, published by the *Daily Province*, one of Vancouver's major dailies, advertised the "History on the Highways" public history program. The pull-out advertisement featured an assortment of caricatures—including a fur trader, a farmer, a prospector, a missionary, a British explorer, and an Indigenous person, among others—smiling together. They hitchhike with their arms extended toward the road, the thumbs of their closed hands pointing upward in the direction of vehicular travel. Here, a highway forms a narrative device linking disparate historical actors together in a seemingly harmonious scene. At the right of the image, five signs tout the presence of "markers" and "historic sites" clustered together along the route. Collectively, these figures and signs narrate stories of BC's local history along the province's infrastructure routes. Finally, a totem pole, representative of Coast Salish wood carvings, sits affixed in the grass, forming the spine of this brochure.

This collection of disparate figures presented in the brochure harks back to Canada's burgeoning consciousness of multiculturalism in the aftermath of the Citizenship Act of 1949. The image belies the country's internment of Japanese Canadians (among other forms of Asian exclusion) in the previous decade, and its ongoing mistreatment of First Nations, Metis, and Inuit people. The depiction of the totem pole is especially contentious since its resignification in this brochure naturalizes theft and desecration. This cultural and religious object was confiscated from First Nations people during the potlatch ban (1885–1951) under an amendment of the Indian Act. Totem poles were then exhibited in museums and circulated across highway routes as

Figure 3. *History on the Highways*, published by the BCGTB in the mid-1950s. Courtesy of Royal BC Museum Archives.

markers of Indigeneity and as a symbol of the province. Its representation in this brochure and its placement toward the "historical" side denies the "place" of Indigenous people in the present and the future, relegating them to a distant past. Ultimately, the totem pole is absorbed into the category of the "scenic," much like viewsheds, lookout points, and winding roads. This brochure makes clear how First Nations motifs, multiculturalism (French and British), and extractive industries were neutralized and used as narrative devices along BC's highways.

At the time, BC's tourism promoters advocated that the province's "Indian lore" was "increasingly uncommon and appeared 'suitably foreign' to visitors from the US."[15] Even the provincial librarian and archivist Willard Ireland stated in 1954 that "the early history of our Province could and should be capitalized for the benefit of our tourist industry."[16] The BCGTB contacted Vancouver-based advertising firms and creative directors, such as R. E. Jefferson of McKim Advertising, Ltd., to "sell" BC's roads and local history.[17] Lyn Harrington, a tourism business writer for *Canadian Business*, praised the province for making use "of the Indian theme in such places as Thunderbird Park in Victoria" and for guaranteeing that "English traditional ways and motifs" offered American tourists a "different" experience.[18]

Figure 4. Print ads from the 1950s by the BCGTB touting "Old Mysteries in a New World," with the slogan "Visit Alluring British Columbia Canada: The Vacation Land That Has Everything." Courtesy of Royal BC Museum Archives.

In these BCGTB promotional posters, "Colonial days" and "Indian customs" are proudly advertised as past traditions (fig. 4). Accompanying imagery touts the allure of British Columbia's "variety" of experiences, from cultural to recreational, in "the vacation-land that has everything!" For example, a young white woman handles a Coast Salish artifact and ceremonial mask in the first poster, framed below by a highway road sign. The second poster features a fluttering Union Jack floating above a recreational setting, with a motoring family taking in the scenery from the front seat of their car. In the third poster, the Union Jack flag is juxtaposed with a carved Coast Salish sculpture and is accompanied by text that boasts the chance to see "old mysteries in a new world." All three posters claim, "No passports needed!," promoting the provincial highway network as a conduit or connector of these varied experiences for the motoring American and Canadian family who wished to travel across the Pacific Northwest and Canada.

Motoring was a radically new way of exploring the interior of the province of BC, and driving made motorists feel like active explorers of the vast landscapes that surrounded them, rather than passive consumers. The promotion of automobile tourism in BC should be located within the larger Keynesian expansion and industrial production of roads and automobiles that occurred in the postwar period in Canada. In 1949, a month after the inauguration of the Hope–Princeton Highway, the government of Canada passed "An Act to Encourage and to Assist in the Construction of a Trans-Canada Highway." This statute authorized provincial governments to build a two-lane highway on a cost-shared basis and was a major postwar attempt to unify the national economy through infrastructure.

Ultimately, the economic benefits from the completed Hope–Princeton Highway resulted in major opportunities for development in BC's southwest interior. As the British Columbia Government Travel Bureau had remarked in its 1940 film *Tourism: A British Columbia Industry*, "The automobile has set the world on wheels. . . . The question is no longer 'Shall we go?' But simply 'Where?'" The Similkameen Valley, south Okanagan, and the Boundary Country in the southwest interior experienced rapid growth in tourism-related development in the postwar years. This included a provincial park system, campgrounds, motels, auto courts, gas stations, restaurants, and other roadside services.

These developments in BC's southwest interior were featured in travelogues created in the 1950s by the BCGTB, which saw the potential of film and moving images as an advertising medium. Under the direction of the clerk-turned-filmmaker Clarence Ferris, the bureau's Photographic Branch developed its production capacity. The typical 1950s travelogue followed a set formula that began by summarizing the region's attractions at the beginning and end, with the body of the film progressing through the district in a strict geographical sequence in which each small city, town, or village encountered is mentioned by name. Films released in the 1950s, such as *Peachtime in the Valley*, *The Fraser Canyon*, and *The New Island Highway*, publicized the "distinctive atmosphere" in the Lower Fraser Valley, the Okanagan-Fraser Canyon Loop, and the Kamloops-Cariboo region.[19]

Collectively, these multipronged state-crafted narratives of the Hope–Princeton Highway forged a new infrastructural imaginary that distorted and rebranded historical memory through scenic byway designations. The creation and expansion of provincial parks and public history campaigns, such as the Stop of Interest signs program, were intimately tied to highway beautification efforts and tourism promotion along provincial roads. Unknown to most motorists of this route, however, were the complex wartime associations of this highway.[20] As an alternate route to the unbuilt Trans-Canada Highway, the Hope–Princeton Highway remains a state-building exercise that fortifies a national infrastructure premised on policing and surveillance. In recent years, acknowledgments of Asian migrant histories of wartime incarceration and forced labor have resurfaced as a provincial tourism effort along this very route.

Forced Labor, Rest, and Resistance

Construction of the Hope–Princeton Highway involved moments of unrest and resistance by road camp workers. Archival fragments such as intercepted letters, photographs, Red Cross reports, and foreman correspondence show how men enacted overt slowdowns and strikes and petitioned for food (such as rice, miso, and soy sauce) and better working conditions.

Figure 5 features a road camp worker lying on his back with his knees bent and his work boots flat on the forest floor. The exact location and date are uncertain.

Figure 5. Road camp worker resting, Hope–Princeton Highway Project [ca. 1940–1949]. Japanese Canadian Research Collection JCPC-03-030. Courtesy of University of British Columbia Library Rare Books and Special Collections.

The man in the photograph is unnamed, and his face is partially obscured by shadows created from the brim of his hat. This anonymous worker was one among many who were interned along the Hope–Princeton Highway route during the war, from 1942 to 1946. The Canadian government mandated that all persons of Japanese descent, including men, women, children, and elders, be forcibly relocated from their homes and businesses in BC coastal areas to the interior of the province. Their property was confiscated and sold by the Office of the Custodian of Enemy Property.

These events unfolded after Canada declared war on Japan following the death of Canadian troops during the Japanese Imperial Army's bombing and occupation of the British Crown colony of Hong Kong, one day after the Pearl Harbor attack.[21] The British Columbia Security Commission (BCSC) developed a road camp program for incarcerated men of Japanese descent, whose forced labor was mandated by an order-in-council.[22] At first, only single, "able-bodied" men between the ages of eighteen and forty-five were forced to work in road camps, but later married men were also solicited for road-building projects. These included Highway 3 (between Hope and Princeton), Highway 1 (Revelstoke-Sicamous Highway), and the Yellowhead–Blue River Highway between Blue River, British Columbia, and Jasper, Alberta, among others. In total 1,800 men of Japanese ancestry served as "enemy alien labor" from 1942 to 1945.[23] Yet the Canadian government referred to these men as "a voluntary civilian corps of Canadian Japanese."[24]

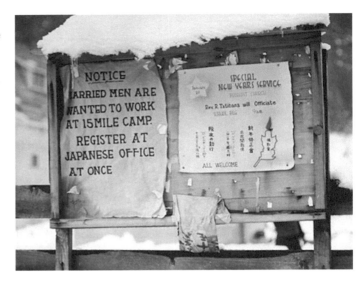

Figure 6. Winter scene of a bulletin board in Tashme Internment Camp in interior BC soliciting married men for the Hope Mile 15 Road Camp. JCCC 2001.3.210 and NNM 2010.23.2.4.740. Courtesy of Japanese Canadian Cultural Center.

The incarcerated road workers on the Hope–Princeton project were severed from their families, who were interned in "self-sufficient camps" at Tashme Internment Camp (fig. 6). Tashme held 2,636 people of Japanese ancestry between 1942 and 1946 and was located within a nexus of six road or labor camps along the 133-kilometer proposed route of the Hope–Princeton Highway. The first group of single men of Japanese descent arrived at the road camps along this route in March 1942. Work proceeded from both ends of the highway. By 1946, "work gangs," or groups of incarcerated men, manually carved out an eighty-nine-mile stretch of road using just picks and shovels. The tar paper shacks that confined these men were eventually disassembled, and their existence along the Hope–Princeton route was erased. Today, these shacks endure in archival photos, architectural and construction drawings, and engineering documents.

The wartime road camp program that held incarcerated men of Japanese descent was based on previous precedents, including Depression-era relief work camps along the same route. The Canadian government also looked to road and railway camps for the Doukhobor people (pacifist populations of Ukrainian descent from the Austro-Hungarian empire), who were interned during World War I and whose forced labor helped to build the infrastructure around Banff National Park in Alberta.[25] In the 1930s, unemployment relief camps run by the Department of National Defense (DND) in rural BC employed young, single, transient Canadian men. In exchange for being clothed, housed, and fed, relief camp workers labored under military-style discipline for an allowance of just twenty cents a day (hence the nickname of the camps as the "Royal 20 Centers").

The men's tar paper shacks were assembled in rows along proposed highway routes (fig. 7). These spaces housed men who performed routine work to establish

Figure 7. Federal Depression-era relief camp for construction of Hope–Princeton Highway, 1933. Local Identifier: HPMP 019A-2. Courtesy of Princeton and District Museum and Archive.

highways, national parks, provincial campgrounds, and recreational facility infra-structure during the Depression years. The mundane and often repetitive tasks of road labor were colloquially referred to as "boondoggles."[26] An initial survey and preliminary roadwork began on the proposed Hope–Princeton Highway route in 1929 and ended abruptly in 1935, after the Relief Camp Worker's Union organized a major BC relief camp strike and the On-to-Ottawa Trek.[27]

During World War II, the Canadian government and the province of British Columbia saw an urgent need for the completion of its highways. The BCSC pro-posed that men of Japanese descent be "put to work" in repurposed Depression-era road camps and in newly built work camps along selected routes.[28] However, man-aging this wartime road-building program along the Hope–Princeton route and elsewhere in BC proved to be a nuisance.[29] The program enrolled both Japanese nationals and civilians of Japanese descent, including elderly men, teenage boys, and men who lacked road-building experience. Prior to the war, Japanese men were primarily employed in fishing and agriculture in Canada. During the wartime road camp program, the BCSC considered many of these men to be "unfit" to per-form the demanding physical labor of road building. The work was strenuous and typically involved scaling rock faces using ropes, cutting down hillsides, filling in low areas with dirt, blasting rocks with dynamite, and installing log culverts.

Regardless of their citizenship status, these enemy aliens "were not to be paid more than the lowest-ranking soldier in the Canadian army."[30] Inmates received between 25 and 35 cents an hour.[31] From that wage, $22.50 was deducted each month for room and board, and for married men, an additional $20.00 was deducted for family support. Most men worked just two to four hours a day, owing to the size of the labor force and available tasks. Men grew increasingly agitated and bored in the Hope–Princeton road camps. They were isolated from their families, who remained interned at Tashme. The Reverend W. R. McWilliams, a United Church minister who worked as a religious minister at the camps, concluded that the road camp scheme "was creating indigents."[32]

Wartime forced labor expanded the carceral geography of the internment camp. Road-building programs in interior BC and in sugar beet fields in Alberta resulted in the wide-scale dispersal of populations of Japanese descent from Canada's West Coast. At road camps, men were grouped into work gangs, each led by a foreman who reported to supervising engineers. The foreman was typically a white man with experience in the military and the police force. They likely had little to no experience on road construction projects. The foremen were also recruited from elsewhere in Canada and, as a result, were unfamiliar with interior BC. Their primary role was to surveil and supervise their assigned work parties. Constables of the Royal Canadian Mounted Police also patrolled these areas to report significant disturbances or indigent behavior.

Mona Oikawa argues that the Canadian government mobilized a particular notion of racialized masculinity and, as a result, employed "racializing discourses depicted Japanese Canadian men as Other in relation to a normative white bourgeois masculinity."[33] Furthermore, she contends that the unitary word *camp* denies the spatial scope of incarceration, forced labor, and dispersal. This singular word obfuscates the extent and materiality of violence that destroyed communal and familial relations during wartime, as well as the ways in which different spaces "produced heterogenous gendered subjects."[34]

Engineering and Construction Service drawings from the Library and Archives Canada (LAC) in Ottawa contain details of the day-to-day construction of the Hope–Princeton Highway. During Red Cross inspections, work gangs were posed in highly staged photographs to reinforce the image of the productive and law-abiding enemy alien. In these federal engineering and construction archives, images of forced labor are roughly stapled and accompanied by hastily typewritten notes that feature one-line descriptions with dates. There is a focus on the productive, law-abiding Japanese Canadian who was "doing his part during the war effort."[35] While the white foremen, engineers, and supervisors are identified by their first and last names, the laborers of Japanese descent, who appear in wide-angle shots, are mostly unnamed and unidentified.

As Oikawa describes, the workers are enrolled against their will in a fiction of white masculinity; even as they are presented as part of the settler project, they are rendered as nameless units of labor, while the images minimize the coercive logic of the camp. The foremen and engineers, in contrast, are featured prominently, and the bulk of archival material consists of correspondence pertaining to the hiring of foremen and subforemen and related personnel issues, including applications, letters of recommendation, and employment offers, which detail information concerning positions, locations, and wages. Typically, files contain foremen reports and correspondence, letters, complaints, engineering specifications, detail drawings, material assessments, and purchase orders. Folders are simply labeled "B.C. Japanese Nationals. Roads. Hope–Princeton" and do not refer to the forced or involuntary aspect of the labor force.

In addition, the spaces inside the road camps are rarely portrayed in Engineering and Construction Service archives, which tend to look beyond the boundaries of the road camp to the conditions of the 133-kilometer pioneer road slowly taking shape. Conditions of the living quarters and the interior activities of the prison road camps are instead best narrated in archival photographs and architectural drawings of camp structures. One notable collection is the Japanese Canadian Blue River Road Camp Collection, which was donated to the Simon Fraser University Labor Archive in 2018. Though it is a different highway project, the architectural typologies and timber construction of the bunk houses and mess buildings display the involvement of Japanese workers as building styles meld traditional Japanese construction-joint detailing with North American timber style construction.

Photographs of the interiors and exteriors of these road camps (fig. 8) offer a glimpse of life inside these ephemeral constructions along the Hope–Princeton Highway project. Records reveal many anxieties and feature foremen frantically communicating with each other to "get the job done faster" by appeasing Japanese men's tastes and accommodating "orders of rice cookers, rice, soy sauce" instead of the standard camp food, which typically included steaks, beans, pies, and sauces. There were also requests for liquor and tobacco as men amused themselves with "Shi-Ko," a Chinese gambling game, well into the evenings. Other forms of leisure, such as gardening, sumo wrestling, and *onsen*-style bathhouse construction, were encouraged by officials to stave off boredom.

While not officially regarded as disturbances—these scenes of rest, leisure, and play were viewed by foremen as "peaceful and quiet post-work activities"—these acts were effective in asserting workers' individual and cultural desires within the camp, against a structuring organization. In addition, these moments of play and leisure disturbed the national imagery of imprisoned enemy aliens who were contributing to the war effort through hard labor. Reports and correspondence reveal that foremen focused their efforts on stifling complaints about food or wages primarily due to fears of an organized strike.

In their correspondence, foremen also corroborated alleged sightings of "supernatural beings and mythical creatures [such as the Sasquatch or Ogopogo]." These folktales were appropriated by BC internees to frighten their out-of-province foremen and cut workdays short.[36] Supervising engineers were furious. They

Figure 8. *Top left*, Camp No. 11 men get the standard lumber camp food: steak, beans, pies, sauces, etc.; *top right*, Hope–Princeton Road Camp 15-mile camp bunkhouse; *bottom left*, sumo wrestling at road camp, Hope–Princeton Highway Project; *bottom right*, workmen at unidentified road camp constructing a traditional bathhouse. Accession numbers LAC RG22.ACC 1997-032 and JCCC 2001.3.182. Courtesy of Library and Archives Canada and Japanese Canadian Cultural Center.

developed manuals distinguishing threats from mythology along these routes, simply cautioning foremen to be watchful of BC grizzly bears. Across road-building projects in interior BC, it was reported:

In almost every Japanese camp a certain number of Japanese, generally the younger generation, make it a point to tantalize and provoke the foremen by purposely slowing up on the work. They do not deliberately refuse to work, but make it a habit to work for possibly half an hour and then sit down for ten or fifteen minutes, to discuss the affairs of the world in general. Many times each day the foremen or straw bosses are forced to beg or attempt to persuade such men to get up and go to work. . . . Without doubt there is a great deal of quiet amusement among the Japanese over the inability of white officials to force them to do an honest day's work.

A certain number of Japanese in almost every camp make it a point to protest against most trivial inconveniences . . . whereas white labourers working under the same conditions would find nothing whatever to complain about. This, I judge, is due to resentment on the part of many Japanese for being placed in camp at all . . . it no doubt is due to a desire to embarrass our officials to the greatest possible extent without going so far as to call for arrest and jail sentences.[37]

The voices of incarcerated Japanese men, while absent from official road construction records, can be found elsewhere. One avenue is written complaints and letters, which were often censored, redacted, or translated from Japanese. For example, on February 19, 1943, internees from various camps expressed concerns to the Canadian representative of the International Red Cross, who reported on the conditions of the interior road camps. Petitions were led by three men: Mitsuo Yokome, Jugoro Fukabori, and Yoshiharu Sugaya. Their complaints included the lack of rice, no electricity or radio, loneliness in the camps, the scarcity of recreational activities, and the inadequacy of the pay scale. These issues were not remedied despite camp-wide complaints.

In successive years, letters exchanged between road workers reveal similar grievances. Private correspondence between road camps was marked "POLITICAL," redacted for "obscene language," and censored for sensitive information but was eventually released to recipients. Three excerpts from such censored letters reveal how the practice of letter writing connected internees across disparate road camps in interior BC as incarcerated road workers were transferred in and out of various highway building projects.

One letter noted:

Since yesterday our camp has not been working. The reason is something like the incident at Yard Creek. On Saturday afternoon one of the boys got sent back to camp and told to go to Tashme 'cause they don't want him. We all got together and decided that if this boy is sent back to Tashme we all want to be sent back too. We told the foreman and now we are waiting for the engineer to come up. This camp is surely the (obscene language). The way it's run by the white guys sure makes me sick. I sure hate the guts of some of these guys. I guess in a few days we'll know what they are going to do with us. Maybe they'll close down the camp like Yard Creek, but we are all ready to go anywhere. I won't write too much detail 'cause the censor might cut this out.[38]

Another letter included:

I guess you read in the Province papers about the 15 mile camp striking for 3 days. Well, we strike from Monday to Thursday. They canned one guy and told him to go back to Tashme, and we didn't like the idea so we striked. He's physically unfit to do hard work for he won't be sent East. I heard Hartley wrote to Commission and the Commission answered back to leave the case alone to the Dept. of Mines & Resources. He still belongs to the Camp but can't get any work. If we had strike until they let the guy come back to work, they would of closed the camp and then bring some guys up from 11 mile. You know this engineer don't give a (obscene language). If we don't like it he tells you he'll close the camp down. From this attitude I figure they want to close the camps.[39]

A final letter excerpt suggested:

There is such a great difference between wages and working conditions here and outside that many of our boys want to go outside to find work, but the engineer in charge here absolutely refuses to let the good workers go. He, on the other hand, forces the lazy ones to go whether they wish it or not. All the men say the only way to get permission to leave is to be lazy. Daki and I have been known as "good boys" since we came here so the whole camp is watching with interest to see if he will let us go as we have requested.[40]

These excerpts offer valuable insights into the day-to-day forced labor and economic conditions, relations with superiors, and growing unrest in these forced labor camps in wartime British Columbia. Furthermore, these letters reveal the consequences of workers' actions, such as the transfer out of a BC road camp into a sugar beet camp in Alberta or a POW camp in Ontario. These modes of correspondence, when read along with highway construction and engineering archives and records from the Department of Mines and Resources and Surveys and Engineering Branch, reveal that the administration and operation of road work camps for interned male Japanese Canadian nationals and civilians was met with resistance.

The following section considers the role of inanimate, immovable objects such as highway road markers and their role in present-day commemorative initiatives to mark legacies of race, mobility, and Indigeneity in British Columbia. This route-marking initiative draws attention to the legacies of these uneven mobilities and to issues of ownership and authorship that are inextricably tied to forging new infrastructural imaginaries.

Route Marking

In the 1960s, the province of British Columbia introduced the Stop of Interest program, a BC Centennial project that aimed to "invite road travelers to reflect on the people, places and events that have helped to shape British Columbia's history."[41] Words, narratives, and other textual references on highway historical road markers forged a new textual landscape across the province (fig. 9). Initially, the government erected signs related to themes of settlement, industry, transportation, and infrastructure in BC. The signs and their distinct aesthetic are iconic to generations of road travelers in BC and are considered heritage features. In the 1960s alone, over 175 signs were installed throughout all regions of the province.

These highway historical markers created a network of heterogeneous, albeit historically grounded sites. The markers provide inscriptions that suggest a visible link to a particular place. While these semiotic devices play a minor role in the construction of spatial and cultural identity, the markers require a certain type of interpretive knowledge for geographic mobility and understanding of place. The Stop of Interest signs can mark the presence of what is and the absence of what used to be, as well as symbolically filling in the gap between the two. Although these markers were becoming more and more prevalent in BC and elsewhere, historians often criticized them for failing to provide any meaningful context and only conveying their messages in a confusing, obscure, and telegraphic style. The texts on these markers, for lack of space, are short and to the point.

Early Stop of Interest signs were authored and authorized by provincial bureaucrats, who decided what events mattered and where they should be memorialized without much regard for the input of local communities. These markers reconstructed or fabricated history and were often the products of overemphasis or "local boosterism."[42] Therefore, not only was erecting a marker a ubiquitous way of historicizing a part of a landscape, but it also became a form of territorial appropriation—of inscribing or imposing authority over a given area.

In 2016, a public nomination process was introduced to democratize BC's Stop of Interest program. This led to a range of new markers proposed by the public, which broadened the original focus on themes of "settlement, industry, transportation, and infrastructure." Over the past few years, signs have been installed to mark the sites of former Indian Residential Schools (the Kamloops Indian Residential School, in September 2019); the earliest Sikh settlements and historic Sikh temples from the early 1900s (Golden Sikhs, in November 2016, and Gur Sikh Temple in Abbotsford, in April 2019); Doukhobor, or Christian pacifist, history; Chinese migrant railroad labor; and Japanese Canadian internment camps, such as the 2017 Tashme Stop of Interest marker installed at the Sunshine Valley RV Resorts and Cabins and the Tashme Museum.[43]

The Tashme camp, which was strategically located near a network of six road camps along the Hope–Princeton Highway from 1943 to 1945, was one site of commemoration.[44] The Tashme Stop of Interest (fig. 10) text reads, "In 1942, over 21,000 Japanese Canadians were unjustly removed from British Columbia's coast. Tashme internment camp held over 2,644 men, women and children who lived in 347 crude tar paper shacks. Despite horrible living conditions, the community organized stores, schools, churches, and a hospital at this site." It features a large white blossom of a Pacific dogwood (*Cornus nuttallii*), which is British Columbia's floral

Figure 9. Stops of Interest ephemera and guidebooks. Courtesy of Google Images and Google Books.

emblem. It is flanked by uppercase text that reads "PROVINCE OF BRITISH COLUMBIA 2017." The sign was erected on the shoulder of Highway 3 on lands owned by the province.

Ultimately, highway road markers have a fraught history of ownership, authorship, and territorialization. They sit in an uneasy position due to the ways that the province has historically used markers of commemoration and of difference along roads and highways. The new signs move away from associations with the scenic or with highway beautification and instead consider ethnic and religious diversity, former carceral spaces, and sites of Indigenous and racialized trauma. Despite this move toward public involvement, this state-sponsored public history initiative still relies on a process of state authorship wherein the plaque text is eventually authorized by provincial officials. The turn to public nominations does not necessarily democratize an already bureaucratic process; rather, the new focus reflects a broader Canadian liberal, multicultural strategy of recognition, inclusion, and reconciliation through symbolic memorials and markers.

However, while efforts are focused on the public nomination and creation of new signs, the "textual politics" of older highway historical markers since the 1960s also deserve public scrutiny. Joanne Hammond, an archaeologist based in Kamloops, BC, who publishes the website Republic of Archaeology, began a Twitter campaign in 2017 to rewrite older, factually incorrect signs. Her Twitter campaign to "decolonize" Stop of Interest signs features images of signs whose texts have been digitally altered using Photoshop to "rewrite the truth."[45] She argues that public still tells "tired, old stories"; she continues:

> We can't choose the history that made this province; it's got a lot of ugly bits
> that we can't undo. But heritage is different. We can choose what we want to
> bring forward with us as our shared heritage. We can tell stories fairly, to try to
> balance the legacy of colonialism. Public history is a big responsibility, because
> it changes the way we think about each other. We *can* be better witnesses to
> the past, in the service of our shared future.[46]

Figure 10. Tashme Stop of Interest, Sunshine Valley, Hope, BC, Highway 3. Hope–Princeton Highway Legacy signage to acknowledge the forced labor of Japanese Canadians interned at Tashme, September 2018 and December 2018. Courtesy of Google Images.

For example, some of her earliest works rewrite the texts of the Eagle Pass and J. W. Trutch Stop of Interest signs to focus attention on Indigenous dispossession caused by infrastructural projects, such as the Canada Pacific Railway and the Alexandra Suspension Bridge led by civil engineers Walter Moberly (at Eagle Pass) and J. W. Trutch (fig. 11). While this truth-telling initiative is commendable as a digital public history project, it does not reckon with the landed and propertied nature of these signs, which continue to sit on provincial lands—highway shoulders, scenic overlooks, and roundabouts.

Hammond's efforts to draw attention to these signs reiterates that provincial roads are charged sites and tools of state power. These signs, among other initiatives, sensationalize the scenic at the expense of histories of land theft, exploitation, and forced labor. The texts of these highway historical markers tell partial histories that are heavily edited to suit the tastes of approval bodies and to appeal to consumer tastes. Ultimately, these signs sit within a longer tradition of highway tourism promotion in the province of British Columbia. Recent attempts to imprint wartime histories of internment and forced labor through this governmental mode of semiotic narration require further interrogation and reflection. As profoundly political devices and placemaking tools, these seemingly anonymous texts shape social, political, and economic contexts by conferring differential and competing symbolic and material values on the land. Instead, how might individual or collective experiences of labor and dissidence in the Hope–Princeton Highway road camps be conveyed beyond a state-led mode of interpretation and preservation?

Toward a Conclusion
This article offers insight into the repurposing of state infrastructure in interior British Columbia into scenic or tourism-based attractions that simultaneously erase histories of incarceration, coerced labor, and land dispossession. The Hope–Princeton

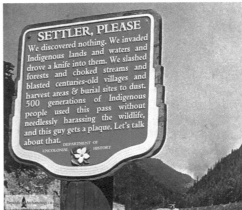

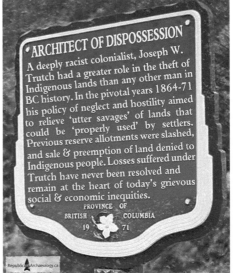

Figure 11. The images at the right are from the Twitter campaign by Joanne Hammond, #rewriteBCsigns, to unsettle infrastructure histories along BC's roads. Courtesy #rewriteBCsigns by Joanne Hammond, Republic of Archaeology.

Highway, while created for public benefit, is an imagined geography that caters to motoring tourists who consume natural and manmade elements of the visual environment in a heavily curated way. The completed route fundamentally altered the geographic imaginary of interior BC and operated within the logic of globalized capital, even while appearing as part of a local landscape. The ongoing political engagement with the Hope–Princeton Highway's labor and land history through the mode of highway road signs demonstrates that the political lives of infrastructure are dynamic and ongoing sites for challenge and revision.

Desiree Valadares is a landscape architect and architectural historian. Her work engages themes of land, territoriality, and empire in the noncontiguous United States and western Canada. Her current project focuses on the heritage politics of World War II confinement landscape preservation in Alaska, Hawaiʻi, and British Columbia. She is assistant professor at University of British Columbia Vancouver in the Geography Department and affiliate faculty in the Asian Canadian and Asian Migration Program.

Notes

I wish to thank members of the Nikkei Working Group—Hana Maruyama, Erin Aoyama, Lisa Doi, Jane Komora, Mika Kennedy, Koji Lau-Ozawa, Nicole Sintetos, Nicole Yakashiro, and Mary Anne Vallianatos—for their critical feedback on early versions of this article. In addition, thanks are extended to Bridget Martin, the special issue editors, and the anonymous reviewers of *Radical History Review* for their commentary on later versions of this article.

1.   The use of cinematic tropes was important given the role of film in supporting the war. Films were sites of escape from the sacrifices of war and were also used to generate sympathy for the war effort. In Canada, the National Film Board became the main producer of both wartime films and informational and instructional films for troops and civilians.

2.   The term *imaginative* or *imagined geographies* refers to the ways in which peoples, cultures, and landscapes are represented. The study of imaginative geographies seeks to unpack the process of their creation and the work they perform in shaping relations between their authors and subjects. The term was popularized by the postcolonial scholar Edward Said in *Orientalism* (1978) to describe how the West has constructed a particular view of the East that exoticized the other and affirmed the Western self. I use the term *infrastructural imaginaries* to consider how competing imaginaries are projected onto newly constructed highway routes.

3.   The Hope–Princeton Highway took approximately 103 years to complete from its beginnings as a fur and gold rush trail. Local historians attribute the long delay to changing government priorities, difficulty in securing road labor, and fluctuations in funding.

4.   For critical histories of Canada's federal road infrastructure, see Michalko, *Obstruction of Justice*; Bennett, "From State-Initiated to Indigenous-Driven Infrastructure"; Carleton, "Justice Delayed Is Justice Denied"; Macfarlane, *Divided Highways*; McDiarmid, *Highway of Tears*; Rymhs, *Roads, Mobility, and Violence*; McKegney, *Masculindians*; and Rhoad, *Those Who Take Us Away*.

5.   For macroscale studies, see Perkins and Neumayer, "Geographies of Educational Mobilities"; Marcu, "Uneven Mobility Experiences"; and de Souza e Silva, "Hybrid Spaces 2.0." For regional-scale studies, see Hernandez, "Uneven Mobilities, Uneven Opportunities"; Barber, "Governing Uneven Mobilities"; and Frey, "Uneven Mobilities."

6.   Pasternak and Dafnos, "How Does a Settler State Secure the Circuitry of Capital?"

7.   Pasternak, "Jurisdiction and Settler Colonialism." See also Adey et al., *Routledge Handbook of Mobilities*; and Boyle and Speed, "From Protection to Coordinated Preparedness."

8.   Chua, "Who Is the 'We'?"; LaDuke and Cowen, "Beyond Wiindigo Infrastructure," 244.

9.   Cowen, *Deadly Life of Logistics*.

10.   Toomey, "Nexus of (Im)mobilities."

11.   Sheller, *New Mobilities Paradigm*. See also Sheller and Urry, "Mobilizing the New Mobilities Paradigm"; Sheller "Uneven Mobility Futures"; Sheller, "Splintered Mobilities"; and Sheller, "Mobile Commoning."

12. Carpio, *Collisions at the Crossroads*; Carpio, Barnd, and Barraclough, "Introduction to the Special Issue."

13. See Day, "Sex, Time, and the Transcontinental Railway"; Karuka, "Railroad Colonialism"; Gonzalez, "Scenic Highways"; and Oikawa, "Cartographies of Violence." See also Ishiguro et al., *Settler Colonialism and Japanese Canadian History*.

14. Magazine ad, quoted in Bradley, *British Columbia by the Road*, 75. See also British Columbia Ministry of Transportation and Infrastructure, "BC Road Trip Time Machine."

15. Dawson, "Consumerism and the Creation of the Tourist Industry."

16. Quoted in Dawson, *Selling British Columbia*, 162.

17. Dawson, Selling British Columbia, 160.

18. Harrington, "The Yankee Dollah!," quoted in Dawson, *Selling British Columbia*, 162.

19. Duffy, *Evergreen Playland*, 4.

20. For critical histories of Canada's federal road infrastructure, see Michalko, *Obstruction of Justice*; Bennett, "From State-Initiated to Indigenous-Driven Infrastructure"; Carleton, "Justice Delayed"; Macfarlane, *Divided Highways*; McDiarmid, *Highway of Tears*; Rymhs, *Roads, Mobility, and Violence*; McKegney, *Masculindians*; and Rhoad, *Those Who Take Us Away*.

21. In total, over twenty-one thousand people of Japanese ancestry, including civilians, were forcibly relocated to internment camps in interior BC and farther inland in Alberta. This was accomplished under Order-in-Council 1665, invoked on March 2, 1942, under the Defense of Canada Regulations of the War Measures Act, which was enacted on January 14, 1942 (a month before the United States enacted a policy of internment on February 19, 1942). The BCSC established a one-hundred-mile "protected area" on the BC West Coast, coinciding with the "exclusion zone" mandated under Executive Order 9066 on the US West Coast. Under Order-in-Council 1665, the Custodian of Enemy Property confiscated internees' property and liquidated all possessions. All seized property was sold, without the owner's consent, to fund wartime internment in Canada.

22. The convention in the American context is to talk about *incarceration*, while in the Canadian context, scholars and community members have historically used the term *internment* or *mass uprooting*. This section uses existing linguistic conventions by adopting the conventional language used in the respective national contexts. The historian Greg Robinson suggests that *confinement* is a term that best captures the broad scope of wartime relocation processes, worrying that *internment* is too narrow a term, given that it is, in his words, "a fancier synonym for 'imprisonment.'" Robinson, *A Tragedy of Democracy*, vii.

23. Shimizu, *Exiles*, 9.

24. Shimizu, *Exiles*, 5.

25. See Kordan and Mahovsky, *A Bare and Impolitic Right*.

26. Waiser, *Park Prisoners*, 52.

27. Fifteen hundred men from the British Columbia relief camps went on strike and congregated in Vancouver. Two months of protests were followed by the decision to take the movement to Ottawa. The action came to be known as the "On-to-Ottawa Trek." The Trekkers were stopped in Regina, and, after a failed attempt to bring the matter to a peaceful end, the Regina Riot occurred. When it was over, 120 Trekkers and citizens had been arrested. For a history of Canada's Depression-era relief camps and subsequent labor strikes in BC, see Liversedge, *Recollections of the On to Ottawa Trek*; Fudge and Tucker, *Labour before the Law*; Barman, *West Beyond the West*; and Neary, *Alan Caswell Collier*.

28. For monographs on BCSC's surveillance and internment operations and the role of the Custodian of Enemy Property in the dispossession and sale of properties belonging to civilians of Japanese descent in Canada, see Sunahara, *Politics of Racism*; Stanger-Ross, *Landscapes of Injustice*; Inouye, *Long Afterlife of Nikkei Wartime Incarceration*; Stanger-Ross and Sugiman, *Witness to Loss*; and Chiu, *Scrutinized!*

29. Stanger-Ross and Sugiman, *Witness to Loss*.

30. Stanger-Ross and Sugiman, *Witness to Loss*.

31. Stanger-Ross and Sugiman, Witness to Loss.

32. Shimizu, *Exiles*, 9.

33. Oikawa, "Cartographies of Violence," 115.

34. Oikawa, "Cartographies of Violence," 113.

35. Shimizu, *Exiles*, 22.

36. Shimizu, *Exiles*, 47.

37. Engineering and Construction – Movement and Control of Japanese Work Camps, 1942–1946, file EC 7-27-1, vol. 211, Records of Parks Canada, Record Group 84, Public Archives of Canada, Ottawa.

38. Japanese Division, Intercepted Letters, 1942–1944, part 2, File 23-2-14, vol. 1527, Records of Labour, Record Group 27, Public Archives of Canada, Ottawa.

39. Japanese Division, Intercepted Letters, 1942–1944, part 1, File 23-2-14, vol. 1527, Records of Labour, Record Group 27, Public Archives of Canada, Ottawa.

40. Japanese Division, Intercepted Letters, 1942–1944, part 3, File 23-2-14, vol. 1527, Records of Labour, Record Group 27, Public Archives of Canada, Ottawa.

41. "Stop of Interest Signs."

42. History is reinvented and rewritten to generate some form of what Loewen calls "local boosterism." See Loewen, *Lies Across America*; Bardet, "Demarcating Territory"; Bright et al., "Heritage Tourism"; Alderman, "'History by the Spoonful'"; Otterstrom and Davis, "Historical Markers"; O'Brien, "Exclusionary Public Memory Documents"; Spencer-Wood, "Empowering Social Justice and Equality"; and Dickey, "'Cameos of History.'"

43. British Columbia, "Stop of Interest Signs Map."

44. These work camps incarcerated men of Japanese descent whose forced labor was mandated under an order-in-council under the Defense of Canada Regulations of the War Measures Act. Since 2017, the Province of British Columbia's Ministry of Transportation and Infrastructure has worked alongside a community organization, the Japanese Canadian Legacy Project Committee, to mark these sites. Highway historical markers were placed at specific locations as part of the existing Stop of Interest program. In September 2018, a Stop of Interest marker and a Highway Legacy sign were installed on Highway 3 at the site of Tashme Internment Camp.

45. Alderman, "'History by the Spoonful'"; CBC News, "Archaeologist 'Decolonizes' BC's Road Signs."

46. Hammond, "Decolonizing BC's Roadside History."

References

Adey, Peter, David Bissell, Kevin Hannam, Peter Merriman, and Mimi Sheller, eds. *The Routledge Handbook of Mobilities*. London: Routledge, Taylor and Francis Group, 2014.

Alderman, Derek H. "'History by the Spoonful' in North Carolina: The Textual Politics of State Highway Historical Markers." *Southeastern Geographer* 52, no. 4 (2012): 355–73.

Barber, Lachlan B. "Governing Uneven Mobilities: Walking and Hierarchized Circulation in Hong Kong." *Journal of Transport Geography* 82 (2020): art. 102622.

Bardet, Pascal. "Demarcating Territory: Historical Markers in the United States." *Miranda*, no. 6 (2012). https://journals.openedition.org/miranda/2920.

Barman, Jean. *The West Beyond the West: A History of British Columbia*. Toronto: University of Toronto Press, 2007.

Bennett, Mia M. "From State-Initiated to Indigenous-Driven Infrastructure: The Inuvialuit and Canada's First Highway to the Arctic Ocean." *World Development* 109 (2018): 134–48.

Boyle, Philip, and Shannon Speed. "From Protection to Coordinated Preparedness: A Genealogy of Critical Infrastructure in Canada." *Security Dialogue* 49, no. 3 (2018): 217–31.

Bradley, Ben. *British Columbia by the Road: Car Culture and the Making of a Modern Landscape*. Vancouver: University of British Columbia Press, 2017.

Bright, Candace Forbes, Kelly N. Foster, Andrew Joyner, and Oceane Tanny. "Heritage Tourism, Historic Roadside Markers and 'Just Representation' in Tennessee, USA." *Journal of Sustainable Tourism* 29, no. 23 (2021): 428–47.

British Columbia. "Stop of Interest Signs Map." Last modified August 31, 2021. https://www2 .gov.bc.ca/gov/content/transportation/driving-and-cycling/traveller-information/stop-of -interest/stop-of-interest-map.

British Columbia Ministry of Transportation and Infrastructure. "BC Road Trip Time Machine: BC Highway 3, Hope to Princeton, 1966." YouTube video, posted September 22, 2016, 11:17. https://www.youtube.com/watch?v=NsBUG3FXZr0&ab_channel=MinistryofTranBC.

Carleton, Sean. "Justice Delayed Is Justice Denied: Highway of Tears and the Missing and Murdered Indigenous Women in Canada." *Canadian Dimension*, October 6, 2015. https:// canadiandimension.com/articles/view/justice-delayed-is-justice-denied.

Carpio, Genevieve. *Collisions at the Crossroads: How Place and Mobility Make Race*. Oakland: University of California Press, 2019.

Carpio, Genevieve, Natchee Blu Barnd, and Laura Barraclough. "Introduction to the Special Issue: Mobilizing Indigeneity and Race within and against Settler Colonialism." *Mobilities* 17, no. 2 (2022): 179–95.

CBC News. "Archaeologist 'Decolonizes' BC's Road Signs via Photoshop." February 13, 2017. https://www.cbc.ca/news/canada/british-columbia/archaeologist-decolonizes-b-c-s-road -signs-via-photoshop-1.3981211.

Chiu, Monica. *Scrutinized! Surveillance in Asian North American Literature*. Honolulu: University of Hawai'i Press, 2014.

Chua, Charmaine. "Who Is the 'We' That the Supply Chain Brings into Relation? Questions on Solidarity and Disruption after the Logistics Revolution." In "Reading Deborah Cowen's The Deadly Life of Logistics: Mapping Violence in Global Trade," *Political Geography* 61 (2017): 263–71.

Cowen, Deborah. *The Deadly Life of Logistics: Mapping Violence in Global Trade*. Minneapolis: University of Minnesota Press, 2014.

Dawson, Michael. "Consumerism and the Creation of the Tourist Industry in British Columbia, 1900–1965." PhD diss., Queen's University, 2001.

Dawson, Michael. *Selling British Columbia: Tourism and Consumer Culture, 1891–1970*. Vancouver: University of British Columbia Press, 2004.

Day, Iyko. "Sex, Time, and the Transcontinental Railway." In *Alien Capital and the Logic of Settler Colonial Capitalism*, 41–63. Durham, NC: Duke University Press, 2016.

de Souza e Silva, Adriana. "Hybrid Spaces 2.0: Connecting Networked Urbanism, Uneven Mobilities, and Creativity, in a (Post) Pandemic World." *Mobile Media and Communication* 11, no. 1 (2023): 59–65.

Dickey, Jennifer. "'Cameos of History' on the Landscape: The Changes and Challenges of Georgia's Historical Marker Program." *Public Historian* 42, no. 2 (2020): 33–55.

Duffy, Dennis J. *Evergreen Playland: A Road Trip through British Columbia.* Victoria: Royal BC Museum, 2008. http://staff.royalbcmuseum.bc.ca/wp-content/uploads/2016/02/EvergreenPlayland.pdf.

Frey, Bronwyn. "Uneven Mobilities: The Everyday Management of App-Based Delivery Work in Germany." *Mobilities* 17, no. 5 (2022): 695–710.

Fudge, Judy, and Eric Tucker. *Labour before the Law: The Regulation of Workers' Collective Action in Canada, 1900–1948.* Toronto: University of Toronto Press, 2001.

Gonzalez, Vernadette Vicuña. "Scenic Highways, Masculinity, Modernity, and Mobility." In *Securing Paradise: Tourism and Militarism in Hawai'i and the Philippines*, 49–71. Durham, NC: Duke University Press, 2013.

Hammond, Joanne. "Decolonizing BC's Roadside History." *Culturally Modified*, November 7, 2017. https://culturallymodified.org/decolonizing-bcs-roadside-history.

Hernandez, Diego. "Uneven Mobilities, Uneven Opportunities: Social Distribution of Public Transport Accessibility to Jobs and Education in Montevideo." *Journal of Transport Geography* 67 (2018): 119–25.

Inouye, Karen. *The Long Afterlife of Nikkei Wartime Incarceration.* Stanford, CA: Stanford University Press, 2018.

Ishiguro, Laura. "Histories of Settler Colonialism: Considering New Currents." *BC Studies*, no. 190 (2016): 5–13.

Ishiguro, Laura, Will Archibald, Nicole Yakashiro, and the LOI Research Collective. *Settler Colonialism and Japanese Canadian History.* Landscapes of Injustice Research Collective Working Paper 3. 2017.

Karuka, Manu. "Railroad Colonialism." In *Empire's Tracks: Indigenous Nations, Chinese Workers, and the Transcontinental Railroad*, 40–59. Berkeley: University of California Press, 2019.

Kordan, Bohdan S., and Craig Mahovsky. *A Bare and Impolitic Right: Internment and Ukrainian-Canadian Redress.* Montreal: McGill-Queen's University Press, 2004.

LaDuke, Winona, and Deborah Cowen. "Beyond Wiindigo Infrastructure." *South Atlantic Quarterly* 119, no. 2 (2020): 243–68.

Liversedge, Ron. *Recollections of the On to Ottawa Trek.* Montreal: McGill-Queens' University Press, 1973.

Loewen, James. *Lies Across America: What Our Historic Sites Get Wrong.* New York: Touchstone, 1999.

Macfarlane, Heather. *Divided Highways: Road Narrative and Nationhood in Canada.* Ottawa: University of Ottawa Press, 2019.

Madokoro, Laura. "'From Citizens to Refugees': Japanese Canadians and the Search for Wartime Sanctuary." *Journal of American Ethnic History* 39, no. 3 (2020): 17–48.

Marcu, Silvia. "Uneven Mobility Experiences: Life Strategy Expectations among Eastern European Undergraduate Students in the UK and Spain." *Geoforum* 58 (2015): 68–75.

McDiarmid, Jessica. *Highway of Tears: A True Story of Racism, Indifference, and the Pursuit of Justice for Missing and Murdered Indigenous Women and Girls.* New York: Atria Books, 2019.

McKegney, Sam, ed. *Masculindians: Conversations about Indigenous Manhood.* Winnipeg: University of Manitoba Press, 2014.

Michalko, Ray. *Obstruction of Justice: The Search for Truth on Canada's Highway of Tears.* Markham, ON: Red Deer Press, 2016.

Miki, Roy. *Redress: Inside the Japanese Canadian Call for Justice*. Vancouver: Raincoast Books, 2004.

Neary, Peter, ed. *Alan Caswell Collier, Relief Stiff: An Artist's Letters from Depression-Era British Columbia*. Vancouver: University of British Columbia Press, 2018.

O'Brien, April L. "Exclusionary Public Memory Documents: Orientating Historical Marker Texts Within a Technical Communication Framework." *Technical Communication Quarterly* 31, no. 2 (2022): 111–25.

Oikawa, Mona. "Cartographies of Violence: Creating Carceral Spaces and Expelling Japanese Canadians from the Nation." In *Cartographies of Violence: Japanese Canadian Women, Memory, and the Subjects of the Internment*, 95–124. Toronto: University of Toronto Press, 2012.

Oikawa, Mona. "Connecting the Internment of Japanese Canadians to the Colonization of Aboriginal Peoples in Canada." In *Aboriginal Connections to Race, Environment, and Traditions*, edited by Rick Riewe and Jill Oakes, 17–26. Winnipeg: University of Manitoba Press, 2006.

Otterstrom, Samuel M., and James A. Davis. "Historical Markers in the Western United States: Regional and Cultural Contrasts." *Journal of Heritage Tourism* 15, no. 5 (2020): 533–53.

Pasternak, Shiri. "Jurisdiction and Settler Colonialism: Where Do Laws Meet?" *Canadian Journal of Law and Society* 29, no. 2 (2014): 145–61.

Pasternak, Shiri, and Tia Dafnos. "How Does a Settler State Secure the Circuitry of Capital?" *Environment and Planning D: Society and Space* 36, no. 4 (2018): 739–57.

Perkins, Richard, and Eric Neumayer. "Geographies of Educational Mobilities: Exploring the Uneven Flows of International Students." *Geographical Journal* 180, no. 3 (2014): 246–59.

Rhoad, Meghan. *Those Who Take Us Away: Abusive Policing and Failures in Protection of Indigenous Women and Girls in Northern British Columbia, Canada*. New York: Human Rights Watch, 2013.

Robinson, Greg. *A Tragedy of Democracy: Japanese Confinement in North America*. New York: Columbia University Press, 2009.

Rymhs, Deena. *Roads, Mobility, and Violence in Indigenous Literature and Art from North America*. Milton, ON: Routledge, 2019.

Said, Edward. *Orientalism*. New York: Pantheon, 1978.

Sheller, Mimi. "Mobile Commoning: Reclaiming Indigenous, Caribbean, Maroon, and Migrant Commons." *Praktyka Teoretyczna* 4, no. 46 (2023): 29–52.

Sheller, Mimi. "The New Mobilities Paradigm for a Live Sociology." *Current Sociology* 62, no. 6 (2014): 789–811. https://doi.org/10.1177/0011392114533211.

Sheller, Mimi. "Splintered Mobilities as Viral Vector: Mobility Justice and Racial Kinopolitics." *Journal of Urban Technology* 29, no. 1 (2022): 161–67.

Sheller, Mimi. "Uneven Mobility Futures: A Foucauldian Approach." *Mobilities* 11, no. 1 (2016): 15–31.

Sheller, Mimi, and John Urry. "Mobilizing the New Mobilities Paradigm." *Applied Mobilities* 1, no. 1 (2016): 10–25.

Shimizu, Yon. *Exiles: An Archival History of the World War II Japanese Road Camps in British Columbia and Ontario*. Wallaceburg, ON: Shimizu Consulting and Publishing, 1993. https://scholar.uwindsor.ca/swoda-windsor-region/9/.

Spencer-Wood, Suzanne M. "Empowering Social Justice and Equality by Developing a Feminist Intersectionality Framework to Increase the Inclusiveness of Detroit Historical Markers." *Michigan Academician* 48, no. 1 (2021): 2–3.

Stanger-Ross, Jordan, ed. *Landscapes of Injustice: A New Perspective on the Internment and Dispossession of Japanese Canadians*. Montreal: McGill-Queens Press, 2020.

Stanger-Ross, Jordan, and Pamela Sugiman, eds. *Witness to Loss: Race, Culpability and Memory in the Dispossession of Japanese Canadians*. Montreal: McGill-Queen's University Press, 2017.

"Stop of Interest Signs." British Columbia, last modified July 2, 2021. https://www2.gov.bc.ca/gov/content/transportation/driving-and-cycling/traveller-information/stop-of-interest.

Sunahara, Ann Gomer. *The Politics of Racism: The Uprooting of Japanese Canadians during the Second World War*. Barnaby, BC: Nikkei National Museum and Cultural Centre, 2020.

Toomey, Nisha. "The Nexus of (Im)mobilities: Hyper, Compelled, and Forced Mobile Subjects." *Mobilities* 17, no. 2 (2022): 269–84.

Vallianatos, Mary Anne. "Marginal Citizens: Interracial Intimacies and the Incarceration of Japanese Canadians, 1942–1949." *Canadian Journal of Law and Society* (2021): 1–19.

Waiser, Bill. *Park Prisoners: The Untold Story of Western Canada's National Parks, 1915–1946*. Saskatoon: Fifth House, 1995.

Yakashiro, Nicole. "Daffodils and Dispossession: Nikkei Settlers, White Possession, and Settler Colonial Property in Bradner, BC, 1914–51." *BC Studies* 211 (Autumn 2021): 49–152.

Yakashiro, Nicole. "'Powell Street Is Dead': Nikkei Loss, Commemoration, and Representations of Place in the Settler Colonial City." *Urban History Review* 48, no. 2 (2021): 32–55.

Abolition Infrastructures

A Conversation on Transformative Justice
with Rachel Herzing and Dean Spade

Bench Ansfield

Over the past two decades, transformative justice has gained momentum as an organized effort to answer contemporary abolitionism's thorniest question: How can a society handle the problem of harm without resorting to punishment? The movement has sought to develop responses to harm and violence that reject retribution and instead emphasize accountability, repair, care, and attention to the systemic roots of violence. If, as Ruth Wilson Gilmore insists, "abolition is presence, not absence," transformative justice (TJ) is an infrastructure project for the abolitionist age.[1] Its practitioners draw blueprints for a world in which justice operates as care work and safety means the absence of hierarchy.

Blueprint or no, the construction of abolition infrastructures has proceeded in a makeshift, prefigurative, and speculative style. While many of its methods have long been practiced by Indigenous communities, TJ as a social movement was born in the early 2000s at the confluence of the renewed anti-prison movement and women of color organizing against violence. The decades since have seen an efflorescence of all forms of abolitionist organization across North America and beyond. And in the wake of the 2020 global uprising, transformative justice concepts have percolated into the public sphere in increasingly potent ways.

In large part because the movement took form in explicit rejection of the state's administration of justice, the work of TJ has most frequently been done on

Radical History Review
Issue 147 (October 2023)   DOI 10.1215/01636545-10637246

an unpaid basis of mutual aid. That this work nearly always happens outside of the confines of the state and capital—and even the 501(c)(3) structure, in most cases—has been one of its defining attributes. Here's a movement that has germinated in collective homes, borrowed office spaces, online forums, activist convenings, and parks—in other words, in the abolitionist commons.

As transformative justice has gained currency over the course of the pandemic, its ideas have been taken up in new realms, including the university, the non-profit, the prison, and the courts. The current moment is ripe for taking stock of where the movement is now and where it is going. What does it look like to build toward abolition infrastructures or infrastructures of collective care? How might an abolitionist theory of the state guide this work?

Who better to unpack these questions than Rachel Herzing and Dean Spade, key architects and builders of the contemporary abolition movement, each of whom bring decades of study and struggle to this work. Herzing is a cofounder of the abolitionist organization Critical Resistance and was a longtime organizer with Creative Interventions and its Storytelling and Organizing Project, which have helped build the scaffolding for the transformative justice movement. She is the coauthor of *How to Abolish Prisons: Lessons from the Movement against Imprisonment* (2023). Spade founded the Sylvia Rivera Law Project, helped organize the Building Accountable Communities Project at the Barnard Center for Research on Women, and is the author of *Mutual Aid: Building Solidarity during this Crisis (and the Next)* (2020).

Bench Ansfield spoke to Herzing and Spade in a wide-ranging conversation about the horizons of abolition in this moment of institutionalization.

Bench Ansfield: *Infrastructure is not typically used as a framework for thinking through transformative justice and abolition in the current moment. I want to begin by asking whether you imagine abolition or transformative justice as infrastructure-building projects. Does this framing hold any resonance for you?*

Rachel Herzing: I don't imagine prison industrial complex (PIC) abolition as a container that's already full of a bunch of stuff. I think of it more as a way of doing things. And with that in mind, I think that there's a way of applying these politics that requires us to build some things as we go, things that don't exist now. And we build them as a way of making the politics practical, of applying the politics to the real world that we live in, and of creating some of the things that we need for those politics to have staying power. So my answer is *probably* in the case of prison industrial complex abolition, and in the case of transformative justice (TJ), I think the answer is more or less the same, though I want to note that abolition and transformative justice are not interchangeable. I think about prison industrial complex abolition as a political praxis and transformative justice as a framework or methodology. And though there are obvious connections between them, I don't think they must be attached to each other, even if they might work well together.

I think that there are certain kinds of things we need to develop or build up in order for that practice—the practice of transformative justice or community accountability—to have the desired effect that we want it to have. As you say, Bench, infrastructure might not be the most natural language for this, but what I'm thinking of is—we need to build some things up to make those practices work well. And those things might be skills, or confidence, or relationships, as much as they are an organization, tool kit, or press release.

Dean Spade: Yes, so much of abolition work is about dismantling infrastructure—stopping the expansion of police stations, courts, jails, databases, or getting them closed. We have seen in the #DefundthePolice efforts how our city councils have this autopilot capacity to endlessly give the cops money, and this same relentless expansion happens at the state and federal levels. We've been told these things will keep us safe, and they don't. They're violent, and they make our lives worse. So the question becomes What *does* make people safer?

I really appreciate what you said, Rachel, about skills. Transformative justice includes a lot of skill building. Many TJ projects are about supporting people to have new relationship skills, more skills for dealing with conflict and finding repair together, more skills for facilitating conversations in groups and communities and making decisions in groups that include everyone's needs and values instead of structuring decision-making through hierarchy and domination.

We need new skills to depart from a system for solving conflict based on a centralized authority that determines who is good and bad. We want to build a decentralized approach to solving conflicts focused on recognizing that everyone is worthy of care and that no one is disposable. What if we all had more skills to solve problems in our communities? Endemic problems like child sexual abuse or sexual assault, gender-based violence—those harms are not going to be solved by a central authority, particularly since the authorities are primary sources of that violence. They'll only be addressed by a multiplicity of localized practices for addressing and preventing harm, which together transform our society. We're talking about undoing that type of brutal authority to hurt and cage and kill. And so I do think it is infrastructure. It is particularly about building complex, flexible, responsive, decentralized infrastructure. This also means, in the world we imagine, having basic infrastructure like housing, childcare, health care, and food for everyone, not based in profit or domination. The prison and policing systems exist to maintain extraction and profit, so when we imagine abolishing them, we are also imagining a new way of life where we all have what we need and no one can hoard it and control us with it.

RH: I take your point, Dean, and I think that though prison industrial complex abolition involves a lot of prison and jail fighting, the targets of TJ also revolve around the locus of the courtroom or the family services building.

The other thing I want to raise is that I want to problematize the idea that—and I'm not suggesting you are saying this necessarily, Dean—but I think when you were talking, this came up for me as a thing that troubles me a little bit, and I haven't exactly figured out how to work it out. So I will rely on the two of you to help me do that. Part of the reason that I made a point of separating transformative justice from prison industrial complex abolition is I think that there's this idea that, when they get mashed together like that, the implication is that the aim of the prison industrial complex really is to fight harm and curb violence. And it's not. That's not its function.

So, when we allow ourselves to be lured into thinking, "well, we have to figure out how to deal with conflict and harm to solve for the prison industrial complex," we're painting ourselves into a corner that we need not paint ourselves into. And I think if we focus on the containment and control aspects of the prison industrial complex, and we really see it for what it is, then we don't get tricked into claiming to fulfill the same social function as the prison industrial complex.

DS: What I've often seen in the local debates about defunding the police, or closing a particular prison or jail is that the opposition will argue that we can't get rid of that jail, or we can't reduce the police budget until you tell us *all* the ways you're going to solve *all* violence.

But we're going to solve violence first and foremost by getting rid of cops and jails because they are a central source of many forms of violence. They are violence. What your point about painting ourselves into a corner made me think of is this really absurd notion that we would have to resolve all violence before broaching abolition. And of course, it would be impossible to resolve violence while the punishment system is in place since *it is violence*.

RH: But I think we get tricked into responding to that, right? I think that's part of what you're raising, Dean. Violence, the management of violence, is a minuscule sliver of what the prison industrial complex takes charge of. Really, it's about managing bodies. Really, it's about legitimacy. Really, it's about suppressing dissent. Really, it's about managing poverty. It has nothing whatsoever to do with violence. And when we take the bait of having to solve for violence, then we cede a lot of terrain to that system.

BA: *To put it into infrastructural terms, what I hear you saying is that we're trying to dismantle the existing system without rebuilding right on top of it. In other words, the task of transformative justice is not to build a new building in the ashes of the complex that we're trying to burn down. As many folks have said, we need to be wary of framing transformative justice as the alternative to the PIC.*[2]

This is where I find infrastructure to be useful. The spark for this conversation was actually something you said in 2019, Rachel. This was years ago, so I won't hold you to it, but what I have down in my notes is something like "We don't need a bunch of neighbor-run centers; what we need is infrastructure." And I think this relates to what you both are saying, especially when we think about transformative justice as being about skill building, which translates into capacity building, which itself can be understood as infrastructure building.

In preparing for this, I was reading The Promise of Infrastructure, *and the introduction describes infrastructure as always bridging between different locations—its work is bridge work.*[3] *So whether we're talking about early aqueducts, or the sewage system, or telephone wires, or the internet, the work of infrastructure is to bridge disparate places. And I was trying to think through what that means for transformative justice.*

What is transformative justice bridging? One possible answer is that it bridges between our uninhabitable present and a possible abolitionist future. Our task is to figure out how to build that bridge with a lot of on-ramps for the abolition-curious without it essentially becoming another tollway in the US highway system. We're trying to figure out how to build this thing and generate momentum without guiding ourselves directly into co-optation.

To phrase this as a question, could you share what you see as the where of transformative justice right now? Where do you see it? With Philly Stands Up, which is the version of it that I know best, we had no offices.[4] *We met in each other's homes. When we were doing accountability processes, we met in the train station, Philly's 30th Street Station, because it was free, it was big, it was always climate controlled. And there was enough space that you could be relatively anonymous. Now that TJ is on the cusp of being institutionalized or taken up inside these different spheres—where it gets confusing for me is I don't know what to imagine as the where of TJ. What do you picture?*

DS: What those of us fighting jails and prisons and police always have to say to our opponents is that the things they think are crime or violence would mostly go away if people just had what they need. So part of the infrastructure that abolitionists or TJ practitioners imagine is just everyone having what they need. Here in Seattle, we have the Seattle Municipal Court, and its job is just to process very poor and unhoused people for things that the city thinks are crimes like peeing outside, sleeping outside—things that happen only because you don't have what you need. So a giant infrastructure question for TJ actually is basic needs—the transportation system, the housing system, childcare, food. It's horrifying that our cities spend half their budgets on policing and courts and jails while people don't have basic needs met. This is also central to conversations about specific kinds of violence. When we ask what trans people who are attacked on the street want and need, our opponents relentlessly suggest police training, and we say that housing is what would make trans people safer. Our opponents want to make our experiences of violence into opportunities to expand police, either justified by punishment or indefensible ideas that police, if properly trained and equipped, would prevent violence. We say stop building the infrastructure of punishment, and let's get people's basic needs met. That will increase safety.

This is part of bridging the uninhabitable present to new social relations— social relations in which people have what they need. When I've taught about abolition and transformative justice, for some students it's really new, and they'll write a paper about how they want to create a transformative justice police force. They'll literally make the same thing again with a new label. This same kind of thinking is present when some people advocate for social workers to replace cops.[5] Let's just have a new set of cops wearing a different outfit. That move makes so much sense because it's really hard to think in a new way. And people want to be able to call something like 911. There's so many gaps in terms of basic necessities, and in terms of relationships, it's really hard for people to picture other ways of solving problems, or to imagine life outside of the fear and isolation that predominate. Even people who hate what the cops are doing feel they don't know what to do about bad things that are happening in their community. This is a very important conversation that is widespread right now, and much needed if people are going to have a chance to imagine beyond the uninhabitable present so that we can create new ways of being together.

I just had this really juicy conversation with Shira Hassan.[6] One of the things we were talking about was that for people who are isolated, such as people who are currently experiencing domestic violence, or who just came to the US, something like 911 is helpful. Something that's very widely known, that is very visible, that's separate from your living situation, that you might know about even if you don't know anyone. But the downside is that most often, the best way to solve conflict and violence is something that draws on community members who know what is going on and have skills for intervening, who stick around, who care about the people involved in the conflict. Community-based interventions are more likely to get the harm to stop. And for very good reasons, people experiencing harm are more likely to reach out to people they know than to strangers like cops or Title IX officers on campus. And community-based interventions are more likely to really address what is going on than a one-size-fits-none punishment response.

So there are questions about the costs and benefits of building new response infrastructure that's more decentralized. What's the danger of people not knowing about it if they are isolated? Or what's the danger of having bigger, more centralized structures and then replicating some of the current dynamics where people are pretty deskilled and just looking for an outside source to deal with conflict, and where those showing up to a scene of harm or violence don't have context or relationships with the people involved?

We need people experimenting a lot to try to figure out what can work. People have always been solving problems in whatever ways we can, because we've always had to, but people are experimenting more and more right now because of the increased call to end cops and prisons and build real solutions. Groups like Interrupting Criminalization are providing a lot of support to people working on these very local experiments.[7]

I was particularly inspired learning about the Confess Project.[8] The Confess Project trains people to support each other's mental health in barbershops and beauty shops—because you're already going to that place—and then you can have someone to talk to who's got some active listening skills and can identify if you need some more intensive support. That's a really different model, where it's brought to you at your barbershop or beauty shop, than a model that's a hotline that anyone in a neighborhood or in a city can call. It's more about disbursing skills to where people need them, and ideally it could grow and prevent a lot of people from reaching a crisis where they needed to call a hotline. But for now most people do not have access to mental health support so many things escalate to crisis.

TJ work ideally happens everywhere. Ideally everyone gains more skills for conflict prevention, giving and receiving feedback, supporting people in crisis, and intervening in harm. TJ is also specific projects that help people in particular situations or communities with particular kinds of crisis. We don't need a one-size-fits-all approach to TJ. But what we do need is a shared assessment of what we're definitely not doing, like policing or imprisonment.

I think that's hard for a lot of people who are new to the analysis, who just want something that maps exactly onto the existing criminal punishment system, which wants us to be as passive as possible and not solve our own problems with each other—something that doesn't require more connection or new skills. It's a tall order to actually know our neighbors, to care about each other, to get better at having hard conversations. Some people don't believe that's possible if they've just heard of it for the first time, and they're accustomed to living in a society where most people are isolated and afraid. There's a lot of growth involved in even trying to imagine these other ways of being. Though I think we all actually do have a lot of practice doing these things in spaces where punishment and exile aren't the only ways to solve problems.

RH: Damn, Dean. You said a mouthful, and now I have a million thoughts going through my head. Where I'll start is—I'm going to stand by what I said in 2019. Bench, I do think that we need an infrastructure for TJ. Dean just spoke to that really well in a bunch of different ways, and you just spoke to that with the example of Philly Stands Up.

There's a mode of thinking around the abolition of the prison industrial complex that says that we have to have all of the what-ifs figured out first, and the what-ifs generally concern crime stopping, or so-called crime stopping. As we've said, many people take the bait. And we feel like we have to answer these questions. "What are you going to do with the litany of things that I'm just making up now that have never happened to me or anybody I know, but TV and movies tell me I should be afraid of them?" This is not to say that there's not real stuff out there, that stuff doesn't happen to people. Harm has happened to me, harm has happened to every last person that I know, so I would never suggest otherwise. But I do think it's a trap to presume that we have to have all of that figured out before we can have more of what we need to live better. We need room for experimentation and practice.

I think we're in a place now where we've become collectively quite romantic about alternatives. And there's this idea that we just need alternatives to policing. And then we get a lot of the stuff that you were describing, Dean, all the replications of what we currently have with different names, rather than How are we going to transform our relationships with each other? Which I think is fundamentally at the heart of what needs to change.

I do think that when people say we just need a bunch more community centers, and everybody just needs to have a place where they can go and macramé after school—I am for community centers, I am for alternatives. But that's not a fix, right? That's not the same kind of fix as having public transportation that works, that runs all night, that is free, that can take you somewhere where you're not vulnerable on the street. A set of community-based programs is never going to do the same work that that could do. Or having streetlights or having high-quality education or having access to medical care. All of those things are not going to be offset by Dean and I running little projects out of our houses, no matter how good Dean and I might be at it. It's just a different scale. I don't think these kinds of projects can replicate the scale of need that we're up against, which doesn't mean we shouldn't have them, which doesn't mean that they don't play a very important role. But it does mean that we can't act as if it's a one-to-one trade-off.

So the infrastructure is important. Having a place to be in—a place that is safe and dry, all of those things, free from the elements, free from harassment—is really important. And so the example that you were giving, Bench, about Philly Stands Up—that's the kind of infrastructure you need, right? Whether that's somebody's house, or whether that's the train station, that's what's necessary to be able to have these complicated conversations, to be able to really get into difficult negotiations with people in a space where they don't feel like everything's going to come collapsing on them and they can participate in those conversations in a real, genuine way.

As for the question of where transformative justice is, I would agree with you, Dean, I think it should be everywhere. If we're applying that framework well, then we're doing it everywhere. And I will confess that I struggle to do it well, everywhere. There are some relationships in my life that I just am like, no thank you. I'm not really trying to resolve a bunch of stuff with you. And I don't think that that's necessarily a complete contradiction of my politics as much as it is a reflection of how hard it is to apply those politics well and consistently. But I think Dean said it really well. If we imagine transformative justice to be a framework or methodology that we apply to the things we're trying to transform, then it could happen anywhere. And I genuinely do think that that's what it takes. Because I think that's part of confidence building. As much as we need skills—and we 100 percent need skills; we need time and space and cover to practice so we can develop those skills—we also need confidence. As we practice, we won't be as prone to take the bait because we know that the thing we try, even if we fuck it up, is likely to be better than what's already on offer. And I don't mean that lightly. I mean we have to build the dynamics between us, such that people can be more confident that if something goes down, they would have a role to play, even if it's not perfect. That's the where. And I feel like we're in a weird place right now, where there's a lot more adoption—maybe it's co-optation—of the language of transformative justice and the idea that people are doing TJ. And sometimes I'm not sure exactly what that means. Organizations spring up, and some may have nonprofit status, or some may be professionalized by absorption into the academy or the state apparatus. These things are happening. Transformative justice is happening in all of those places. And I'm not yet ready to say that we should just oppose all of those sites of practice. My guess is that something useful is happening there; maybe it's worth salvaging the nuggets before we burn the house down. But I also want to acknowledge that its growing ubiquity means that sometimes it'll flow into these other sites, where it might get more constrained. Or it might get overlaid with the very things that we're trying to get it out from under already.

BA: *I want to follow up about this question of abolition and the state. What is the relationship between the practice of transformative justice and the state? I think that if TJ has had an orientation toward the state up to this point, it's mostly been one of refusal or abstention—seeing itself as a challenge to state authority, or a reimagining of our social relations outside of the state. And yet, the state is there just as infrastructure is there. And one question that might be helpful to think through is—when the movement started calling itself transformative justice, it was at a moment when it was happening in such small pockets that it was almost easy to eschew the state apparatus altogether. And so my question is about what has changed in the last few years. What's the current terrain of struggle? How has it shifted since 2005 or 2007, when we saw the first flowering of self-identified TJ projects?*

The US state is obviously too vast to consider in its totality. But I am starting to wonder about my own possibly knee-jerk posture of "we exist outside of the state," which has been the easiest posture, at least in my work with Philly Stand Up. We simply didn't work with the cops, courts, or prisons. That was crystal clear. Our only engagement with the state was in joining local decarceration efforts. What do you think about this question of state engagement?

RH: I think I had a similar orientation, Bench, around the punishment system: no engagement whatsoever. And, for most of my time doing this work, I've been way too purist about it: "I'm going to take the high ground here." And I think there's a reason for that. I'm not trying to disparage positions that I took, because I had legitimate concerns. I think you have a much, much harder time trying to dismantle the punishment system if you're engaging the punishment system—because you give it legitimacy.

And that's still a tension that I have today with comrades who believe in police accountability bodies. Some of the smartest people I know believe that these accountability bodies could work toward the purpose of abolition. I don't think they can. That was a line that I have drawn historically: no engagement with cops or guards.

But I believe in hospitals. I've had my life saved in a hospital. And it was not a private hospital. And I like the idea that I might be able to send somebody to a hospital if they need help, particularly if I have some reassurance that the people there have good common sense around not engaging the punishment system. There are plenty of medical spaces that are no-cop zones, or they have parts of the hospital where cops can't go.

I believe in education. I think people should be able to go to school. I would like schools to be high-quality schools, and I would like people to be learning things that are useful to them. But even schools can be used by the punishment system and frequently are used by the punishment system. I'm not of the opinion that there's something inherently punishing about schools. I think schools have frequently been manipulated to do that, but I don't think the practice of education *has* to be coercive and punishing. And for that purpose, I would like people to be able to go to school.

So I don't have a set of hard and fast rules when it comes to all state institutions. I was trying to think if there is any nugget at all inside of the punishment system that might be of use, and I cannot think of one. But I am not, I'm not ready to forego the state altogether. I do not believe that all states are the same. I also do not believe that the state is a static form. And I do think that there are possibilities—I just said a few of those. I do not think the US state needs to be the model of what a state is. I think there are other forms that it could take.

DS: When I learned the term *transformative justice,* what was significant for me was its refusal to involve the cops and the courts. And that was important to say because there were a lot of restorative justice projects happening (not all restorative justice does this) that were working with the court system—a restorative circle with police officers and the survivor of the harm and the harm doer. Those processes are often complementary to the existing system or even an expansion of the system because they hire new staff to put people through those processes. Such "alternatives" can be good PR for the criminalization system while it continues to harass, arrest, and imprison the same populations.

That is why *transformative justice* was such a significant new term—a way of talking about alternatives that explicitly refused to collaborate with cops and prosecutors. To me that refusal doesn't mean we don't touch those systems. Abolitionists tangle with really difficult things like how to do prison education programs where you have to go through the Department of Corrections without being co-opted as good PR for the DOC—and while facing the limits they put on your program. Abolitionism isn't about purity in being allergic to government formations, or even criminal punishment system formations. It's knowing why you're there, having criteria for how you will engage. We are here to dismantle, we are here to support criminalized people, we are here to not let this system use our models to replicate or expand itself. It's hard work. We need to collectively debate our tactics, we need to make mistakes and learn. That is abolitionist and transformative justice method.

Abolition and TJ work on college campuses can look like campaigning to get your campus to stop working with city police and to get rid of your campus police. Or putting together survivor support groups or doing deep education around consent and sexuality and gender-based violence with the campus community. There are countless strategies for the countless harms happening in any given community. It's about taking where we are as the site of intervention, but not necessarily investing in the idea that our campus is going to become a thing that delivers our liberation. Let's organize here where we are. Just because we mess with institutions or use institutions as sites of organizing doesn't mean we are uncritically embracing them as the world we're building.

On the question of the state, to me, prisons are fundamental to the nation-state form. In my opinion, if we get what we want, which is to end capitalism, militaries, prisons, borders, and police, in my opinion we will not have this thing called the nation-state. I am often surprised when other abolitionists are not anarchists, because this seems obvious to me. It makes for a compelling conversation amongst abolitionists, which I am excited to see happening a lot right now.

I firmly believe that we can have the things we need in the world like health care, electricity, and transportation without extraction, without profit. And actually, we'd have them much better if they were governed by people who use them, if they were not for anybody's profit. I learned this through different forms of women-of-color feminist and disability justice frameworks that are critical of institutionalization, that are concerned about distribution of well-being. Through these lineages I figured out that I want to abolish the state form that was invented to facilitate extraction and uses violence to maintain it.

That doesn't mean I think the state is going to disappear quickly, just like I don't think that prisons, policing, militaries, and borders are disappearing quickly.

Nevertheless, abolition helps me discern the directions I want to head towards, and the directions to avoid. For instance, because I'm an abolitionist, I know I don't want trans cops as a way to deal with transphobia. Anarchism offers a parallel compass— helps me know that what I am building towards is no state, and helps me assess and debate with others whether given tactics are on the right path or are strengthening what we are trying to dismantle. I think there's something wrong with small groups of people (elites) deciding the life circumstances of huge groups of people that they don't know. That's what states are. The US is a particularly horrible one where the government is a farce and elites rule through a corrupt electoral and judicial system designed to establish and maintain a colonial, white supremacist extraction machine under a pretense of democracy. But I think that centralized state power is a problem beyond the US too.

Being an anarchist does not mean avoiding engaging with the governments we live under. We get into city councils and defund the cops. We oppose new criminalizing laws and new criminalization expansion projects. This is not a purity thing—not about ignoring current governments. It's about what we are imagining we are going towards. Our task is to build our capacity for collective self-determination. Are we ready to run our own lives together? We've lived in this pacifying and conquering societal model of a nation-state that requires extraction from us, and assures us we're incapable of meeting our own needs together. Everything we need we have to get through the racist, capitalist, fossil-fuel based, profit-centered food, energy, housing, health care, and childcare systems. We want to be liberated from those systems and create ways of surviving that are run by the people who live with and through them.

The rest of our lives will be marked by mounting crisis and disaster as ecological crisis mounts. The state forms we live under now respond to crisis and disaster with militarization and control. They show up to the hurricane with a lot of guns, not with water, housing, and medicine. We can see how they managed the pandemic— letting millions die, enriching a few people, making a vaccine for profit so that most of the world can't get it. They're terrible at managing disaster. And they've created a disaster pipeline that we are going to be living in for the rest of our lives.

And so the question is not What's my fantasy for how we could live? Because that's not really on the menu. The question is How does what I believe about the state help me prepare with others for what's coming? What do I do if I know they're going to show up with guns and cages to all the disasters, and I know they're going to divert as much money (which they extracted from us) away from our well-being as possible, so that after each disaster, we're actually in worse condition? How should we prepare for the next disaster, to have the most possible skills and tools for what's coming? This is beyond the fantasy that if we just got the right people in office, I would never need those skills and tools because the state will take care of me. That help is not coming. It's beyond the eleventh hour, and we don't have Medicare for All or the

Green New Deal (both of which are inadequate), they keep growing the immigration enforcement system, we don't have relief from constant warfare, no matter who's president. For me this is not an absolutism around whether or not we should do electoral work. We should be looking for political opportunities everywhere, but we should be very skeptical of the idea that getting the right people into the government will change much.

The bigger goal for me is maximum mobilization of the people to take up active roles in their own lives and in their communities. Achieving that is very place-based and based on local political conditions. Once we release the fantasy that the state is going to be the source of care and support, it's not as if we turn our backs on it or don't use the electric grid (for now). Instead, it's about enacting social relations that better prepare us for disaster and distribute resources better. We have to figure out how to do that within the actual conditions we're in, with food and energy systems that are going to collapse in our lifetimes. These systems *already* collapse in places where disaster is more advanced, in particular communities and for particular populations—like in Puerto Rico, inside prisons and jails, in the poorest neighborhoods. What did we learn about centralized electricity systems from the California fires in 2018 and the fallout of Hurricane Maria in Puerto Rico? What could we learn about COVID from how it unfolded in prisons? What did we learn about the nature of prisons and about the nature of disaster from Katrina? From all the different disasters we're living through?

Abolitionists are increasingly debating the question of the state. I am finding those debates thoughtful and caring and important for this phase of our work. Nobody's got the answers for what will happen next. We are all assessing the crises. Just as abolition and TJ challenge us to place our faith in human potential, this question of the state asks us: Do we believe we could do for ourselves better than a centralized state organized by white supremacy and capitalism is doing for us?

BA: *In my experience, transformative justice, from the start, has had an anti-authoritarian bent, if not an explicitly anarchist orientation toward the state. I'm thinking about Rachel's point that the state isn't a static form; it changes over time. And in this moment, as the state and its adjacent institutions are potentially warming up to the idea of transformative justice, I want to think a bit more about our orientation toward these institutions. Dean, you draw this useful parallel between how abolitionism helps define the direction we're going over the long term, even if it's not immediately achievable. And anarchism plays a similar role for you. So how would a more full-throated embrace of anarchism potentially reconfigure transformative justice work, especially since anti-authoritarianism has been part of TJ from the start? The other side of this question is whether the state form has any potential role in what Rachel called the essential work of transformative justice, which is transforming our relationships with each other.*

RH: I've been thinking a lot, Bench, about what you laid out here. And I appreciate the provocations and the questions. And I will lead with something that I think is probably obvious, which is that I am not an anarchist, I do not hold anarchist politics, and so I can't speak to what a "full-throated embrace" of anarchism might get us.

I do imagine myself to have anti-authoritarian politics, so I don't think that those two have to be tied together. If we're imagining a transformation of relationships, I don't think we need to rely on the state to make those possible. But I don't know that the state completely precludes us from being able to transform our relationships to each other. In my recent experience of abolitionists' critiques of the state, a lot of those operate from the presumption that the state form must be tied to capitalism, and while I think the reverse is true—that capitalism relies very heavily and maybe requires a state form in order to function—I'm not sure that I believe there is not a state formation that couldn't operate outside of capitalism. We have global examples to draw from there. Abolitionist politics requires us to think very expansively and creatively about what's possible. We're imagining what doesn't already exist. And we apply pretty broad and visionary politics toward that end. So maybe that's a full-throated embrace that I'm interested in: a genuine interrogation of what would happen if we applied ourselves to thinking as expansively as possible about what structures we could put in place in service of anti-authoritarian politics. What supports for service provision and governance could be established that don't replicate and fuel the exploitation and divisions inherent in a capitalist state? And maybe that's just too contradictory to be possible, but I'm willing to take up the task of imagining what else.

The other thing that I think is important in terms of my thinking around this stuff is to remember that prison industrial complex abolition is not a finished project, or a project that has a definite end point. It's processual and more like a horizon that moves us in the direction of the future we seek. Because I'm imagining prison industrial complex abolition as a horizon that we're moving toward, there's a way that thinking about a static state formation that looks essentially like the United States state form in this period doesn't allow for the creativity or flexibility required by this kind of horizon thinking. What else could be possible?

DS: I want to speak to what Rachel is asking about whether it's the right idea to reject the possibility that we could have some kind of state formation more conducive to what we're all dreaming about, or whether it's lacking imagination to dismiss such an idea. And this brings up a question that's been very central to me for many years: What is state formation?

I feel clear that the United States is a racial project founded in colonialism and slavery, that it's not redeemable, that it's based in these fundamental structures of oppression and exploitation and extraction, that it's a military imperialist project. I'm clear that the United States is not a salvageable project. But then I still have bigger questions about state formations generally. That's a different kind of question. It's been useful to read the writing of Peter Gelderloos, a nonacademic anarchist theorist and activist/organizer whose work is full of instructive examples from all across time, all over the world. I also go back to Peter Kropotkin's book *Mutual Aid*, along with many other writers thinking about this question, including Harsha Walia and William C. Anderson.9

Where my own investigation of these questions has led me is that state formation requires the conquering of people and the centralization of governance, such that you lose power over your own life and your basic necessities. State formation requires extraction by elites, requires the concentration of wealth, and requires warfare—and this is always to the detriment of ordinary people. People have resisted the historical processes by which states came to exist all along. People have not wanted to be ruled by people they don't know, they have not wanted to pay taxes to somebody far away so that elites could build a military, they have not wanted to be forced to be conscripted to those militaries, they have not wanted to be subject to surveillance and police work from those faraway rulers. State builders had to conquer people to force them into states, and there has always been resistance to this kind of rule. People had health care, ways of educating youth, all kinds of infrastructure before states were built that eventually replaced many of those ways of doing things with something mandated by a central authority run by elites.

What people do when there isn't that form of state power, and what we do to survive while living under that form of state power (which is extractive to the point of being deadly for many populations) is that we practice mutual aid. Capitalism is about removing our ability to collectively create and maintain the conditions of our lives, and instead everything that makes our lives go becomes a source of profit. Even in states that are not considered capitalist, having to go through state systems for basic necessities is a site of control and domination. Because we live in a time period defined by mounting crises, more people are talking about and trying out mutual aid now. We're faced with what is fundamentally an infrastructure question: How can we build the networks and methods and practices to provide the basic necessities for each other's survival as the disasters unfold and as much of the infrastructure crumbles or fails? And how can we dismantle the infrastructure designed to extract from and subdue us?

When I hear you saying, Rachel, can we think more creatively and expansively about what the state could be, to me it just sounds like—couldn't we just think of a really good prison? I know that's not what you're saying, but that's how it strikes me because I am so convinced that nation-states are not designed to be life-giving, just as I am convinced the project of caging people is not redeemable.

When we look at the history of mutual aid work done by movements before us, from the Underground Railroad to the Young Lords, one thing we see is that governments criminalize mutual aid. Governments try to stamp it out because they need us all to be forced into wage labor, to get our necessities through the market. That is how they control us and keep enriching elites at our expense. People have a hard time imagining being able to build enough of our own survival infrastructure because we are so dependent on capitalist methods for accessing housing, food, energy, etc. It's a huge imagination project, even though their systems are breaking down around us. They are terrible at providing people with what we need; the ways they provide it hurt and kill people and are endangering all life on earth. We have to imagine what it would look like for us to provide each other with everything we need—not through a centralized state formation but through the means that humans have most often used throughout human history: sharing, collaboration, and subsistence projects.

To me, the centralized state is fundamentally at odds with the collective self-determination and liberation that abolitionists imagine. State formations emerge and flourish under capitalism because they enable the types of racialized control and authority capitalism requires. I can't imagine a state formation that isn't articulating those kinds of control, and I don't know why I would want to. Why would it be liberatory to imagine a governance power that necessarily creates elite rule? It is through my abolitionist politics that I have come to understand what the state is, what state formation is, and how incompatible it is with liberation and collective self-determination.

This exchange features two key thinkers and movement leaders, **Rachel Herzing** and **Dean Spade**, who have both played a profound role in the abolitionist left over the last two decades. Herzing is cofounder of the abolitionist organization Critical Resistance and was a longtime organizer with Creative Interventions and its Storytelling and Organizing Project, which have helped build the scaffolding for the transformative justice movement. She is coauthor of *How to Abolish Prisons: Lessons from the Movement against Imprisonment* (with Justin Piché, 2023). Spade founded the Sylvia Rivera Law Project, helped organize the Building Accountable Communities Project at the Barnard Center for Research on Women, and is author of *Mutual Aid: Building Solidarity during This Crisis (and the Next)* (2020). The conversation is moderated by **Bench Ansfield**, a historian of racial capitalism with over a decade of experience with the veteran transformative justice organization Philly Stands Up.

Notes

1. Gilmore, "Keynote Conversation."
2. See, e.g., Kaba, *We Do This 'til We Free Us*, 136.
3. Anand, Gupta, and Appel, *Promise of Infrastructure*, 14.
4. Philly Stands Up was a transformative justice and abolitionist collective active from 2004 to 2015.
5. For a pointed critique of this position, see the Abolition and Disability Justice Collective, "Reforms to Avoid."
6. Shira Hassan is the former director of the Young Women's Empowerment Project and a longtime leader in the transformative justice movement.

7. Interrupting Criminalization, a project of Mariame Kaba and Andrea J. Ritchie, "aims to interrupt and end the growing criminalization and incarceration of women, girls, trans, and gender nonconforming people of color." See www.interruptingcriminalization.com.
8. For more on the Confess Project, see https://www.theconfessprojectofamerica.org.
9. Kropotkin, *Mutual Aid*; Walia, *Border and Rule*; Anderson, *The Nation on No Map*.

References

Abolition and Disability Justice Collective. "Reforms to Avoid." https://abolitionanddisability justice.com/reforms-to-oppose (accessed April 24, 2023).

Anand, Nikhil, Akhil Gupta, and Hannah Appel, eds. *The Promise of Infrastructure.* Durham, NC: Duke University Press, 2018.

Anderson, William C. *The Nation on No Map: Black Anarchism and Abolition*. Chico, CA: AK Press, 2021.

Gilmore, Ruth Wilson. "Keynote Conversation." Making and Unmaking Mass Incarceration conference, University of Mississippi, December 5, 2019. tweeted by Micah Herskind, https://twitter.com/micahinATL/status/1202728202424213505?s=20&t=Ts-Jt74Fgz4_niqOdzUyKA.

Kaba, Mariame. *We Do This 'til We Free Us: Abolitionist Organizing and Transforming Justice.* Edited by Tamara K. Nopper. Chicago: Haymarket Books, 2021.

Kropotkin, Peter. *Mutual Aid: A Factor of Evolution*. New York: McClure Phillips, 1902.

Walia, Harsha. *Border and Rule: Global Migration, Capitalism, and the Rise of Racist Nationalism*. Chicago: Haymarket Books, 2021.

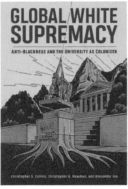

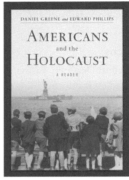

Keep up to date on new scholarship

Issue alerts are a great way to stay current on all the cutting-edge scholarship from your favorite Duke University Press journals. This free service delivers tables of contents directly to your inbox, informing you of the latest groundbreaking work as soon as it is published.

To sign up for issue alerts:

1. Visit **dukeu.press/register** and register for an account. You do not need to provide a customer number.

2. After registering, visit **dukeu.press/alerts**.

3. Go to "Latest Issue Alerts" and click on "Add Alerts."

4. Select as many publications as you would like from the pop-up window and click "Add Alerts."

read.dukeupress.edu/journals

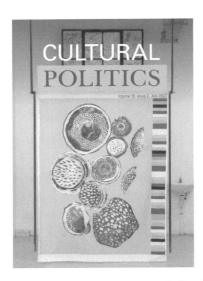